Imaginations

Kora in Hell
Spring and All
The Great American Novel
The Descent of Winter
A Novelette and Other Prose

By William Carlos Williams

The Autobiography
The Build-up
Collected Earlier Poems
Collected Later Poems
The Embodiment of Knowledge
The Farmers' Daughters
I Wanted to Write a Poem
Imaginations
In the American Grain
In the Money
Interviews with W. C. Williams
Kora in Hell: Improvisations†
Many Loves and Other Plays
Paterson, Books 1-5
Pictures from Brueghel and Other Poems
A Recognizable Image
The Selected Essays
Selected Poems
A Voyage to Pagany
White Mule
The William Carlos Williams Reader

† *City Lights Books*

WILLIAM CARLOS WILLIAMS

Imaginations

Kora in Hell
Spring and All
The Great American Novel
The Descent of Winter
A Novelette and Other Prose

edited with introductions by
Webster Schott

A NEW DIRECTIONS BOOK

ACKNOWLEDGMENTS
Excerpts from *I Wanted to Write a Poem* by William Carlos Williams,
quoted in Webster Schott's introductions, are reprinted by permission
of The Beacon Press, Copyright © 1958 by William Carlos Williams.

First published clothbound in 1970
First published as ND Paperbook 329 in 1971

Manufactured in the United States of America
Published simultaneously in Canada by George J. McLeod, Ltd., Toronto

New Directions Books are published for James Laughlin
by New Directions Publishing Corporation,
80 Eighth Avenue, New York 10011

SEVENTH PRINTING

Contents

Acknowledgments

Without the encouragement, help, patience of several others, this book would never have been completed. Most important were James Laughlin, Dr. Williams's friend and publisher and enthusiastic critic, and Florence Williams, Williams's remarkable wife and friend to all who value his work. Before his death Winfield Townley Scott helped me to see Williams clearer. Conrad Knickerbocker asked the right questions. Emily Mitchell Wallace's efforts in *A Bibliography of William Carlos Williams* made everything easier. Dee Danner Barwick typed and retyped much of the manuscript and commented intelligently. Editing the early Williams would have been drudgery without the help of Barbara Harr. Nan Schott tolerated anxiety and listened. David E. Scherman first understood what I have tried to say here about William Carlos Williams.

The introduction originally appeared, with minor changes, in *The American Scholar*.

Kansas City, Mo.   w.s.

Introduction

Beautiful Blood, Beautiful Brain

And approaching the end of the novel in his mind as he sat there with his wife sleeping alone in the next room he could feel that something unusual had happened. Something had grown up in his life dearer than—It, as the end. The words from long practice had come to be leaves, trees, the corners of his house—such was the end. He had progressed leaving the others behind him.

—The Great American Novel

WILLIAM CARLOS WILLIAMS forces the kinds of questions we address to natural disasters, reports of miracles and works of genius. How? Why? From what inexplicable source?

He was an American original. In his 79 years Williams led at least two lives, and at manic intensity. For some forty years he practiced medicine—obstetrics and pediatrics—in the small industrial town of Rutherford, New Jersey. He saw by his own account a million and a half patients and delivered 2,000 babies. This was from 1910 until 1951, before the era of doctoring by answering service and beginning the medical day with a call to the stockbroker. Williams worked like a slave at medicine. It brought him neither fortune nor special rank. Instead, it gave him and us that other life beyond value, a life of art.

While stealing time between patients, catching images and ideas between house calls, scribbling at midnight, William Carlos Williams laid the foundation of the most consequential one-man body of modern literature in American history—a total of 49 books in every literary form we know and in forms we still have trouble classifying. He wrote some 600 poems, four full-length plays, an opera libretto, 52 short stories, four novels, a book of essays and criticism, his autobiography, a biography of his mother, an American history, a book of letters. He translated a medieval Spanish novel. He wrote the five-volume epic-spectacular poem *Paterson* over a period of three decades. Williams's most important work had been done by the time he retired from medicine in 1951. When he died 12 years later, after a series of crippling strokes, William Carlos Williams had no peer as the total American writer.

Not our time but another time will fix Williams's place in American literature. For the present he stands first among his contemporaries. If the public did not draw him to its bosom as it did the performing Robert Frost or canonize him as it did T. S. Eliot, the new young poets of his era paid him the perfect homage. They became like him. Not Ezra Pound or E. E. Cummings, but finally William Carlos Williams freed American poetry from the irons of rhyme and meter. His disciples of liberation ranged from formal poets like Winfield Townley Scott and Karl Shapiro to insurgents like Charles Olson and Robert Duncan. He was the instrument of change. Without him one cannot account for contemporary American poetry.

If Williams left tingling elegances to Wallace Stevens and academic grace to W. H. Auden, he chose larger. He seized experience and turned it into poetry hot with the blood of life. His was a found art that raised everything it touched—trees and birds, people and dogs, water and fruit, love and flowers—to a level of startled awareness. It was an art so embedded in his own personality and manner of living even Williams could never translate it into a coherent system of aesthetics readily available to others.

William Burroughs once told the critic Conrad Knickerbocker there is no such thing as will power, only need. Driving William Carlos Williams was a need for both medicine and literature that exceeded the definitions of commitment. He turned his moods into work: "Periodicity of psychological and imaginative energy," he said in a notebook in 1930. "Work *all* the time—manic depression but learn to use yourself: when up drive in—when down assume the clerk—there's plenty of room for both." He pursued both medicine and art simultaneously. "Time meant nothing to me," he said in his autobiography. "I might be in the middle of some flu epidemic, the phone ringing day and night, madly, not a moment free. That made no difference . . . Five minutes, ten minutes can always be found. I had my typewriter in my office desk. All I needed to do was pull up the leaf . . . and I was ready to go . . . I worked at top speed. If a patient came in at the door while I was in the middle of a sentence, bang would go the machine—I was a physician. When the last patient left, up would come the machine . . . Finally, after 11 at night, when the last patient had been put to bed, I would always find the time to bang out 10 or 12 pages. In fact, I couldn't rest until I had freed my mind from the obsessions which had been tormenting me all day . . . Having scribbled I could rest."

Medicine fired and fed the poet. Art informed the doctor: "To treat a man as material for a work of art makes him somehow come alive for me." It also held him together: "Most of my life has been lived in hell—a hell of repression lit by flashes of inspiration, when a poem such as this or that would appear." There was not only space, but absolute necessity, for both writer and physician in Williams.

Mostly we know William Carlos Williams as the titan who created *Paterson,* as the revolutionary miniaturist of "The Red Wheelbarrow," or as the magnificent autumnal lover of "Asphodel That Greeny Flower." This is the artist commanding his powers. To know the doctor searching for his art and testing it, the artist tasting life and suffering it, or to know the literary heretic rationalizing his schism and anticipating the future, we need more. We need the socially introspective journal writer of "The Descent of Winter." We need the iconoclastic and privately published (usually in France) doctor-poet of such strange and troubled books as *Kora in Hell, The Great American Novel, A Novelette,* and *Spring and All*. Qualified fictions that probe the idea of fiction, not wholly poetry but set with the jewels of poetry, they are William Carlos Williams's books of primary belief. They are also crisis books. Crisis books because they show Williams immediately after his first poems, barely known and desperately struggling to erect a platform of ideas from which he could make sense to himself and whoever would read him. They show him breaking through a thicket of words and emotions to a belief in his own worth that was never shaken. A belief that poured the concrete of *Paterson* and gave Williams his heirs.

These are difficult books, these four, and not to be wished onto desert minds. They churn with giant ideas and powerful feelings, often pursued with the fragile butterfly net of intuition. There are no narrative lines except those in Williams's head. No conventions except those Williams invented as he went along. No genuflections to formality or propriety. Williams had no time and less taste for that. He was writing these books in search of a faith, not an audience. From 300 to 1,000 copies of each were printed. Fewer were sold. The radical present and the revolutionary future were Williams's goal, not an invitation into the lace-curtained living room of America. "I'll write whatever I damn please," he said in his preface to *Kora*, "whenever I damn please and as I damn please and it'll be good if the authentic spirit of change is on it."

This doesn't mean Williams was living in splendid isolation among the Dantesque vistas of industrial New Jersey. The aesthetic upheavals of the post-World-War-I period (when all of these books were written) lifted Williams too. His appetite for art was gargantuan. He consumed music, drama, painting, literature as if they were food. He visited France and Switzerland briefly. Through friends he had lines out to dadaism, surrealism, furturism, objectivism, imagism, cubism, cacophonous music. These convulsions of aesthetics caught Williams at a crucial time—his late 30's and early 40's—and he was struggling between discontent and assertion, self-examination and self-discovery. He was put down by poets who counted—Eliot, Stevens, Hilda Doolittle, even his old college pal Ezra Pound. As a physician he found meanness and stupidity thwarting his medicine and life itself. The nights looked like corpses, he says in *Kora*. It was hard to tell loss from gain and all beauty stood upon "the edge of the deflowering."

So Williams wrote, as always, to keep his sanity by extending the world he saw into the one that bloomed in his imagination. In *The Great American Novel* he ruminated over such vexing questions as what makes a novel? where are its sources? how does it become American? what should language do? One of the first anti-novels written in America, the work becomes a commentary on its own construction. The luminous *Kora in Hell* grew out of compulsion. Like Kora, the Greek goddess of spring who was captured and taken to hell, Williams "thought of myself as Springtime and I felt I was on my way to Hell (but I didn't get very far)." After a year of writing every day he had created an underground classic, one of the earliest models for contemporary prose poetry. Williams wrote *Spring and All* as a travesty on the typographically chaotic literature of the time (1923). He also wanted to push on with the freedom he had found in *Kora*. Thus he framed some of his finest poems—"The Red Wheelbarrow," "By the Road to the Contagious Hospital," "The Sea That Encloses Her Young Body"—in eccentric prose sermons on their principles. Years later Williams said that *Spring and All* "made sense to me, at least to my disturbed mind—because it was disturbed at that time—but I doubt it made sense to anyone else." *A Novelette* was another piece of imaginative prose written "for personal satisfaction" and to learn more about the problems of prose. He had "abandoned all hope of getting American readers of a special sort." Remembering *Kora*, Williams sat down, faced the page, and poured himself out in automatic paragraphs. He broke rules, defied

logic, and charged his psychic battery. By dint of rhetoric
if not force of argument, he also managed to wed his the-
ories of art to his ideas about matrimony. With *The
Descent of Winter*, a journal he never saw fit to push be-
yond its first appearance in 1928 in Ezra Pound's *The Exile*,
Williams seemed to throw poetry, fiction, social insight and
critical commentary onto paper as if attempting to exorcise
depression via the act of creating. Art was Williams's ther-
apy. Several fine poems glorify this nearly forgotten work.
But the most instructive thing about *The Descent of Win-
ter* is Williams's great sense of urgency. Time was running
out for art as it was running out for him as he wrote. Poetry
must make contact with hard facts and authentic feelings or
else become rhetorical trash atop the junk heap of industri-
alization.

These works tell us as much about the how and why of
William Carlos Williams as anything he wrote. All speak in
the voices of autobiography, and they reveal an immensely
complicated man: energetic, compassionate, socially con-
scious, depressive, urbane, provincial, tough, fastidious, ca-
pricious, independent, dedicated, completely responsive. To
the charge that he contradicted himself, Walt Whitman
replied that he embraced multitudes. So did Williams. He
was the complete human being, and all of the qualities of
his personality were fused in his writing. He possessed to
the full those traits we associate with the myth of the
American: ingenuity, lusty enthusiasm, and an absolute
faith in the new. Yet despite all the riches of his personality
and the fluids of exegesis embalming his writing in scholar-
ship, Williams's writing came from a simple source—his
belief in the imagination.

Long after these works, near the end of his career, Wil-
liams turned inward in "Asphodel That Greeny Flower" to
seek out those truths that had held firm. He said:

> It is difficult
> to get the news from poems
> yet men die miserably every day
> for lack
> of what is found there.

He was speaking of the power of the imagination to hold human beings to life and propel them onward. *Kora, The Great American Novel, Spring and All, A Novelette, The Descent of Winter* are documents of that discovery. Williams made it for himself; it became the foundation of all his poetry, fiction, drama. And he extended it as a means of evaluating all other art.

Williams knew one reality. He created another reality to make the first manageable. Against the practice of medicine, following "the poor defeated body into gulfs and grottoes," he posed his flights of imagination into the intensity of living things, the splendors of association and dislocation. If these books are "about" anything—as opposed to being the things they are themselves—they are about the powers of the imagination to sustain and expand human consciousness. "To refine, to clarify, to intensify that eternal moment in which we alone live there is but a single force—the imagination," Williams says in *Spring and All*. "The only realism in art is of the imagination." It makes blackness beautiful. "The birth of the imagination is like waking from a nightmare. Never was the night so beneficent." In a mysterious psychoanalytic transaction with the self, imagination "gives the feeling of completion by revealing the oneness of experience, it rouses rather than stupefies the intelligence by demonstrating the importance of personality, by showing the individual, depressed before it, that his life is valuable—when completed by the imagination. And then only."

Words, language, the means of speaking the imagination, were also the barrier to penetrating the imagination. "Words are the flesh of yesterday," Williams says in *The*

Great American Novel. "Progress is to get—But how can words get. Let them get drunk. Bah. Words are words." Worse yet, our words were English words trying to do American work. Struggling against the dead cultural whale of Europe, the American imagination had to recreate "everything afresh in the likeness of that which it was." Using spoken, heard American English the imagination "affirms reality most powerfully . . . it creates a new object, a play, a dance which is not a mirror up to nature."

What did such theories mean in action? That Williams would see life brand-new but all of a piece. The hums of a dynamo and the screams of a woman in anguish are fused in the energy of the present. The discovery and exploration of America parallel Williams's search for the new speech to create the New World's art. Erotic juice flows through all things. A little car purrs to itself at the thought of night and longs to be a woman. Imagining turns words into things. It lifts them from beneath the nose and hurls them fresh as rain against Williams's consciousness. The poems of *Spring and All* turn from print into the things, the events themselves. Sun streams. Roses bloom. "Say it, no ideas but in things," Williams demanded. And his writing snaps pictures like a marvelous image machine.

Williams found a system that worked for him. The imagination became source of calm, art, union with the universe. Riding along in his car with a yellow pad and pencil on the seat, stopping for locomotives, swerving to avoid ash carts, Williams plunged his mind into the deluge of objects and actions around him. He snatched poetry from the instant. He may have been the first writer in the world to fashion art from the dreaminess of driving a car. Swift, fragmentary, compressed, his technique was the product of his circumstance. He had to write his way because his medicine gave him no choice. Ringing telephones and waiting patients allowed no deliberation over sonnets or villanelles. Williams had to make art straight from common speech and uncommon imagination or no art at all. Succeeding at art and succeeding at life through art, Williams believed he had nailed truth down. What worked for him had to work for everyone. He was drunk with enthusiasm—sometimes even irrational—in celebrating what the imagination could do. He behaved like a prophet. Reading these early works now, we know he was.

In the last half of the twentieth century we've learned we can be free only through the senses, and we've been struck by a sensual revolution. Industrialization triggered it. Technology completed it. William Carlos Williams anticipated it. Williams was our forebear, and if our time had any saintly men he was among them.

We live in a world where no one, neither God nor Caesar, is in charge. Our evils appear to be giants beyond personal reach. Our acts of holiness are performed by advisory committees. Daily existence often seems to be a demoralizing routine of psychological drudgery, physical tedium, and socially induced guilt. Our words usually mean something else. Like Dr. Zhivago, we think we may be dying of lies. Our actions are slow to cause effect. Yet the largest and swiftest action of all may precede the last action—storms of fire and rains of fatal dust. For most of us the world is unmanageable. There is little we can do except feel, see, hear—sense.

"The Poet should be forever at the ship's prow," Williams said. And he was. Driven to the edge of despair ("I had recourse to the expedient of letting life go completely," he says in *Spring and All*) for all kinds of reasons—his private life, his trips into the hells around him, his sense of America's loss—Williams retreated to the senses and found a piece of freedom through the imagination. He says in *The Descent of Winter* that "the perfect type of the man of action is the suicide," but Williams goes on searching for inner action through his imagination. He didn't tell us the bitterness of loss could be halted by the imagination. "On the contrary," he said in *Kora*, "it [the loss] is intensified, resembling thus possession itself. But he who has no power of the imagination cannot even know the full of his injury." To Williams the ability to imagine became the ability to survive. It was a need as urgent as sexual hunger: "The imagination will not down . . . If it is not a dance, a song, it becomes an outcry, a protest. If it is not flamboyance it becomes deformity; if it is not art, it becomes crime. Men and women cannot be content any more than children, with the mere facts of a humdrum life—the imagination must adorn and exaggerate life, must give it splendor and grotesqueness, beauty and infinite depth."

Williams was discovering his program for modern American literature and his means of coping with brute reality. What he found has become a part of our own equipment for survival. He couldn't state the proposition as succinctly and clearly as we might like. He thought he heard the music of the soul and was in a hurry to get to its source. But he had all the component ideas for a working scheme of life in our modern industrialized society. Knowledge is endless and reality must ride on the imagination. The power to fantasize, to recreate, is the power to arrest the mercantile-mechanical crush on the sensibilities. To live the American life we must discover the American experience. We must either grow on the new or starve on the bones of the old. To make art, find the essential moment, seek primary quality: not a representation, but a separate existence in a mass of copies.

Williams's speculations and excursions in these writings open onto a vast sea. He was driven to create them because, like the great artists Camus sought, he lived to the full. Nothing was alien to him. His medicine took him to the tangled nerve centers of his fellow men. He found his way back to order and joy through perfect visions. He told us we would have to do it too. "All beauty comes from beautiful blood and a beautiful brain," Walt Whitman said. Read William Carlos Williams and know it is true.

Kansas City, Mo.   w.s.

Kora in Hell: Improvisations

To
Flossie

Introduction

Kora in Hell: Improvisations

ONE OF William Carlos Williams's own favorite books, *Kora in Hell: Improvisations* was first published in Boston in 1920. "It is the one book I have enjoyed referring to more than any of the others," he said in 1957. "It reveals myself to me and perhaps that is why I have kept it to myself." Until now it has not been republished complete with its prologue.

In *I Wanted to Write a Poem*, Williams tells how he composed the book:

"I had no book in mind when I began the Improvisations. For a year I used to come home and no matter how late it was before I went to bed I would write something . . . and at the end of the year there were 365 entries. Even if I had nothing in my mind at all I put something down, and as may be expected, some of the entries were pure nonsense and were rejected when the time for publication came. They were a reflection of the day's happenings more or less, and what I had to do with them. Some were unintelligible to a stranger and I knew that I would have to interpret them. I was groping around to find a way to include the interpretations when I came upon a book [Ezra] Pound had left in the house, *Varie Poesie Dell' Abate Pietro Metastasio*, Venice, 1795. I took the method used by the Abbot of drawing a line to separate my material. First came the *Improvisations*, those more or less incomprehensible statements, then the dividing line and, in italics, my interpretations of the Improvisations. . . .

"I am indebted to Pound for the title. We had talked about Kora, the Greek parallel of Persephone, the legend of Springtime captured and taken to Hades. I thought of

myself as Springtime and I felt I was on my way to Hell
(but I didn't go very far). This was what the *Improvisa-
tions* were trying to say. . . .

"Finally, when it was all done, I thought of the Pro-
logue which is really an Epilogue. I felt I had to give some
indication of myself to the people I knew; sound off, tell
the world—especially my intimate friends—how I felt
about them. All my gripes to other poets, all my loyalties
to other poets, are here in the Prologue . . . When I was
halfway through the Prologue, "Prufrock" appeared. I had
a violent feeling that [T.S.] Eliot had betrayed what I be-
lieved in. He was looking backward; I was looking for-
ward. He was a conformist, with wit, learning which I did
not possess. He knew French, Latin, Arabic, god knows
what. I was interested in that. But I felt he had rejected
America and I refused to be rejected and so my reaction
was violent. I realized the responsibility I must accept. I
knew he would influence all subsequent American poets
and take them out of my sphere. I had envisaged a new
form of poetic composition, a form for the future. It was
a shock to me that he was so tremendously successful; my
contemporaries flocked to him—away from what I wanted.
It forced me to be successful."

In a form that did influence the future, the prose poetry
of *Kora* is an extraordinary combination of aphorism, ro-
manticism, philosophizing, obscurity, obsession, exhorta-
tion, reverie, beautiful lines and scary paragraphs. Although
Kora's official literary status has lagged behind its actual
effect, young writers have known better. They've carried
the City Lights version around for years. Karl Shapiro
wrote *The Bourgeois Poet* remembering it. It's a luxury of
William Carlos Williams, a soul book. Williams celebrates
and castigates the imagination. He finds the erotic inform-
ing events and arguments. Through all the darkness of de-
pression, his spirit leaps at the sight or thought of woman-
hood. Williams writes swiftly, naturally, as a bird flies. He
becomes utterly despondent and irrepressibly joyous.

There are problems. Williams repeats himself. Gaps yawn between what Williams thinks he puts into the prose poems and what he says prompted them. Some *Improvisations* needing explanations lack them. But the book expands its reader. Surely it expanded Williams. The sensibilities of the poems that would follow *Kora* are first freed here, and Williams anticipates the method of creating those poems.

Williams "danced" as he could. Both his poetic form and his prose style came as a result of his writing habits. Quick, snatched, not disciplined by the continuous rewriting of the sedentary academician, his work had the freshness of the instant. By the time he had leisure to do otherwise, Williams had established his technique. Much of his critical writing was to become rationalization and justification for a method that was forecast by *Kora*. For Williams the method was both inevitable and essential. *Kora* became one of his frequent points of reference.

Asked in later life what had been the strongest influence on his writing, Williams said medical case histories. *Kora in Hell* must be read to comprehend the bond between Williams's profession and his art. It is entry to the passions— hot, cold, and finally controlled—that joined the doctor and the poet.

w.s.

Prologue

The Return of the Sun

Her voice was like rose-fragrance waltzing in the wind.
She seemed a shadow, stained with shadow colors,
Swimming through waves of sunlight . . .

THE SOLE precedent I can find for the broken style of my
prologue is *Longinus on the Sublime* and that one far-
fetched.

When my mother was in Rome on that rare journey for-
ever to be remembered, she lived in a small pension near the
Pincio Gardens. The place had been chosen by my brother
as one notably easy of access, being in a quarter free from
confusion of traffic, on a street close to the park, and fur-
thermore the tram to the American Academy passed at the
corner. Yet never did my mother go out but she was in fear
of being lost. By turning to the left when she should have
turned right, actually she did once manage to go so far
astray that it was nearly an hour before she extricated her-
self from the strangeness of every new vista and found a
landmark.

There has always been a disreputable man of picturesque
personality associated with this lady. Their relations have
been marked by the most rollicking spirit of comradeship.
Now it has been William, former sailor in Admiral Dewey's
fleet at Manila, then Tom O'Rourck who has come to her to
do odd jobs and to be cared for more or less when drunk or
ill, their Penelope. William would fall from the grape arbor
much to my mother's amusement and delight and to his
blustering discomfiture or he would stagger to the back
door nearly unconscious from bad whiskey. There she
would serve him with very hot and very strong coffee, then

6

put him to scrubbing the kitchen floor, into his suddy-pail pouring half a bottle of ammonia which would make the man gasp and water at the eyes as he worked and became sober.

She has always been incapable of learning from benefit or disaster. If a man cheat her she will remember that man with a violence that I have seldom seen equaled, but so far as that could have an influence on her judgment of the next man or woman, she might be living in Eden. And indeed she is, an impoverished, ravished Eden but one indestructible as the imagination itself. Whatever is before her is sufficient to itself and so to be valued. Her meat though more delicate in fiber is of a kind with that of Villon and La Grosse Margot:

> *Vente, gresle, gelle, j'ai mon pain cuit!*

Carl Sandburg sings a Negro cotton picker's song of the boll weevil. Verse after verse tells what they would do to the insect. They propose to place it in the sand, in hot ashes, in the river, and other unlikely places but the boll weevil's refrain is always: "That'll be ma HOME! That'll be ma HOOME!"

My mother is given over to frequent periods of great depression being as I believe by nature the most light-hearted thing in the world. But there comes a grotesque turn to her talk, a macabre anecdote concerning some dream, a passionate statement about death, which elevates her mood without marring it, sometimes in a most startling way.

Looking out at our parlor window one day I said to her: "We see all the shows from here, don't we, all the weddings and funerals?" (They had been preparing a funeral across the street, the undertaker was just putting on his overcoat.) She replied: "Funny profession that, burying the dead people. I should think they wouldn't have any delusions of life left." W.—Oh yes, it's merely a profession. M.—Hm. And how they study it! They say sometimes people look terrible and they come and make them look fine. They push things

into their mouths! (Realistic gesture) W.—Mama! M.—
Yes, when they haven't any teeth.

By some such dark turn at the end she raises her story out
of the commonplace: "Look at that chair, look at it!" [The
plasterers had just left.] "If Mrs. J. or Mrs. D. saw that they
would have a fit." W.—Call them in, maybe it will kill
them. M.—But they're not near as bad as that woman, you
know, her husband was in the chorus—has a little daughter
Helen. Mrs. B., yes. She once wanted to take rooms here. I
didn't want her. They told me: 'Mrs. Williams, I heard
you're going to have Mrs. B. *She* is particular.' She said so
herself. Oh no! Once she burnt all her face painting under
the sink.

Thus, seeing the thing itself without forethought or after-
thought but with great intensity of perception, my mother
loses her bearings or associates with some disreputable per-
son or translates a dark mood. She is a creature of great
imagination. I might say this is her sole remaining quality.
She is a despoiled, molted castaway but by this power she
still breaks life between her fingers.

Once when I was taking lunch with Walter Arensberg at
a small place on 63rd Street I asked him if he could state
what the more modern painters were about, those roughly
classed at that time as "cubists": Gleizes, Man Ray, Demuth,
Duchamp—all of whom were then in the city. He replied
by saying that the only way man differed from every other
creature was in his ability to improvise novelty and, since
the pictorial artist was under discussion, anything in paint
that is truly new, truly a fresh creation, is good art. Thus,
according to Duchamp, who was Arensberg's champion at
the time, a stained-glass window that had fallen out and lay
more or less together on the ground was of far greater in-
terest than the thing conventionally composed *in situ*.

We returned to Arensberg's sumptuous studio where he
gave further point to his remarks by showing me what ap-
peared to be the original of Duchamp's famous "Nude De-
scending a Staircase." But this, he went on to say, is a full-

sized photographic print of the first picture with many new touches by Duchamp himself and so by the technique of its manufacture as by other means it is a novelty!

Led on by these enthusiasms Arensberg has been an indefatigable worker for the yearly salon of the Society of Independent Artists, Inc. I remember the warmth of his description of a pilgrimage to the home of that old Boston hermit who, watched over by a forbidding landlady (evidently in his pay), paints the cigar-box-cover-like nudes upon whose fingers he presses actual rings with glass jewels from the five-and-ten-cent store.

I wish Arensberg had my opportunity for prying into jaded households where the paintings of Mama's and Papa's flowertime still hang on the walls. I propose that Arensberg be commissioned by the Independent Artists to scour the country for the abortive paintings of those men and women who without master or method have evolved perhaps two or three unusual creations in their early years. I would start the collection with a painting I have by a little Englishwoman, A. E. Kerr, 1906, that in its unearthly gaiety of flowers and sobriety of design possesses exactly that strange freshness a spring day approaches without attaining, an expansion of April, a thing this poor woman found too costly for her possession—she could not swallow it as the Negroes do diamonds in the mines. Carefully selected, these queer products might be housed to good effect in some unpretentious exhibition chamber across the city from the Metropolitan Museum of Art. In the anteroom could be hung perhaps photographs of prehistoric rock-paintings and etchings on horn: galloping bisons and stags, the hind feet of which have been caught by the artist in such a position that from that time until the invention of the camera obscura, a matter of six thousand years or more, no one on earth had again depicted that most delicate and expressive posture of running.

The amusing controversy between Arensberg and Duchamp on one side, and the rest of the hanging committee on the other as to whether the porcelain urinal was to be admitted to the Palace Exhibition of 1917 as a representative piece of American sculpture, should not be allowed to slide into oblivion.

One day Duchamp decided that his composition for that day would be the first thing that struck his eye in the first hardware store he should enter. It turned out to be a pickax which he bought and set up in his studio. This was his composition. Together with Mina Loy and a few others Duchamp and Arensberg brought out the paper, *The Blind Man,* to which Robert Carlton Brown, with his vision of suicide by diving from a high window of the Singer Building, contributed a few poems.

In contradistinction to their south, Marianne Moore's statement to me at the Chatham parsonage one afternoon— my wife and I were just on the point of leaving—sets up a north: My work has come to have just one quality of value in it: I will not touch or have to do with those things which I detest. In this austerity of mood she finds sufficient freedom for the play she chooses.

Of all those writing poetry in America at the time she was here Marianne Moore was the only one Mina Loy feared. By divergent virtues these two women have achieved freshness of presentation, novelty, freedom, break with banality.

When Margaret Anderson published my first improvisations Ezra Pound wrote me one of his hurried letters in which he urged me to give some hint by which the reader of good will might come at my intention.

Before Ezra's permanent residence in London, on one of his trips to America—brought on I think by an attack of jaundice—he was glancing through some book of my father's. "It is not necessary," he said, "to read everything in a book in order to speak intelligently of it. Don't tell everybody I said so," he added.

During this same visit my father and he had been reading and discussing poetry together. Pound has always liked my father. "I of course like your old man and I have drunk his Goldwasser." They were hot for an argument that day. My parent had been holding forth in downright sentences upon my own "idle nonsense" when he turned and became equally vehement concerning something Ezra had written: what in heaven's name Ezra meant by "jewels" in a verse that had come between them. These jewels,—rubies, sapphires, amethysts and whatnot, Pound went on to explain with great determination and care, were the backs of books as they stood on a man's shelf. "But why in heaven's name don't you say so then?" was my father's triumphant and crushing rejoinder.

The letter:

. . . God knows I have to work hard enough to escape, not *propagande*, but getting centered in *propagande*. And America? What the h—l do you a blooming foreigner know about the place. Your *père* only penetrated the edge, and you've never been west of Upper Darby, or the Maunchunk switchback.

Would H., with the swirl of the prairie wind in her underwear, or the Virile Sandburg recognize you, an effete easterner as a REAL American? INCONCEIVABLE!!!!!

My dear boy you have never felt the woop of the PEEraries. You have never seen the projecting and protuberant Mts. of the SIerra Nevada. WOT can you know of the country?

You have the naive credulity of a Co. Clare emigrant. But I *(der grosse Ich)* have the virus, the bacillus of the land in my blood, for nearly three bleating centuries.

(Bloody snob. 'eave a brick at 'im!!!) . . .

I was very glad to see your wholly incoherent unamerican poems in the L.R.

Of course Sandburg will tell you that you miss the "big drifts," and Bodenheim will object to your not being sufficiently decadent.

You thank your bloomin gawd you've got enough Spanish blood to muddy up your mind, and prevent the current American ideation from going through it like a blighted colander.

The thing that saves your work is opacity, and don't forget it. Opacity is NOT an American quality. Fizz, swish, gabble, and verbiage, these are *echt americanisch*.

And alas, alas, poor old Masters. Look at Oct. *Poetry*.

Let me indulge the American habit of quotation:

"Si le cosmopolitisme littéraire gagnait encore et qu'il réussit
à éteindre ce que les différences de race ont allumé de haine de
sang parmi les hommes, j'y verrais un gain pour la civilisation et
pour l'humanité tout entière. . . .

"L'amour excessif d'une patrie a pour immédiat corollaire
l'horreur des patries étrangères. Non seulement on craint de
quitter la jupe de sa maman, d'aller voir comment vivent les
autres hommes, de se mêler à leur luttes, de partager leurs tra-
vaux, non seulement on reste chez soi, mais on finit par fermer
sa porte.

"Cette folie gagne certains littérateurs et le même professeur,
en sortant d'expliquer le Cid ou Don Juan, rédige de gracieuses
injures contre Ibsen et l'influence, hélas, trop illusoire, de son
oeuvre, pourtant toute de lumière et de beauté." et cetera. Lie
down and compose yourself.

I like to think of the Greeks as setting out for the colonies
in Sicily and the Italian peninsula. The Greek temperament
lent itself to a certain symmetrical sculptural phase and to a
fat poetical balance of line that produced important work
but I like better the Greeks setting their backs to Athens.
The ferment was always richer in Rome, the dispersive ex-
plosion was always nearer, the influence carried further and
remained hot longer. Hellenism, especially the modern sort,
is too staid, too chilly, too little fecundative to impregnate
my world.

Hilda Doolittle before she began to write poetry or at
least before she began to show it to anyone would say:
"You're not satisfied with me, are you Billy? There's some-
thing lacking, isn't there?" When I was with her my feet
always seemed to be sticking to the ground while she would
be walking on the tips of the grass stems.

Ten years later as assistant editor of the *Egoist* she refers
to my long poem, "March," which thanks to her own and
her husband's friendly attentions finally appeared there in a
purified form:

14 *Aug.* 1916

Dear Bill:—
I trust you will not hate me for wanting to delete from your
poem all the flippancies. The reason I want to do this is that

the beautiful lines are so very beautiful—so in the tone and spirit of your *Postlude*—(which to me stands, a Nike, supreme among your poems). I think there is *real* beauty—and real beauty is a rare and sacred thing in this generation—in all the pyramid, Ashur-ban-i-pal bits and in the Fiesole and in the wind at the very last.

I don't know what you think but I consider this business of writing a very sacred thing!—I think you have the "spark"—am sure of it, and when you speak *direct* are a poet. I feel in the hey-ding-ding touch running through your poem a derivative tendency which, to me, is not *you*—not your very self. It is as if you were *ashamed* of your Spirit, ashamed of your inspiration!—as if you mocked at your own song. It's very well to *mock* at yourself—it is a spiritual sin to mock at your inspiration—

Hilda

Oh well, all this might be very disquieting were it not that "sacred" has lately been discovered to apply to a point of arrest where stabilization has gone on past the time. There is nothing sacred about literature, it is damned from one end to the other. There is nothing in literature but change and change is mockery. I'll write whatever I damn please, whenever I damn please and as I damn please and it'll be good if the authentic spirit of change is on it.

But in any case H. D. misses the entire intent of what I am doing no matter how just her remarks concerning that particular poem happen to have been. The hey-ding-ding touch *was* derivative, but it filled a gap that I did not know how better to fill at the time. It might be said that that touch is the prototype of the improvisations.

It is to the inventive imagination we look for deliverance from every other misfortune as from the desolation of a flat Hellenic perfection of style. What good then to turn to art from the atavistic religionists, from a science doing slavey service upon gas engines, from a philosophy tangled in a miserable sort of dialect that means nothing if the full power of initiative be denied at the beginning by a lot of baying and snapping scholiasts? If the inventive imagination must look, as I think, to the field of art for its richest discoveries today it will best make its way by compass and follow no path.

But before any material progress can be accomplished there must be someone to draw a discriminating line between true and false values.

The true value is that peculiarity which gives an object a character by itself. The associational or sentimental value is the false. Its imposition is due to lack of imagination, to an easy lateral sliding. The attention has been held too rigid on the one plane instead of following a more flexible, jagged resort. It is to loosen the attention, my attention since I occupy part of the field, that I write these improvisations. Here I clash with Wallace Stevens.

The imagination goes from one thing to another. Given many things of nearly totally divergent natures but possessing one-thousandth part of a quality in common, provided that be new, distinguished, these things belong in an imaginative category and not in a gross natural array. To me this is the gist of the whole matter. It is easy to fall under the spell of a certain mode, especially if it be remote of origin, leaving thus certain of its members essential to a reconstruction of its significance permanently lost in an impenetrable mist of time. But the thing that stands eternally in the way of really good writing is always one: the virtual impossibility of lifting to the imagination those things which lie under the direct scrutiny of the senses, close to the nose. It is this difficulty that sets a value upon all works of art and makes them a necessity. The senses witnessing what is immediately before them in detail see a finality which they cling to in despair, not knowing which way to turn. Thus the so-called natural or scientific array becomes fixed, the walking devil of modern life. He who even nicks the solidity of this apparition does a piece of work superior to that of Hercules when he cleaned the Augean stables.

Stevens' letter applies really to my book of poems, *Al Que Quiere* (which means, by the way, "To Him Who Wants It") but the criticism he makes of that holds good for each of the improvisations if not for the *oeuvre* as a whole.

It begins with a postscript in the upper left hand corner: "I think, after all, I should rather send this than not, although it is quarrelsomely full of my own ideas of discipline."

April 9

My dear Williams:

. . . .

What strikes me most about the poems themselves is their casual character. . . . Personally I have a distaste for miscellany. It is one of the reasons I do not bother about a book myself.

[*Wallace Stevens is a fine gentleman whom Cannell likened to a Pennsylvania Dutchman who has suddenly become aware of his habits and taken to "society" in self-defense. He is always immaculately dressed. I don't know why I should always associate him in my mind with an imaginary image I have of Ford Madox Ford.*]

. . . My idea is that in order to carry a thing to the extreme necessity to convey it one has to stick to it; . . . Given a fixed point of view, realistic, imagistic or what you will, everything adjusts itself to that point of view; and the process of adjustment is a world in flux, as it should be for a poet. But to fidget with points of view leads always to new beginnings and incessant new beginnings lead to sterility.

(This sounds like Sir Roger de Coverley)

A single manner or mood thoroughly matured and exploited is that fresh thing . . . etc.

One has to keep looking for poetry as Renoir looked for colors in old walls, woodwork and so on.

Your place is

—among children

Leaping around a dead dog.

A book of that would feed the hungry . . .

Well a book of poems is a damned serious affair. I am only objecting that a book that contains your particular quality should contain anything else and suggesting that if the quality were carried to a communicable extreme, in intensity and volume, etc. . . . I see it all over the book, in your landscapes and portraits, but dissipated and obscured. Bouquets for brides and Spenserian compliments for poets . . . There are a very few men who have anything native in them or for whose work I'd

give a Bolshevik ruble. . . . But I think your tantrums not half
mad enough.

[*I am not quite clear about the last sentence but I presume he
means that I do not push my advantage through to an over-
whelming decision. What would you have me do with my
Circe, Stevens, now that I have double-crossed her game, marry
her? It is not what Odysseus did.*]

I return Pound's letter . . . observe how in everything he does
he proceeds with the greatest positiveness, etc.

Wallace Stevens

I wish that I might here set down my "Vortex" after the
fashion of London, 1913, stating how little it means to me
whether I live here, there or elsewhere or succeed in this,
that or the other so long as I can keep my mind free from
the trammels of literature, beating down every attack of its
retiarii with my *mirmillones*. But the time is past.

I thought at first to adjoin to each improvisation a more
or less opaque commentary. But the mechanical interference
that would result makes this inadvisable. Instead I have
placed some of them in the preface where without losing
their original intention (see reference numerals at the be-
ginning of each) they relieve the later text and also add
their weight to my present fragmentary argument.

V. No. 2. By the brokenness of his composition the poet
makes himself master of a certain weapon which he could
possess himself of in no other way. The speed of the emo-
tions is sometimes such that thrashing about in a thin exal-
tation or despair many matters are touched but not held,
more often broken by the contact.

II. No. 3. The instability of these improvisations would
seem such that they must inevitably crumble under the at-
tention and become particles of a wind that falters. It would
appear to the unready that the fiber of the thing is a thin
jelly. It would be these same fools who would deny tough
cords to the wind because they cannot split a storm endwise
and wrap it upon spools. The virtue of strength lies not in
the grossness of the fiber but in the fiber itself. Thus a poem
is tough by no quality it borrows from a logical recital of

events nor from the events themselves but solely from that
attenuated power which draws perhaps many broken things
into a dance giving them thus a full being.

It is seldom that anything but the most elementary com-
munications can be exchanged one with another. There are
in reality only two or three reasons generally accepted as
the causes of action. No matter what the motive it will sel-
dom happen that true knowledge of it will be anything
more than vaguely divined by some one person, some half a
person whose intimacy has perhaps been cultivated over the
whole of a lifetime. We live in bags. This is due to the gross
fiber of all action. By action itself almost nothing can be
imparted. The world of action is a world of stones.

XV. No. 1. Bla! Bla! Bla! Heavy talk is talk that waits
upon a deed. Talk is servile that is set to inform. Words
with the bloom on them run before the imagination like the
saeter girls before Peer Gynt. It is talk with the patina of
whim upon it makes action a bootlicker. So nowadays poets
spit upon rhyme and rhetoric.

The stream of things having composed itself into wiry
strands that move in one fixed direction, the poet in desper-
ation turns at right angles and cuts across current with
startling results to his hangdog mood.

XI. No. 2. In France, the country of Rabelais, they
know that the world is not made up entirely of virgins.
They do not deny virtue to the rest because of that. Each
age has its perfections but the praise differs. It is only stupid
when the praise of the gross and the transformed would be
minted in unfit terms such as suit nothing but youth's sweet-
ness and frailty. It is necessary to know that laughter is the
reverse of aspiration. So they laugh well in France, at
Coquelin and the *Petoman*. Their girls, also, thrive upon the
love-making they get, so much so that the world runs to
Paris for that reason.

XII. No. 2B. It is chuckleheaded to desire a way through
every difficulty. Surely one might even communicate with
the dead—and lose his taste for truffles. Because snails are

slimy when alive and because slime is associated (errone-
ously) with filth, the fool is convinced that snails are de-
testable when, as it is proven every day, fried in butter with
chopped parsley upon them, they are delicious. This is both
sides of the question: the slave and the despoiled of his
senses are one. But to weigh a difficulty and to turn it aside
without being wrecked upon a destructive solution bespeaks
an imagination of force sufficient to transcend action. The
difficulty has thus been solved by ascent to a higher plane.
It is energy of the imagination alone that cannot be laid
aside.

Rich as are the gifts of the imagination bitterness of
world's loss is not replaced thereby. On the contrary it is
intensified, resembling thus possession itself. But he who has
no power of the imagination cannot even know the full of
his injury.

VIII. No. 3. Those who permit their senses to be de-
spoiled of the things under their noses by stories of all man-
ner of things removed and unattainable are of frail imagina-
tion. Idiots, it is true nothing is possessed save by dint of
that vigorous conception of its perfections which is the
imagination's special province but neither is anything pos-
sessed which is not extant. A frail imagination, unequal to
the tasks before it, is easily led astray.

IV. No. 2. Although it is a quality of the imagination that
it seeks to place together those things which have a com-
mon relationship, yet the coining of similes is a pastime of
very low order, depending as it does upon a nearly vege-
table coincidence. Much more keen is that power which
discovers in things those inimitable particles of dissimilarity
to all other things which are the peculiar perfections of the
thing in question.

But this loose linking of one thing with another has
effects of a destructive power little to be guessed at: all
manner of things are thrown out of key so that it ap-
proaches the impossible to arrive at an understanding of
anything. All is confusion, yet it comes from a hidden de-

sire for the dance, a lust of the imagination, a will to accord two instruments in a duet.

But one does not attempt by the ingenuity of the joiner to blend the tones of the oboe with the violin. On the contrary the perfections of the two instruments are emphasized by the joiner; no means is neglected to give to each the full color of its perfections. It is only the music of the instruments which is joined and that not by the woodworker but by the composer, by virtue of the imagination.

On this level of the imagination all things and ages meet in fellowship. Thus only can they, peculiar and perfect, find their release. This is the beneficent power of the imagination.

Age and youth are great flatterers. Brooding on each other's obvious psychology neither dares tell the other outright what manifestly is the truth: your world is poison. Each is secure in his own perfections. Monsieur Eichorn used to have a most atrocious body odor while the odor of some girls is a pleasure to the nostril. Each quality in each person or age, rightly valued, would mean the freeing of that age to its own delights of action or repose. Now an evil odor can be pursued with praiseworthy ardor leading to great natural activity whereas a flowery skinned virgin may and no doubt often does allow herself to fall into destructive habits of neglect.

XIII. No. 3. A poet witnessing the chicory flower and realizing its virtues of form and color so constructs his praise of it as to borrow no particle from right or left. He gives his poem over to the flower and its plant themselves, that they may benefit by those cooling winds of the imagination which thus returned upon them will refresh them at their task of saving the world. But what does it mean, remarked his friends?

VII. *Coda*. It would be better than depriving birds of their song to call them all nightingales. So it would be better than to have a world stript of poetry to provide men with some sort of eyeglasses by which they should be unable to read any verse but sonnets. But fortunately although there are many sorts of fools, just as there are many birds which sing and many sorts of poems, there is no need to please them.

All schoolmasters are fools. Thinking to build in the young the foundations of knowledge they let slip their minds that the blocks are of gray mist bedded upon the wind. Those who will taste of the wind himself have a mark in their eyes by virtue of which they bring their masters to nothing.

All things brought under the hand of the possessor crumble to nothingness. Not only that: He who possesses a child if he cling to it inordinately becomes childlike, whereas, with a twist of the imagination, himself may rise into comradeship with the grave and beautiful presences of antiquity. But some have the power to free, say a young matron pursuing her infant, from her own possessions, making her kin to Yang Kuei-fei because of a haunting loveliness that clings about her knees, impeding her progress as she takes up her matronly pursuit.

As to the sun what is he, save for his light, more than the earth is: the same mass of metals, a mere shadow? But the winged dawn is the very essence of the sun's self, a thing cold, vitreous, a virtue that precedes the body which it drags after it.

The features of a landscape take their position in the imagination and are related more to their own kind there than to the country and season which has held them hitherto as a basket holds vegetables mixed with fruit.

VI. No. 1. A fish swimming in a pond, were his back white and his belly green, would be easily perceived from above by hawks against the dark depths of water and from below by larger fish against the penetrant light of the sky. But since his belly is white and his back green he swims about in safety. Observing this barren truth and discerning at once its slavish application to the exercises of the mind, a young man, who has been sitting for some time in contemplation at the edge of a lake, rejects with scorn the parochial deductions of history and as scornfully asserts his defiance.

XIV. No. 3. The barriers which keep the feet from the dance are the same which in a dream paralyze the effort to escape and hold us powerless in the track of some murderous pursuer. Pant and struggle but you cannot move. The birth of the imagination is like waking from a nightmare. Never does the night seem so beneficent.

The raw beauty of ignorance that lies like an opal mist over the west coast of the Atlantic, beginning at the Grand Banks and extending into the recesses of our brains—the children, the married, the unmarried—clings especially about the eyes and the throats of our girls and boys. Of a Sunday afternoon a girl sits before a mechanical piano and, working it with her hands and feet, opens her mouth and sings to the music—a popular tune, ragtime. It is a serenade. I have seen a young Frenchman lean above the piano and looking down speak gently and wonderingly to one of our girls singing such a serenade. She did not seem aware of what she was singing and he smiled an occult but thoroughly bewildered smile—as of a man waiting for a fog to lift, meanwhile lost in admiration of its enveloping beauty—fragments of architecture, a street opening and closing, a mysterious glow of sunshine.

VIII. No. 1. A man of note upon examining the poems of his friend and finding there nothing related to his immediate understanding laughingly remarked: After all, literature is communication while you, my friend, I am afraid, in attempting to do something striking, are in danger of achieving mere preciosity.——But inasmuch as the fields of the mind are vast and little explored, the poet was inclined only to smile and to take note of that hardening infirmity of the imagination which seems to endow its victim with great solidity and rapidity of judgment. But he thought to himself: And yet of what other thing is greatness composed than a power to annihilate half-truths for a thousandth part of accurate understanding. Later life has its perfections as well as that bough-bending time of the mind's florescence with which I am so discursively taken.

I have discovered that the thrill of first love passes! It even becomes the backbone of a sordid sort of religion if not assisted in passing. I knew a man who kept a candle burning before a girl's portrait day and night for a year— then jilted her, pawned her off on a friend. I have been reasonably frank about my erotics with my wife. I have never or seldom said, my dear I love you, when I would rather say: My dear, I wish you were in Tierra del Fuego. I have discovered by scrupulous attention to this detail and by certain allied experiments that we can continue from time to time to elaborate relationships quite equal in quality, if not greatly superior, to that surrounding our wedding. In fact, the best we have enjoyed of love together has come after the most thorough destruction or harvesting of that which has gone before. Periods of barrenness have intervened, periods comparable to the prison music in *Fidelio* or to any of Beethoven's pianissimo transition passages. It is at these times our formal relations have teetered on the edge of a debacle to be followed, as our imaginations have permitted, by a new growth of passionate attachment dissimilar in every member to that which has gone before.

It is in the continual and violent refreshing of the idea that love and good writing have their security.

Alfred Kreymborg is primarily a musician, at best an innovator of musical phrase:

> We have no dishes
> to eat our meals from.
> We have no dishes
> to eat our meals from
> because we have no dishes
> to eat our meals from
>
> . . . .
>
> We need no dishes
> to eat our meals from,
> we have fingers
> to eat our meals from.

Kreymborg's idea of poetry is a transforming music that has much to do with tawdry things.

Few people know how to read Kreymborg. There is no modern poet who suffers more from a bastard sentimental appreciation. It is hard to get his things from the page. I have heard him say he has often thought in despair of marking his verse into measures as music is marked. Oh, well—

The man has a bare irony, the gift of rhythm and *Others*. I smile to think of Alfred stealing the stamps from the envelopes sent for return of mss., to the *Others* office! The best thing that could happen for the good of poetry in the United States today would be for someone to give Alfred Kreymborg a hundred thousand dollars. In his mind there is the determination for freedom brought into relief by a crabbedness of temper that makes him peculiarly able to value what is being done here. Whether he is bull enough for the work I am not certain, but that he can find his way that I know.

A somewhat petulant English college friend of my brother's once remarked that Britons make the best policemen the world has ever witnessed. I agree with him. It is silly to go into a puckersnatch because some brass-button-minded nincompoop in Kensington flies off the handle and speaks openly about our United States prize poems. This Mr. Jepson—"Anyone who has heard Mr. J. read Homer and discourse on Catullus would recognize his fitness as a judge and respecter of poetry"—this is Ezra!—this champion of the right is not half a fool. His epithets and phrases—slipshod, rank bad workmanship of a man who has shirked his job, lumbering fakement, cumbrous artificiality, maundering dribble, rancid as *Ben Hur*—are in the main well-merited. And besides, he comes out with one fairly lipped cornet blast: the only distinctive U. S. contributions to the arts have been ragtime and buck-dancing.

Nothing is good save the new. If a thing have novelty it stands intrinsically beside every other work of artistic excellence. If it have not that, no loveliness or heroic proportion or grand manner will save it. It will not be saved above all by an attenuated intellectuality.

But all U. S. verse is not bad according to Mr. J., there is T. S. Eliot and his "Love Song of J. Alfred Prufrock."

But our prize poems are especially to be damned not because of superficial bad workmanship, but because they are rehash, repetition—just as Eliot's more exquisite work is rehash, repetition in another way of Verlaine, Baudelaire, Maeterlinck—conscious or unconscious—just as there were Pound's early paraphrases from Yeats and his constant later cribbing from the Renaissance, Provence and the modern French: Men content with the connotations of their masters.

It is convenient to have fixed standards of comparison: All antiquity! And there is always some everlasting Polonius of Kensington forever to rate highly his eternal Eliot. It is because Eliot is a subtle conformist. It tickles the palate of this archbishop of procurers to a lecherous antiquity to hold up Prufrock as a New World type. Prufrock, the nibbler at sophistication, endemic in every capital, the not quite (because he refuses to turn his back), is "the soul of that modern land," the United States!

> Blue undershirts,
> Upon a line,
> It is not necessary to say to you
> Anything about it—

I cannot question Eliot's observation. Prufrock is a masterly portrait of the man just below the summit, but the type is universal; the model in his case might be Mr. J.

No. The New World is Montezuma or, since he was stoned to death in a parley, Guatemozin who had the city of Mexico leveled over him before he was taken.

For the rest, there is no man even though he dare who can make beauty his own and "so at last live," at least there is no man better situated for that achievement than another. As Prufrock longed for his silly lady, so Kensington longs for its Hardanger dairymaid. By a mere twist of the imagination, if Prufrock only knew it, the whole world can be inverted (why else are there wars?) and the mermaids be set warbling to whoever will listen to them. Seesaw and blindman's buff converted into a sort of football.

But the summit of United States achievement, according to Mr. J.—who can discourse on Catullus—is that very beautiful poem of Eliot's, "La Figlia che Piange": just the right amount of everything drained through, etc., etc., etc., etc., the rhythm delicately studied and—IT CONFORMS! *ergo*, here we have "the very fine flower of the finest spirit of the United States."

Examined closely this poem reveals a highly refined distillation. Added to the already "faithless" formula of yesterday we have a conscious simplicity:

"Simple and faithless as a smile and shake of the hand."

The perfection of that line is beyond cavil. Yet, in the last stanza, this paradigm, this very fine flower of U.S. art is warped out of alignment, obscured in meaning even to the point of an absolute unintelligibility by the inevitable straining after a rhyme, the very cleverness with which this straining is covered being a sinister token in itself.

"And I wonder how they should have been together!"

So we have no choice but to accept the work of this fumbling conjurer.

Upon the Jepson filet Eliot balances his mushroom. It is the latest touch from the literary cuisine, it adds to the pleasant outlook from the club window. If to do this, if to be a Whistler at best, in the art of poetry, is to reach the height of poetic expression then Ezra and Eliot have approached it and *tant pis* for the rest of us.

The Adobe Indian hag sings her lullaby:

> The beetle is blind
> The beetle is blind
> The beetle is blind
> The beetle is blind, etc., etc.

and Kandinsky in his, *Ueber das Geistige in der Kunst,* sets
down the following axioms for the artist:

> Every artist has to express himself.
> Every artist has to express his epoch.
> Every artist has to express the pure and eternal
> qualities of the art of all men.

So we have the fish and the bait, but the last rule holds
three hooks at once—not for the fish, however.

I do not overlook De Gourmont's plea for a meeting of
the nations, but I do believe that when they meet Paris
will be more than slightly abashed to find parodies of the
middle ages, Dante and *langue d'oc* foisted upon it as the
best in United States poetry. Even Eliot, who is too fine an
artist to allow himself to be exploited by a blockheaded
grammaticaster, turns recently toward "one definite false
note" in his quatrains, which more nearly approach Amer-
ica than ever "La Figlia che Piange" did. Ezra Pound is a
Boscan who has met his Navagiero.

One day Ezra and I were walking down a back lane in
Wyncote. I contended for bread, he for caviar. I became
hot. He, with fine discretion, exclaimed: "Let us drop it.
We will never agree, or come to an agreement." He spoke
then like a Frenchman, which is one who discerns.

Imagine an international congress of poets at Paris or Ver-
sailles, Remy de Gourmont (now dead) presiding, poets all
speaking five languages fluently. Ezra stands up to represent
U. S. verse and De Gourmont sits down smiling. Ezra begins
by reading "La Figlia che Piange." It would be a pretty pas-
time to gather into a mental basket the fruits of that read-
ing from the minds of the ten Frenchmen present; their
impressions of the sort of United States that very fine flower
was picked from. After this Kreymborg might push his
way to the front and read "Jack's House."

E. P. is the best enemy United States verse has. He is
interested, passionately interested—even if he doesn't know
what he is talking about. But of course he does know what

he is talking about. He does not, however, know every-
thing, not by more than half. The accordances of which
Americans have the parts and the colors but not the com-
pletions before them pass beyond the attempts of his
thought. It is a middle-aging blight of the imagination.

I praise those who have the wit and courage, and the
conventionality, to go direct toward their vision of perfec-
tion in an objective world where the signposts are clearly
marked, viz., to London. But confine them in hell for their
paretic assumption that there is no alternative but their own
groove.

Dear fat Stevens, thawing out so beautifully at forty! I
was one day irately damning those who run to London
when Stevens caught me up with his mild: "But where in
the world will you have them run to?"

Nothing that I should write touching poetry would be
complete without Maxwell Bodenheim in it, even had he not
said that the *Improvisations* were "perfect," the best things
I had ever done; for that I place him, Janus, first and last.

Bodenheim pretends to hate most people, including Pound
and Kreymborg, but that he really goes to this trouble I
cannot imagine. He seems rather to me to have the virtue of
self-absorption so fully developed that hate is made im-
possible. Due to this, also, he is an unbelievable physical
stoic. I know of no one who lives so completely in his
pretenses as Bogie does. Having formulated his world nei-
ther toothache nor the misery to which his indolence re-
duces him can make head against the force of his imagina-
tion. Because of this he remains for me a heroic figure,
which, after all, is quite apart from the stuff he writes and
which only concerns him. He is an Isaiah of the butterflies.

Bogie was the young and fairly well acclaimed genius
when he came to New York four years ago. He pretended
to have fallen in Chicago and to have sprained his shoulder.
The joint was done up in a proper Sayre's dressing and
there really looked to be a bona-fide injury. Of course he
couldn't find any work to do with one hand so we all

chipped in. It lasted a month! During that time Bogie spent a week at my house at no small inconvenience to Florence, who had two babies on her hands just then. When he left I expressed my pleasure at having had his company. "Yes," he replied, "I think you have profited by my visit." The statement impressed me by its simple accuracy as well as by the evidence it bore of that fullness of the imagination which had held the man in its tide while we had been together.

Charley Demuth once told me that he did not like the taste of liquor, for which he was thankful, but that he found the effect it had on his mind to be delightful. Of course Li Po is reported to have written his best verse supported in the arms of the Emperor's attendants and with a dancing girl to hold his tablet. He was also a great poet. Wine is merely the latch-string.

The virtue of it all is in an opening of the doors, though some rooms of course will be empty, a break with banality, the continual hardening which habit enforces. There is nothing left in me but the virtue of curiosity, Demuth puts in. The poet should be forever at the ship's prow.

An acrobat seldom learns really a new trick, but he must exercise continually to keep his joints free. When I made this discovery it started rings in my memory that keep following one after the other to this day.

I have placed the following *Improvisations* in groups, somewhat after the A.B.A. formula, that one may support the other, clarifying or enforcing perhaps the other's intention.

The arrangement of the notes, each following its poem and separated from it by a ruled line, is borrowed from a small volume of Metastasio, *Varie Poesie Dell' Abate Pietro Metastasio*, Venice, 1795.

September 1, 1918   —William Carlos Williams

Prologue to City Lights Edition

IN 1920 when the *Kora in Hell* was originally published by The Four Seas Co., of Boston, I was a young man, full of yeast that was soon to flower as the famous outburst of literature and painting marking the early years of the present century. The notorious Armory Show had taken place in 1913, seven years earlier, James Joyce's *Ulysses* was to appear in 1922.

The legend of the Rape of Persephone, or Kora, had been familiar to me from my beginnings and its significance to the pagan world. March had always been my favorite month, the month of the first robin's songs signaling the return of the sun to these latitudes; I existed through the tough winter months of my profession as a physician only for that. So that scribbling in the dark, leaving behind on my desk, often past midnight, the sheets to be filed away later, at the end of a year I had assembled a fairly bulky manuscript.

What to do with it? It would mean nothing to a casual reader. I added notes of explanation, often more dense than the first writing. The whole seemed satisfactory to me when I gathered it together because to explain further what I intended would be tautological, the surface appearance of the whole would please all the ablest I was approaching.

But what was such a form to be called? I was familiar with the typically French prose poem, its pace was not the same as my own compositions. What I had permitted myself could not by any stretch of the imagination be called verse. Nothing to do but put it down as it stood, trusting to the generous spirit of the age to find a place for it. In the same spirit I added the original prologue, omitted in this edition, entirely separated from the rest of the text, which was an intensely private avowal, to give it a public front.

The book as soon as it was printed entered a world which I didn't feel I could betray so that I did not at first want it to be republished. It remained more or less of a secret document for my own wonder and amusement known to few others. Lawrence Ferlinghetti offered to reprint it in the Pocket Poets Series. I'll be glad to see the book again in a cheap form this time in which my friends can make the most of it. The one thing I possibly regret is the absence of Stuart Davis's attractive frontispiece and the dust jacket at which I more than once laughed heartily showing as it did a human ovum surrounded by spermatozoa black and white.

March, 1957   —William Carlos Williams

Kora in Hell: Improvisations

I

1

Fools HAVE big wombs. For the rest?—here is penny-royal if one knows to use it. But time is only another liar, so go along the wall a little further: if blackberries prove bitter there'll be mushrooms, fairy-ring mushrooms, in the grass, sweetest of all fungi.

2

For what it's worth: Jacob Louslinger, white haired, stinking, dirty bearded, cross eyed, stammer tongued, broken voiced, bent backed, ball kneed, cave bellied, mucous faced—deathling,—found lying in the weeds "up there by the cemetery." "Looks to me as if he'd been bumming around the meadows for a couple of weeks." Shoes twisted into incredible lilies: out at the toes, heels, tops, sides, soles. Meadow flower! ha, mallow! at last I have you. (Rot dead marigolds—an acre at a time! Gold, are you?) Ha, clouds will touch world's edge and the great pink mallow stand singly in the wet, topping reeds and—a closet full of clothes and good shoes and my-thirty-year's-master's-daughter's two cows for me to care for and a winter room with a fire in it—. I would rather feed pigs in Moonachie and chew calamus root and break crab's claws at an open fire: age's lust loose!

3

Talk as you will, say: "No woman wants to bother with children in this country";—speak of your Amsterdam and

the whitest aprons and brightest doorknobs in Christendom.
And I'll answer you: Gleaming doorknobs and scrubbed
entries have heard the songs of the housemaids at sun-up
and—housemaids are wishes. Whose? Ha! the dark canals
are whistling, whistling for who will cross to the other
side. If I remain with hands in pocket leaning upon my
lamppost—why—I bring curses to a hag's lips and her
daughter on her arm knows better than I can tell you—best
to blush and out with it than back beaten after.

———————

*In Holland at daybreak, of a fine spring morning, one
sees the housemaids beating rugs before the small houses
of such a city as Amsterdam, sweeping, scrubbing the low
entry steps and polishing doorbells and doorknobs. By night
perhaps there will be an old woman with a girl on her arm,
histing and whistling across a deserted canal to some late
loiterer trudging aimlessly on beneath the gas lamps.*

II

I

Why go further? One might conceivably rectify the
rhythm, study all out and arrive at the perfection of a tiger
lily or a china doorknob. One might lift all out of the ruck,
be a worthy successor to—the man in the moon. Instead
of breaking the back of a willing phrase why not try to
follow the wheel through—approach death at a walk, take
in all the scenery. There's as much reason one way as the
other and then—one never knows—perhaps we'll bring back
Eurydice—this time!

———————

*Between two contending forces there may at all times
arrive that moment when the stress is equal on both sides
so that with a great pushing a great stability results giving*

*a picture of perfect rest. And so it may be that once upon
the way the end drives back upon the beginning and a stop-
page will occur. At such a time the poet shrinks from the
doom that is calling him forgetting the delicate rhythms of
perfect beauty, preferring in his mind the gross buffetings
of good and evil fortune.*

2

Ay dio! I would say so much were it not for the tunes
changing, changing, darting so many ways. One step and
the cart's left you sprawling. Here's the way! and—you're
hip bogged. And there's blame of the light too: when eyes
are humming birds who'll tie them with a lead string? But
it's the tunes they want most,—send them skipping out at
the tree tops. Whistle then! who'd stop the leaves swarm-
ing; curving down the east in their braided jackets? Well
enough—but there's small comfort in naked branches when
the heart's not set that way.

*A man's desire is to win his way to some hilltop. But
against him seem to swarm a hundred jumping devils. These
are his constant companions, these are the friendly images
which he has invented out of his mind and which are in-
viting him to rest and to disport himself according to hidden
reasons. The man being half a poet is cast down and longs
to rid himself of his torment and his tormentors.*

3

When you hang your clothes on the line you do not
expect to see the line broken and them trailing in the mud.
Nor would you expect to keep your hands clean by putting
them in a dirty pocket. However and of course if you are a
market man, fish, cheeses and the like going under your
fingers every minute in the hour you would not leave off

the business and expect to handle a basket of fine laces without at least mopping yourself on a towel, soiled as it may be. Then how will you expect a fine trickle of words to follow you through the intimacies of this dance without— oh, come let us walk together into the air awhile first. One must be watchman to much secret arrogance before his ways are tuned to these measures. You see there is a dip of the ground between us. You think you can leap up from your gross caresses of these creatures and at a gesture fling it all off and step out in silver to my finger tips. Ah, it is not that I do not wait for you, always! But my sweet fellow —you have broken yourself without purpose, you are— Hark! it is the music! Whence does it come? What! Out of the ground? Is it this that you have been preparing for me? Ha, goodbye, I have a rendezvous in the tips of three birch sisters. *Encouragez vos musiciens!* Ask them to play faster. I will return—later. Ah you are kind. —and I? must dance with the wind, make my own snow flakes, whistle a contrapuntal melody to my own fugue! Huzza then, this is the dance of the blue moss bank! Huzza then, this is the mazurka of the hollow log! Huzza then, this is the dance of rain in the cold trees.

III

1

So far away August green as it yet is. They say the sun still comes up o'mornings and it's harvest moon now. Always one leaf at the peak twig swirling, swirling and apples rotting in the ditch.

2

My wife's uncle went to school with Amundsen. After he, Amundsen, returned from the south pole there was a Scandinavian dinner, which bored Amundsen like a boyhood friend. There was a young woman at his table, silent and aloof from the rest. She left early and he   restless at some impalpable delay   apologized suddenly and went off with two friends, his great, lean bulk twitching agilely. One knew why the poles attracted him. Then my wife's mother told me the same old thing, how a girl in their village jilted him   years back. But the girl at the supper! Ah—that comes later when   we are wiser   and older.

3

What can it mean to you that a child wears pretty clothes and speaks three languages or that its mother goes to the best shops? It means: July has good need of his blazing sun. But if you pick one berry from the ash tree I'd not know it again for the same no matter how the rain washed. Make my bed of witchhazel twigs, said the old man, since they bloom on the brink of winter.

There is neither beginning nor end to the imagination but it delights in its own seasons reversing the usual order at will. Of the air of the coldest room it will seem to build the hottest passions. Mozart would dance with his wife, whistling his own tune to keep the cold away and Villon ceased to write upon his Petit Testament only when the ink was frozen. But men in the direst poverty of the imagination buy finery and indulge in extravagant moods in order to piece out their lack with other matter.

IV

I

Mamselle Day, Mamselle Day, come back again! Slip your clothes off! —the jingling of those little shell ornaments   so deftly fastened—! The streets are turning in their covers. They smile with shut eyes. I have been twice to the

moon since supper but she has nothing to tell me. Mam-
selle   come back! I will be wiser this time.

———————

*That which is past is past forever and no power of the
imagination can bring it back again. Yet inasmuch as there
are many lives being lived in the world, by virtue of sadness
and regret we are enabled to partake to some small degree
of those pleasures we have missed or lost but which others
more fortunate than we are in the act of enjoying.*

If one should catch me in this state! —wings would go
at a bargain. Ah but to hold the world in the hand then—
Here's a brutal jumble. And if you move the stones, see the
ants scurry. But it's queen's eggs they take first, tax their
jaws most. Burrow, burrow, burrow! there's sky that way
too   if the pit's deep enough—so the stars tell us.

———————

*It is an obsession of the gifted that by direct onslaught
or by some back road of the intention they will win the
recognition of the world. Cézanne. And inasmuch as some
men have had a bare recognition in their lives the fiction is
continued. But the sad truth is that since the imagination
is nothing, nothing will come of it. Thus those necessary
readjustments of sense which are the everyday affair of the
mind are distorted and intensified in these individuals so
that they frequently believe themselves to be the very
helots of fortune, whereas nothing could be more ridiculous
than to suppose this. However their strength will revive if
it may be and finding a sweetness on the tongue of which
they had no foreknowledge they set to work again with
renewed vigor.*

2

How smoothly the car runs. And these rows of celery,
how they bitter the air—winter's authentic foretaste. Here

among these farms how the year has aged, yet here's last
year and the year before and all years. One might rest here
time without end, watch out his stretch and see no other
bending than spring to autumn, winter to summer and earth
turning into leaves and leaves into earth and—how restful
these long beet rows—the caress of the low clouds—the
river lapping at the reeds. Was it ever so high as this, so
full? How quickly we've come this far. Which way is north
now? North now? why that way I think. Ah there's the
house at last, here's April, but—the blinds are down! It's
all dark here. Scratch a hurried note. Slip it over the sill.
Well, some other time.

How smoothly the car runs. This must be the road. Queer
how a road juts in. How the dark catches among those
trees! How the light clings to the canal! Yes, there's one
table taken, we'll not be alone. This place has possibilities.
Will you bring *her* here? Perhaps—and when we meet on
the stair, shall we speak, say it is some acquaintance—or
pass silent? Well, a jest's a jest but how poor this tea is.
Think of a life in this place, here in these hills by these
truck farms. Whose life? Why there, back of you. If a
woman laughs a little loudly one always thinks that way
of her. But how she bedizens the country-side. Quite an old
world glamour. If it were not for—but one cannot have
everything. What poor tea it was. How cold it's grown.
Cheering, a light is that way among the trees. That
heavy laugh! How it will rattle these branches in six weeks'
time.

3

The frontispiece is her portrait and further on—the
obituary sermon: she held the school upon her shoulders.
Did she. Well—turn in here then:—we found money in
the blood and some in the room and on the stairs. My God
I never knew a man had so much blood in his head! —and
thirteen empty whisky bottles. I am sorry but those who

come this way meet strange company. This is you see death's canticle.

———————

A young woman who had excelled at intellectual pursuits, a person of great power in her sphere, died on the same night that a man was murdered in the next street, a fellow of very gross behavior. The poet takes advantage of this to send them on their way side by side without making the usual unhappy moral distinctions.

V

I

Beautiful white corpse of night actually! So the northwest winds of death are mountain sweet after all! All the troubled stars are put to bed now: three bullets from wife's hand none kindlier: in the crown, in the nape and one lower: three starlike holes among a million pocky pores and the moon of your mouth: Venus, Jupiter, Mars, and all stars melted forthwith into this one good white light over the inquest table,—the traditional moth beating its wings against it—except there are two here. But sweetest are the caresses of the county physician, a little clumsy perhaps—*mais*—! and the Prosecuting Attorney, Peter Valuzzi and the others, waving green arms of maples to the tinkling of the earliest ragpicker's bells. Otherwise—: kindly stupid hands, kindly coarse voices, infinitely soothing, infinitely detached, infinitely beside the question, restfully babbling of how, where, why and night is done and the green edge of yesterday has said all it could.

———————

Remorse is a virtue in that it is a stirrer up of the emotions but it is a folly to accept it as a criticism of conduct. So to accept it is to attempt to fit the emotions of a certain

*state to a preceding state to which they are in no way re-
lated. Imagination though it cannot wipe out the sting of
remorse can instruct the mind in its proper uses.*

2

It is the water we drink. It bubbles under every hill.
How? Agh, you stop short of the root. Why, caught and
the town goes mad. The haggard husband pirouettes in
tights. The wolf-lean wife is rolling butter pats: it's a clock
striking the hour. Pshaw, they do things better in Bangkok,
—here too, if there's heads together. But up and leap at
her throat! Bed's at fault! Yet—I've seen three women pros-
trate, hands twisted in each other's hair, teeth buried where
the hold offered,—not a movement, not a cry more than
a low meowling. Oh call me a lady and think you've caged
me. Hell's loose every minute, you hear? And the truth is
there's not an eye clapped to either way but someone
comes off the dirtier for it. Who am I to wash hands and
stand near the wall? I confess freely there's not a bitch
littered in the pound but my skin grows ruddier. Ask me
and I'll say: curfew for the ladies. Bah, two in the grass
is the answer to that gesture. Here's a text for you: Many
daughters have done virtuously but thou excellest them
all! And so you do, if the manner of a walk means anything.
You walk in a different air from the others,—though your
husband's the better man and the charm won't last a fort-
night: the street's kiss parried again. But give thought to
your daughters' food at mating time, you good men. Send
them to hunt spring beauties beneath the sod this winter,—
otherwise: hats off to the lady! One can afford to smile.

3

Marry in middle life and take the young thing home.
Later in the year let the worst out. It's odd how little the
tune changes. Do worse—till your mind's turning, then

rush into repentance and the lady grown a hero while the clock strikes.

Here the harps have a short cadenza. It's sunset back of the new cathedral and the purple river scum has set seaward. The car's at the door. I'd not like to go alone tonight. I'll pay you well. It's the king's-evil. Speed! Speed! The sun's self's a chancre low in the west. Ha, how the great houses shine—for old time's sake! For sale! For sale! The town's gone another way. But I'm not fooled that easily. *Fort sale! Fort sale!* if you read it aright. And Beauty's own head on the pillow, *à la Maja Desnuda! O Duquesa de Alba! Duquesa de Alba!* Never was there such a lewd wonder in the streets of Newark! Open the windows—but all's boarded up here. Out with you, you sleepy doctors and lawyers you,—the sky's afire and Calvary Church with its snail's horns up, sniffing the dawn—o' the wrong side! Let the trumpets blare! *Tutti i instrumenti!* The world's bound homeward.

A man whose brain is slowly curdling due to a syphilitic infection acquired in early life calls on a friend to go with him on a journey to the city. The friend out of compassion goes, and, thinking of the condition of his unhappy companion, falls to pondering on the sights he sees as he is driven up one street and down another. It being evening he witnesses a dawn of great beauty striking backward upon the world in a reverse direction to the sun's course and not knowing of what else to think discovers it to be the same power which has led his companion to destruction. At this he is inclined to scoff derisively at the city's prone stupidity and to make light indeed of his friend's misfortune.

VI

1

Of course history is an attempt to make the past seem stable and of course it's all a lie. Nero must mean Nero or the game's up. But—though killies have green backs and white bellies, *zut!* for the bass and hawks! When we're tired of swimming we'll go climb in the ledgy forest. Confute the sages.

2

Quarrel with a purple hanging because it's no column from the Parthenon. Here's splotchy velvet set to hide a door in the wall and there—there's the man himself praying! Oh quarrel whether 'twas Pope Clement raped Persephone or—did the devil wear a mitre in that year? Come, there's much use in being thin on a windy day if the cloth's cut well. And oak leaves will not come on maples, nor birch trees either—that is provided—, but pass it over, pass it over.

———————

A woman of good figure, if she be young and gay, welcomes the wind that presses tight upon her from forehead to ankles revealing the impatient mountains and valleys of her secret desire. The wind brings release to her. But the wind is no blessing to all women. At the same time it is idle to quarrel over the relative merits of one thing and another, oak leaves will not come on maples. But there is a deeper folly yet in such quarreling: the perfections revealed by a Rembrandt are equal whether it be question of a laughing Saskia or an old woman cleaning her nails.

3

Think of some lady better than Rackham draws them: mere fairy stuff—some face that would be your face, were you of the right sex, some twenty years back of a still morning, some Lucretia out of the Vatican turned Carmelite, some double image cast over a Titian Venus by two eyes quicker than Titian's hands were, some strange daughter of an inn-keeper,—some . . . Call it a net to catch love's twin doves and I'll say the sky's blue. Whisk the thing away now? What's the sky now?

By virtue of works of art the beauty of woman is released to flow whither it will up and down the years. The imagination transcends the thing itself. Kaffirs admire what they term beauty in their women but which is in official parlance a deformity. A Kaffir poet to be a good poet would praise that which is to him praiseworthy and we should be scandalized.

VII

I

It is still warm enough to slip from the weeds into the lake's edge, your clothes blushing in the grass and three small boys grinning behind the derelict hearth's side. But summer is up among the huckleberries near the path's end and snakes' eggs lie curling in the sun on the lonely summit. But—well—let's wish it were higher after all these years staring at it deplore the paunched clouds glimpse the sky's thin counter-crest and plunge into the gulch. Sticky cobwebs tell of feverish midnights. Crack a rock (what's a thousand years!) and send it crashing among the oaks! Wind a pine tree in a grey-worm's net and play it for a trout; oh—but it's the moon does that! No, summer has

gone down the other side of the mountain. Carry home
what we can. What have you brought off? Ah here are
thimbleberries.

———————

*In middle life the mind passes to a variegated October.
This is the time youth in its faulty aspirations has set for
the achievement of great summits. But having attained the
mountain top one is not snatched into a cloud but the
descent proffers its blandishments quite as a matter of
course. At this the fellow is cast into a great confusion and
rather plaintively looks about to see if any has fared better
than he.*

2

The little Polish Father of Kingsland does not under-
stand, he cannot understand. These are exquisite differences
never to be resolved. He comes at midnight through mid-
winter slush to baptize a dying newborn; he smiles suavely
and shrugs his shoulders: a clear middle A touched by a
master—but he cannot understand. And Benny, Sharon,
Henrietta, and Josephine, what is it to them? Yet jointly
they come more into the way of the music. And white
haired Miss Ball! The empty school is humming to her
little melody played with one finger at the noon hour but it
is beyond them all. There is much heavy breathing, many
tight shut lips, a smothered laugh whiles, two laughs crack-
ing together, three together sometimes and then a burst of
wind lifting the dust again.

———————

*Living with and upon and among the poor, those that
gather in a few rooms, sometimes very clean, sometimes
full of vermin, there are certain pestilential individuals,
priests, school teachers, doctors, commercial agents of one
sort or another who though they themselves are full of
graceful perfections, nevertheless contrive to be so com-*

*placent of their lot, floating as they are with the depth of a
sea beneath them, as to be worthy only of amused con-
tempt. Yet even to these sometimes there rises that which
they think in their ignorance is a confused babble of aspir-
ing voices not knowing what ancient harmonies these are
to which they are so faultily listening.*

3

What I like best's the long unbroken line of the hills
there. Yes, it's a good view. Come, let's visit the orchard.
Here's peaches twenty years on the branch. Not ripe yet!?
Why—! Those hills! Those hills! But you'd be young
again! Well, fourteen's a hard year for boy or girl, let
alone one older driving the pricks in, but though there's
more in a song than the notes of it and a smile's a pretty
baby when you've none other—let's not turn backward.
Mumble the words, you understand, call them four brothers,
strain to catch the sense but have to admit it's in a language
they've not taught you, a flaw somewhere,—and for an-
swer: well, that long unbroken line of the hills there.

——————

*Two people, an old man and a woman in early middle
life, are talking together upon a small farm at which the
woman has just arrived on a visit. They have walked to
an orchard on the slope of a hill from which a distant range
of mountains can be clearly made out. A third man, piecing
together certain knowledge he has of the woman with
what is being said before him is prompted to give rein to
his imagination. This he does and hears many oblique sen-
tences which escape the others.*

Coda

Squalor and filth with a sweet cur nestling in the grimy
blankets of your bed and on better roads striplings dream-

ing of wealth and happiness. Country life in America! The cackling grackle that dartled at the hill's bottom have joined their flock and swing with the rest over a broken roof toward Dixie.

VIII

I

Some fifteen years we'll say I served this friend, was his valet, nurse, physician, fool and master: nothing too menial, to say the least. Enough of that: so.

Stand aside while they pass. This is what they found in the rock when it was cracked open: this fingernail. Hide your face among the lower leaves, here's a meeting should have led to better things but—it is only one branch out of the forest and night pressing you for an answer! Velvet night weighing upon your eye-balls with gentle insistence; calling you away: Come with me, now, tonight! Come with me! now tonight . . .

———————

In great dudgeon over the small profit that has come to him through a certain companionship a poet addresses himself and the loved one as if it were two strangers, thus advancing himself to the brink of that discovery which will reward all his labors but which he as yet only discerns as a night, a dark void coaxing him whither he has no knowledge.

2

You speak of the enormity of her disease, of her poverty. Bah, these are the fiddle she makes tunes on and it's tunes bring the world dancing to your house-door, even on this swamp side. You speak of the helpless waiting, waiting till the thing squeeze her windpipe shut. Oh, that's best

of all, that's romance—with the devil himself a hero. No
my boy. You speak of her man's callous stinginess. Yes, my
God, how can he refuse to buy milk when it's alone milk
that she can swallow now? But how is it she picks market
beans for him day in, day out, in the sun, in the frost? You
understand? You speak of so many things, you blame me
for my indifference. Well, this is you see my sister and
death, great death is robbing her of life. It dwarfs most
things.

------

*Filth and vermin though they shock the over-nice are
imperfections of the flesh closely related in the just imagi-
nation of the poet to excessive cleanliness. After some years
of varied experience with the bodies of the rich and the
poor a man finds little to distinguish between them, bulks
them as one and bases his working judgments on other
matters.*

3

Hercules is in Hacketstown doing farm labor. Look at
his hands if you'll not believe me. And what do I care if
yellow and red are Spain's riches and Spain's good blood.
Here yellow and red mean simply autumn! The odor of
the poor farmer's fried supper is mixing with the smell
of the hemlocks, mist is in the valley hugging the ground
and over Parsippany—where an oldish man leans talking
to a young woman—the moon is swinging from its star.

IX

1

Throw that flower in the waste basket, it's faded. And
keep an eye to your shoes and fingernails. The fool you
once laughed at has made a fortune! There's small help in
a clutter of leaves either, no matter how they gleam.

Punctilio's the thing. A nobby vest. Spats. Lamps carry far, believe me, in lieu of sunshine!

Despite vastness of frontiers, which are as it were the fringes of a flower full of honey, it is the little things that count! Neglect them and bitterness drowns the imagination.

2

The time never was when he could play more than mattress to the pretty feet of this woman who had been twice a mother without touching the meager pollen of their marriage intimacy. What more for him than to be a dandelion that could chirp with crickets or do a onestep with snow flakes? The tune is difficult but not impossible to the middle aged whose knees are tethered faster to the mind than they are at eighteen when any wind sets them clacking. What a rhythm's here! One would say the body lay asleep and the dance escaped from the hair tips, the bleached fuzz that covers back and belly, shoulders, neck and forehead. The dance is diamantine over the sleeper who seems not to breathe! One would say heat over the end of a roadway that turns down hill. ¡Cesa!

One may write music and music but who will dance to it? The dance escapes but the music, the music—projects a dance over itself which the feet follow lazily if at all. So a dance is a thing in itself. It is the music that dances but if there are words then there are two dancers, the words pirouetting with the music.

3

One has emotions about the strangest things: men—women himself the most contemptible. But to struggle with

ants for a piece of meat,—a mangy cur to swallow beetles
and all—better go slaughter one's own kind in the name of
peace—except when the body's not there maggots swarm
in the corruption. Oh let him have it. Find a cleaner fare for
wife and child. To the sick their sick. For us heads bowed
over the green-flowered asphodel. Lean on my shoulder
little one, you too. I will lead you to fields you know
nothing of. There's small dancing left for us any way you
look at it.

———————

*A man who enjoyed his food, the company of his chil-
dren and especially his wife's alternate caresses and tongue
lashings felt his position in the town growing insecure due
to a successful business competitor. Being thus stung to the
quick he thinks magnanimously of his own methods of deal-
ing with his customers and likens his competitor to a dog
that swallows his meat with beetles or maggots upon it,
that is, any way so he gets it.*

*Being thus roused the man does not seek to outdo his
rival but grows heavily sad and thinks of death and his lost
pleasures thus showing himself to be a person of discern-
ment. For by so doing he gives evidence of a bastard sort
of knowledge of that diversity of context in things and
situations which the great masters of antiquity looked to for
the inspiration and distinction of their compositions.*

X

I

If I could clap this in a cage and let that out we'd see
colored wings then to blind the sun but—the good ships
are anchored up-stream and the gorged seagulls flap heavily.
At sea! At sea! That's where the waves beat kindliest. But
no, singers are beggars or worse cannot man a ship songs

are their trade. Ku-whee! Ku-whee! It's a wind in the look-out's nest talking of Columbus, whom no sea daunted, Columbus, chained below decks, bound homeward.

They built a replica of Columbus's flagship the Santa Maria and took it from harbor to harbor along the North Atlantic seaboard. The insignificance of that shell could hardly be exaggerated when comparison was made with even the very least of our present day sea-going vessels. Thus was the magnificence of enterprise and the hardihood of one Christopher Columbus celebrated at this late date.

2

You would learn—if you knew even one city—where people are a little gathered together and where one sees—it's our frontier you know—the common changes of the human spirit: our husbands tire of us and we—let us not say we go hungry for their caresses but for caresses—of a kind. Oh I am no prophet. I have no theory to advance, except that it's well nigh impossible to know the wish till after. Cross the room to him if the whim leads that way. Here's drink of an eye that calls you. No need to take the thing too seriously. It's something of a will-o'-the-wisp I acknowledge. All in the pressure of an arm—through a fur coat often. Something of a dancing light with the rain beating on a cab window. Here's nothing to lead you astray. What? Why you're young still. Your children? Yes, there they are. Desire skates like a Hollander as well as runs pickaninny fashion. Really, there's little more to say than: flowers in a glass basket under the electric glare; the carpet is red, mostly, a hodge-podge of zig-zags that pass for Persian fancies. Risk a *double entendre*. But of a sudden the room's not the same! It's a strange blood sings under some skin. Who will have the sense for it? The men sniff suspiciously;

you at least my dear had your head about you. It was a
tender nibble but it really did you credit. But think of what
might be! It's all in the imagination. I give you no more
credit than you deserve, you will never rise to it, never be
more than a rose dropped in the river—but acknowledge
that there is, ah there is a— You are such a clever knitter.
Your hands please. Ah, if I had your hands.

---

*A woman of marked discernment finding herself among
strange companions wishes for the hands of one of them and
inasmuch as she feels herself refreshed by the sight of these
perfections she offers in return those perfections of her
own which appear to her to be most appropriate to the
occasion.*

3

Truth's a wonder. What difference is it how the best
head we have greets his first born these days? What weight
has it that the bravest hair of all's gone waiting on cheap
tables or the most garrulous lives lonely by a bad neighbor
and has her south windows pestered with caterpillars? The
nights are long for lice combing or moon dodging—and the
net comes in empty again. Or there's been no fish in this
fiord since Christian was a baby. Yet up surges the good
zest and the game's on. Follow at my heels, there's little to
tell you you'd think a stoopsworth. You'd pick the same
faces in a crowd no matter what I'd say. And you'd be
right too. The path's not yours till you've gone it alone a
time. But here's another handful of west wind. White of
the night! White of the night. Turn back till I tell you a
puzzle: What is it in the stilled face of an old menderman
and winter not far off and a darky parts his wool, and
wenches wear of a Sunday? It's a sparrow with a crumb in
his beak dodging wheels and clouds crossing two ways.

Virtue is not to be packed in a bag and carried off to the rag mill. Perversions are righted and the upright are reversed, then the stream takes a bend upon itself and the meaning turns a livid purple and drops down in a whirlpool without so much as fraying a single fibre.

XI

I

Why pretend to remember the weather two years back? Why not? Listen close then repeat after others what they have just said and win a reputation for vivacity. Oh feed upon petals of edelweiss! one dew drop, if it be from the right flower, is five years' drink!

Having once taken the plunge the situation that preceded it becomes obsolete which a moment before was alive with malignant rigidities.

2

When beldams dig clams their fat hams (it's always beldams) balanced near Tellus's hide, this rhinoceros pelt, these lumped stones—buffoonery of midges on a bull's thigh—invoke,—what you will: birth's glut, awe at God's craft, youth's poverty, evolution of a child's caper, man's poor inconsequence. Eclipse of all things; sun's self turned hen's rump.

Cross a knife and fork and listen to the church bells! It is the harvest moon's made wine of our blood. Up over the dark factory into the blue glare start the young poplars. They whisper: It is Sunday! It is Sunday! But the laws of the country have been stripped bare of leaves. Out over the marshes flickers our laughter. A lewd anecdote's the chase. On through the vapory heather! And there at banter's edge the city looks at us sidelong with great eyes—lifts to its lips heavenly milk! Lucina, O Lucina! beneficent cow, how have we offended thee?

Hilariously happy because of some obscure wine of the fancy which they have drunk four rollicking companions take delight in the thought that they have thus evaded the stringent laws of the county. Seeing the distant city bathed in moonlight and staring seriously at them they liken the moon to a cow and its light to milk.

XII

I

The browned trees are singing for my thirty-fourth birthday. Leaves are beginning to fall upon the long grass. Their cold perfume raises the anticipation of sensational revolutions in my unsettled life. Violence has begotten peace, peace has fluttered away in agitation. A bewildered change has turned among the roots and the Prince's kiss as far at sea as ever.

To each age as to each person its perfections. But in these things there is a kind of revolutionary sequence. So that a man having lain at ease here and advanced there as time progresses the order of these things becomes inverted. Thinking to have brought all to one level the man finds his foot striking through where he had thought rock to be and stands firm where he had experienced only a bog hitherto. At a loss to free himself from bewilderment at this discovery he puts off the caress of the imagination.

2

The trick is never to touch the world anywhere. Leave yourself at the door, walk in, admire the pictures, talk a few words with the master of the house, question his wife a little, rejoin yourself at the door—and go off arm in arm listening to last week's symphony played by angel hornsmen from the benches of a turned cloud. Or if dogs rub too close and the poor are too much out let your friend answer them.

The poet being sad at the misery he has beheld that morning and seeing several laughing fellows approaching puts himself in their way in order to hear what they are saying. Gathering from their remarks that it is of some sharp business by which they have all made an inordinate profit, he allows his thoughts to play back upon the current of his own life. And imagining himself to be two persons he eases his mind by putting his burdens upon one while the other takes what pleasure there is before him.

Something to grow used to; a stone too big for ox haul, too near for blasting. Take the road round it or—scrape away, scrape away: a mountain's buried in the dirt! Marry a gopher to help you! Drive her in! Go yourself down along the lit pastures. Down, down. The whole family take shovels, babies and all! Down, down! Here's Tenochtitlán! here's a strange Darien where worms are princes.

3

But for broken feet beating, beating on worn flagstones I would have danced to my knees at the fiddle's first run. But here's evening and there they scamper back of the world chasing the sun round! And it's daybreak in Calcutta! So lay aside, let's draw off from the town and look back awhile. See, there it rises out of the swamp and the mists already blowing their sleepy bagpipes.

———————

Often a poem will have merit because of some one line or even one meritorious word. So it hangs heavily on its stem but still secure, the tree unwilling to release it.

XIII

1

Their half sophisticated faces gripe me in the belly. There's no business to be done with them either way. They're neither virtuous nor the other thing, between which exist no perfections. Oh, the mothers will explain that they are good girls. But these never guess that there's more sense in a sentence heard backward than forward most times. A country whose flowers are without perfume and whose girls lack modesty—the saying goes—. Dig deeper *mon ami*, the rock maidens are running naked in the dark cellars.

———————

In disgust at the spectacle of an excess of ripe flesh that, in accordance with the local custom of the place he is in, will be left to wither without ever achieving its full enjoyment, a young man of the place consoles himself with a vision of perfect beauty.

2

I'll not get it no matter how I try. Say it was a girl in black I held open a street door for. Let it go at that. I saw a man an hour earlier I liked better much better. But it's not so easy to pass over. Perfection's not a thing you'll let slip so easily. What a body. The little flattened buttocks;

the quiver of the flesh under the smooth fabric! Agh, it isn't that I want to go to bed with you. In fact what is there to say? except the mind's a queer nereid sometimes and flesh is at least as good a gauze as words are: something of that. Something of mine—yours—hearts on sleeves? Ah *zut* what's the use? It's not that I've lost her again either. It's hard to tell loss from gain anyway.

3

The words of the thing twang and twitter to the gentle rocking of a high-laced boot and the silk above that. The trick of the dance is in following now the words, *allegro*, now the contrary beat of the glossy leg: Reaching far over as if—But always she draws back and comes down upon the word flatfooted. For a moment we—but the boot's costly and the play's not mine. The pace leads off anew. Again the words break it and we both come down flatfooted. Then—near the knee, jumps to the eyes, catching in the hair's shadow. But the lips take the rhythm again and again we come down flatfooted. By this time boredom takes a hand and the play's ended.

XIV

1

The brutal Lord of All will rip us from each other— leave the one to suffer here alone. No need belief in god or hell to postulate that much. The dance: hands touching, leaves touching—eyes looking, clouds rising—lips touching, cheeks touching, arm about . . . Sleep. Heavy head, heavy arm, heavy dream—: Of Ymir's flesh the earth was made and of his thoughts were all the gloomy clouds created. Oya!

Out of bitterness itself the clear wine of the imagination will be pressed and the dance prosper thereby.

2

To you! whoever you are, wherever you are! (But I know where you are!) There's Dürer's "Nemesis" naked on her sphere over the little town by the river—except she's too old. There's a dancing burgess by Tenier and Villon's *maîtresse*—after he'd gone bald and was skin pocked and toothless: she that had him ducked in the sewage drain. Then there's that miller's daughter of "buttocks broad and breastes high." Something of Nietzsche, something of the good Samaritan, something of the devil himself,—can cut a caper of a fashion, my fashion! Hey you, the dance! Squat. Leap. Hips to the left. Chin—ha!— sideways! Stand up, stand up *ma bonne!* you'll break my backbone. So again!—and so forth till we're sweat soaked.

———————

Some fools once were listening to a poet reading his poem. It so happened that the words of the thing spoke of gross matters of the everyday world such as are never much hidden from a quick eye. Out of these semblances, and borrowing certain members from fitting masterpieces of antiquity, the poet began piping up his music, simple fellow, thinking to please his listeners. But they getting the whole matter sadly muddled in their minds made such a confused business of listening that not only were they not pleased at the poet's exertions but no sooner had he done than they burst out against him with violent imprecations.

3

It's all one. Richard worked years to conquer the descending cadence, idiotic sentimentalist. Ha, for happiness!

is he being sarcastic or not?

This tore the dress in ribbons from her maid's back and not spared the nails either; wild anger spit from her pinched eyes! This is the better part. Or a child under a table to be dragged out coughing and biting, eyes glittering evilly. I'll have it my way! Nothing is any pleasure but misery and brokenness. THIS is the only up-cadence. This is where the secret rolls over and opens its eyes. Bitter words spoken to a child ripple in morning light! Boredom from a bed-room doorway thrills with anticipation! The complaints of an old man dying piecemeal are starling chirrups. Coughs go singing on springtime paths across a field; corruption picks strawberries and slow warping of the mind, blacking the deadly walls—counted and recounted—rolls in the grass and shouts ecstatically. All is solved! The moaning and dull sobbing of infants sets blood tingling and eyes ablaze to listen. Speed sings in the heels at long nights tossing on coarse sheets with burning sockets staring into the black. Dance! Sing! Coil and uncoil! Whip yourselves about! Shout the deliverance! An old woman has infected her blossomy grand-daughter with a blood illness that every two weeks drives the mother into hidden songs of agony, the pad-footed mirage of creeping death for music. The face muscles keep pace. Then a darting about the compass in a tarantelle that wears flesh from bones. Here is dancing! The mind in tatters. And so the music wistfully takes the lead. *Ay de mí, Juana la Loca, reina de España, esa está tu canta, reina mía!*

XV

I

'N! cha! cha! cha! destiny needs men, so make up your mind. Here's an oak filling the wind's space. Out with him!

By carefully prepared stages come down through the vulgarities of a cupiscent girlhood to the barren distinction of this cold six A.M. Her pretty, pinched face is a very simple tune but it carries now a certain quasi-maidenly distinction. It's not at least what you'd have heard six years back when she was really virgin.

Often when the descent seems well marked there will be a subtle ascent over-ruling it so that in the end when the degradation is fully anticipated the person will be found to have emerged upon a hilltop.

2

Such an old sinner knows the lit-edged clouds. No spring days like those that come in October. Strindberg had the eyes for Swan White! So make my bed with yours, tomorrow . . . ? Tomorrow . . . the hospital.

Seeing his life at an end a miserable fellow, much accustomed to evil, wishes for the companionship of youth and beauty before he dies and in exchange thinks to proffer that praise which due to the kind of life he has led he is most able to give.

3

Here's a new sort of April clouds: whiffs of dry snow on the polished roadway that, curled by the wind, lie in feathery figures. Oh but April's not to be hedged that simply. She was a Scotch lady and made her own butter and they grew their own rye. It was the finest bread I ever tasted. And how we used to jump in the hay! When he lost his money she kept a boarding house . . . But this is nothing to the story that should have been written could he have had time to jot it all down: of how Bertha's lips

are turned and her calf also and how she weighs 118
pounds. Do I think that is much? Hagh! And her other
perfections. Ruin the girl? Oh there are fifty niceties that—
being virtuous, oh glacially virtuous—one might consider,
i.e. whose touch is the less venomous and by virtue of what
sanction? Love, my good friends, has never held sway in
more than a heart or two here and there since—? All
beauty stands upon the edge of the deflowering. I confess I
wish my wife younger. This is the lewdest thought possible:
it makes mockery of the spirit, say you? Solitary poet who
speaks his mind and has not one fellow in a virtuous world!
I wish for youth! I wish for love—! I see well what passes
in the street and much that passes in the mind. You'll say
this has nothing in it of chastity. Ah well, chastity is a lily
of the valley that only a fool would mock. There is no
whiter nor no sweeter flower—but once past, the rankest
stink comes from the soothest petals. Heigh-ya! A crib from
our mediæval friend Shakespeare.

---

*That which is heard from the lips of those to whom we
are talking in our day's-affairs mingles with what we see
in the streets and everywhere about us as it mingles also
with our imaginations. By this chemistry is fabricated a
language of the day which shifts and reveals its meaning as
clouds shift and turn in the sky and sometimes send down
rain or snow or hail. This is the language to which few ears
are tuned so that it is said by poets that few men are ever
in their full senses since they have no way to use their
imaginations. Thus to say that a man has no imagination is
to say nearly that he is blind or deaf. But of old poets would
translate this hidden language into a kind of replica of the
speech of the world with certain distinctions of rhyme and
meter to show that it was not really that speech. Nowadays
the elements of that language are set down as heard and the
imagination of the listener and of the poet are left free to
mingle in the dance.*

XVI

I

Per le pillole d'Ercole! I should write a happy poem to-
night. It would have to do with a bare, upstanding fellow
whose thighs bulge with a zest for—say, a zest! He tries his
arm. Flings a stone over the river. Scratches his bare back.
Twirls his beard, laughs softly and stretches up his arms in
a yawn. —stops in the midst—looking! A white flash over
against the oak stems! Draws in his belly. Looks again. In
three motions is near the stream's middle, swinging for-
ward, hugh, hugh, hugh, hugh, blinking his eyes against the
lapping wavelets! Out! and the sting of the thicket!

---

*The poet transforms himself into a satyr and goes in
pursuit of a white skinned dryad. The gaiety of his mood
full of lustihood, even so, turns back with a mocking jibe.*

2

Giants in the dirt. The gods, the Greek gods, smothered
in filth and ignorance. The race is scattered over the world.
Where is its home? Find it if you've the genius. Here
Hebe with a sick jaw and a cruel husband,—her mother left
no place for a brain to grow. Herakles rowing boats on
Berry's Creek! Zeus is a country doctor without a taste for
coin jingling. Supper is of a bastard nectar on rare nights
for they will come—the rare nights! The ground lifts and
out sally the heroes of Sophokles, of Æschylus. They go
seeping down into our hearts, they rain upon us and in the
bog they sink again down through the white roots, down—
to a saloon back of the rail-road switch where they have
that girl, you know, the one that should have been Venus

by the lust that's in her. They've got her down there among
the railroad men. A crusade couldn't rescue her. Up to jail
—or call it down to Limbo—the Chief of Police our Pluto.
It's all of the gods, there's nothing else worth writing of.
They are the same men they always were—but fallen. Do
they dance now, they that danced beside Helicon? They
dance much as they did then, only, few have an eye for it,
through the dirt and fumes.

---

*When they came to question the girl before the local
judge it was discovered that there were seventeen men
more or less involved so that there was nothing to do but
to declare the child a common bastard and send the girl
about her business. Her mother took her in and after the
brat died of pneumonia a year later she called in the police
one day. An officer opened the bedroom door. The girl was
in bed with an eighteenth fellow, a young roaming loafer
with a silly grin to his face. They forced a marriage which
relieved the mother of her burden. The girl was weak
minded so that it was only with the greatest difficulty that
she could cover her moves, in fact she never could do so
with success.*

3

Homer sat in a butcher's shop one rainy night and
smelt fresh meat near him so he moved to the open window.
It is infinitely important that I do what I well please in the
world. What you please is that I please what you please
but what I please is well rid of you before I turn off from
the path into the field. What I am, why that they made me.
What I do, why that I choose for myself. Reading shows,
you say. Yes, reading shows reading. What you read is
what they think and what they think is twenty years old or
twenty thousand and it's all one to the little girl in the
pissoir. Likewise to me. But the butcher was a friendly

fellow so he took the carcass outside thinking Homer to be no more than any other beggar.

A man's carcass has no more distinction than the carcass of an ox.

XVII

I

Little round moon up there—wait awhile—do not walk so quickly. I could sing you a song—: Wine clear the sky is and the stars no bigger than sparks! Wait for me and next winter we'll build a fire and shake up twists of sparks out of it and you shall see yourself in the ashes, young—as you were one time.

It has always been the fashion to talk about the moon.

2

This that I have struggled against is the very thing I should have chosen—but all's right now. They said I could not put the flower back into the stem nor win roses upon dead briars and I like a fool believed them. But all's right now. Weave away, dead fingers, the darkies are dancing in Mayaguez—all but one with the sore heel and sugar cane will soon be high enough to romp through. Haia! leading over the ditches, with your skirts flying and the devil in the wind back of you—no one else. Weave away and the bitter tongue of an old woman is eating, eating, eating venomous words with thirty years' mould on them and all shall be eaten back to honeymoon's end. Weave and pangs of agony and pangs of loneliness are beaten backward into the love kiss, weave and kiss recedes into kiss and kisses into looks and looks into the heart's dark—and over again and over again and time's pushed ahead in spite of all that. The petals that fell bearing me under are lifted one by one. That which kissed my flesh for priest's lace so that I could not touch it—weave and you have lifted it   and I am glimpsing light chinks among the notes! Backward, and my hair is crisp with purple sap and the last crust's broken.

A woman on the verge of growing old kindles in the mind of her son a certain curiosity which spinning upon itself catches the woman herself in its wheel, stripping from her the accumulations of many harsh years and shows her at last full of an old time suppleness hardly to have been guessed by the stiffened exterior which had held her fast till that time.

3

Once again   the moon   in a glassy twilight. The gas jet in the third floor window is turned low, they have not drawn the shade, sends down a flat glare upon the lounge's cotton-Persian cover where   the time passes with clumsy carresses. Never in this *milieu* has one stirred himself to turn up the light. It is costly to leave a jet burning at all. Feel your way to the bed. Drop your clothes on the floor and creep in. Flesh becomes so accustomed to the touch   she will not even waken. And so hours pass and not a move. The room too falls asleep and the street outside falls mumbling into a heap of black rags   morning's at seven—

Seeing a light in an upper window the poet by means of the power he has enters the room and of what he sees there brews himself a sleep potion.

XVIII

I

How deftly we keep love from each other. It is no trick at all: the movement of a cat that leaps a low barrier. You have—if the truth be known—loved only one man and that was before my time. Past him you have never thought nor desired to think. In his perfections you are perfect. You are likewise perfect in other things. You present to me the surface of a marble. And I, we will say, loved also before your time. Put it quite obscenely. And I have my perfections. So here we present ourselves to each other naked. What have we effected? Say we have aged a little together and you have borne children. We have in short thriven as the world goes. We have proved fertile. The children are apparently healthy. One of them is even whimsical and one has an unusual memory and a keen eye. But—it is not that we have not felt a certain rumbling, a certain stirring of the earth, but what has it amounted to? Your first love and mine were of different species. There is only one way out. It is for me to take up my basket of words and for you to sit at your piano, each his own way, until I have, if it so be that good fortune smile my way, made a shrewd bargain at some fair and so by dint of heavy straining supplanted in your memory the brilliance of the old firmhold. Which is impossible. Ergo: I am a blackguard.

The act is disclosed by the imagination of it. But of first importance is to realize that the imagination leads and the deed comes behind. First Don Quixote then Sancho Panza. So that the act, to win its praise, will win it in diverse fashions according to the way the imagination has taken. Thus a harsh deed will sometimes win its praise through laughter and sometimes through savage mockery, and a deed of

*simple kindness will come to its reward through sarcastic
comment. Each thing is secure in its own perfections.*

2

After thirty years staring at one true phrase he discov-
ered that its opposite was true also. For weeks he laughed
in the grip of a fierce self derision. Having lost the false-
hood to which he'd fixed his hawser he rolled drunkenly
about the field of his environment before the new direction
began to dawn upon his cracked mind. What a fool ever to
be tricked into seriousness. Soft hearted, hard hearted.
Thick crystals began to shoot through the liquid of his
spirit. Black, they were: branches that have lain in a fog
which now a wind is blowing away. Things more. Fatigued
as you are watch how the mirror sieves out the extraneous:
in sleep as in waking. Summoned to his door by a tinkling
bell he looked into a white face, the face of a man con-
vulsed with dread, saw the laughter back of its drawn
alertness. Out in the air: the sidesplitting burlesque of a
sparkling midnight stooping over a little house on a sand-
bank. The city at the horizon blowing a lurid red against
the flat cloud. The moon masquerading for a tower clock
over the factory, its hands in a gesture that, were time real,
would have settled all. But the delusion convulses the leafless
trees with the deepest appreciation of the mummery: inso-
lent poking of a face upon the half-lit window from which
the screams burst. So the man alighted in the great silence,
with a myopic star blinking to clear its eye over his hat top.
He comes to do good. Fatigue tickles his calves and the
lower part of his back with solicitous fingers, strokes his
feet and his knees with appreciative charity. He plunges
up the dark steps on his grotesque deed of mercy. In his
warped brain an owl of irony fixes on the immediate ob-
ject of his care as if it were the thing to be destroyed,
guffaws at the impossibility of putting any kind of value

on the object inside or of even reversing or making less
by any other means than induced sleep—which is no solu-
tion—the methodical gripe of the sufferer. Stupidity
couched in a dingy room beside the kitchen. One room
stove-hot, the next the dead cold of a butcher's ice box.
The man leaned and cut the baby from its stem. Slop in
disinfectant, roar with derision at the insipid blood stench:
hallucination comes to the rescue on the brink of serious-
ness: the gas-stove flame is starblue, violets back of
L'Horloge at Lancy. The smile of a spring morning trickles
into the back of his head and blinds the eyes to the irrita-
tion of the poppy red flux. A cracked window blind lets in
Venus. Stars. The hand-lamp is too feeble to have its own
way. The vanity of their neck stretching, trying to be large
as a street-lamp sets him roaring to himself anew. And
rubber gloves, the color of moist dates, the identical glisten
and texture: means a balloon trip to Fez. So one is a ridicu-
lous savior of the poor, with fatigue always at his elbow
with a new jest, the newest smutty story, the prettiest de-
fiance of insipid pretenses that cannot again assert divine
right—nonsensical gods that are fit to lick shoes clean: and
the great round face of Sister Pelagia straining to keep com-
posure against the jaws of a body louse. In at the back
door. We have been a benefactor. The cross laughter has
been denied us but one cannot have more than the appe-
tite sanctions.

3

Awake early to the white blare of a sun flooding in side-
wise. Strip and bathe in it. Ha, but an ache tearing at your
throat—and a vague cinema lifting its black moon blot all
out. There's no walking barefoot in the crisp leaves now-
adays. There's no dancing save in the head's dark. Go
draped in soot; call on modern medicine to help you: the
coal man's blowing his thin dust up through the house!

Why then, a new step lady! I'll meet you—you know where—o' the dark side! Let the wheel click.

———————

In the mind there is a continual play of obscure images which coming between the eyes and their prey seem pictures on the screen at the movies. Somewhere there appears to be a mal-adjustment. The wish would be to see not floating visions of unknown purport but the imaginative qualities of the actual things being perceived accompany their gross vision in a slow dance, interpreting as they go. But inasmuch as this will not always be the case one must dance nevertheless as he can.

XIX

I

Carry clapping bundles of lath-strips, adjust, dig, saw on a diagonal, hammer a thousand ends fast and discover afterward the lattice-arbor top's two clean lines in a dust of dew. There are days when leaves have knife's edges and one sees only eye-pupils, fixes every catch-penny in a shop window and every wire against the sky but—goes puzzled from vista to vista in his own house staring under beds for God knows what all.

———————

A lattice screen say fifty feet long by seven high, such a thing as is built to cut off some certain part of a yard from public view, is surprisingly expensive to put up. The wooden strips alone, if they are placed at all close together must be figured solid, as if it were a board fence. Then there are the posts, the frames, the trimming, the labor and last of all the two coats of paint. Is it a wonder the artisan cannot afford more than the luxury of these calculations.

2

Imperceptibly your self shakes free in all its brutal significance, feels its subtle power renewed and abashed at its covered lustihood breaks to the windows and draws back before the sunshine it sees there as before some imagined figure that would be there if—ah if— But for a moment your hand rests upon the palace window sill, only for a moment.

3

It is not fair to be old, to put on a brown sweater. It is not just to walk out of a November evening bare headed and with white hair in the wind. Oh the cheeks are ruddy enough and the grin broad enough, it's not that. Worse is to ride a wheel, a glittering machine that runs without knowing to move. It is no part of the eternal truth to wear white canvas shoes and a pink coat. It is a damnable lie to be fourteen. The curse of God is on her head! Who can speak of justice when young men wear round hats and carry bundles wrapped in paper. It is a case for the Supreme Court to button a coat in the wind, no matter how icy. Lewd to touch an arm at a crossing; the shame of it screams to the man in a window. The horrible misery brought on by the use of black shoes is more than the wind will ever swallow. To move at all is worse that murder, worse than Jack the Ripper. It lies, walking, spitting, breathing, coughing lies that bloom, shine sun, shine moon. Unfair to see or be seen, snatch-purses work. Eat hands full of ashes, angels have lived on it time without end. Are you better than an angel? Let judges giggle to each other over their benches and use dirty towels in the anteroom. Gnaw, gnaw, gnaw! at the heads of felons . . . There was a baroness lived in Hungary bathed twice monthly in virgin's blood.

A mother will love her children most grotesquely. I do not mean by that more than the term "perversely" perhaps more accurately describes. Oh I mean the most commonplace of mothers. She will be most willing toward that daughter who thwarts her most and not toward the little kitchen helper. So where one is mother to any great number of people she will love best perhaps some child whose black and peculiar hair is an exact replica of that of the figure of Velázquez's Infanta Maria Teresa or some Italian matron whose largeness of manner takes in the whole street. These things relate to inner perfections which it would be profitless to explain.

XX

1

Where does this downhill turn up again? Driven to the wall you'd put claws to your toes and make a ladder of smooth bricks. But this, this scene shifting that has clipped the clouds' stems and left them to flutter down; heaped them at the feet, so much hay, so much bull's fodder. (*Au moins,* you cannot deny you have the clouds to grasp now, *mon ami!*) Climb now? The wall's clipped off too, only its roots are left. Come, here's an iron hoop from a barrel once held nectar to gnaw spurs out of.

2

You cannot hold spirit round the arms but it takes lies for wings, turns poplar leaf and flutters off—leaving the old stalk desolate. There's much pious pointing at the sky but on the other side few know how youth's won again, the pesty spirit shed each ten years for more skin room. And who'll say what's pious or not pious or how I'll sing praise to God? Many a morning, were't not for a cup of coffee, a man would be lonesome enough no matter how his child gambols. And for the boy? There's no craft in him; it's this or that, the thing's done and tomorrow's another day. But if you push him too close, try for the butterflies, you'll have a devil at the table.

3

One need not be hopelessly cast down because he cannot cut onyx into a ring to fit a lady's finger. You hang your head. There is neither onyx nor porphyry on these roads—only brown dirt. For all that, one may see his face in a flower along it—even in this light. Eyes only and for a flash only. Oh, keep the neck bent, plod with the back to the split dark! Walk in the curled mudcrusts to one side, hands hanging. Ah well . . . Thoughts are trees! Ha, ha, ha, ha! Leaves load the branches and upon them white night sits kicking her heels against the stars.

A poem can be made of anything. This is a portrait of a disreputable farm hand made out of the stuff of his environment.

XXI

I

There's the bathtub. Look at it, caustically rejecting its smug proposal. Ponder removedly the herculean task of a bath. There's much cameraderie in filth but it's no' that. And change is lightsome but it's not that either. Fresh linen with a dab here, there of the wet paw serves me better. Take a stripling stroking chin-fuzz, match his heart against that of grandpa watching his silver wane. When these two are compatible I'll plunge in. But where's the edge

lifted between sunlight and moonlight. Where does lamp-
light cease to nick it? Here's hot water.

---

*It is the mark of our civilization that all houses today
include a room for the relief and washing of the body, a
room ingeniously appointed with water-vessels of many
and curious sorts. There is nothing in antiquity to equal
this.*

2

Neatness and finish; the dust out of every corner! You
swish from room to room and find all perfect. The house
may now be carefully wrapped in brown paper and sent
to a publisher. It is a work of art. You look rather askance
at me. Do not believe I cannot guess your mind, yet I have
my studies. You see, when the wheel's just at the up turn
it glimpses horizon, zenith, all in a burst, the pull of the
earth shaken off, a scatter of fragments, significance in a
burst of water striking up from the base of a fountain.
Then at the sickening turn toward death the pieces are
joined into a pretty thing, a bouquet frozen in an ice-
cake. *This* is art, *mon cher*, a thing to carry up with you on
the next turn; a very small thing, inconceivably feathery.

---

*Live as they will together a husband and wife give each
other many a sidelong glance at unlikely moments. Each
watches the other out of the tail of his eye. Always it
seems some drunkenness is waiting to unite them. First
one then the other empties some carafe of spirits forgetting
that two lumps of earth are neither wiser nor sadder. . . .
A man watches his wife clean house. He is filled with
knowledge by his wife's exertions. This is incomprehensi-
ble to her. Knowing she will never understand his excite-
ment he consoles himself with the thought of art.*

3

The pretension of these doors to broach or to conclude our pursuits, our meetings,—of these papered walls to separate our thoughts of impossible tomorrows and these ceilings—that are a jest at shelter . . . It is laughter gone mad—of a holiday—that has frozen into this—what shall I say? Call it, this house of ours, the crystal itself of laughter, thus peaked and faceted.

It is a popular superstition that a house is somehow the possession of the man who lives in it. But a house has no relation whatever to anything but itself. The architect feels the rhythm of the house drawing his mind into opaque partitions in which doors appear, then windows and so on until out of the vague or clearcut mind of the architect the ill-built or deftly-built house has been empowered to draw stone and timbers into a foreappointed focus. If one shut the door of a house he is to that extent a carpenter.

Coda

Outside, the north wind, coming and passing, swelling and dying, lifts the frozen sand   drives it arattle against the lidless windows   and we   my dear   sit   stroking the cat stroking the cat and smiling sleepily, prrrrr.

A house is sometimes wine. It is more than a skin. The young pair listen attentively to the roar of the weather. The blustering cold takes on the shape of a destructive presence. They loosen their imaginations. The house seems protecting them. They relax gradually as though in the keep of a benevolent protector. Thus the house becomes a wine which has drugged them out of their senses.

XXII

1

This is a slight stiff dance to a waking baby whose arms have been lying curled back above his head upon the pillow, making a flower—the eyes closed. Dead to the world! Waking is a little hand brushing away dreams. Eyes open. Here's a new world.

———————

There is nothing the sky-serpent will not eat. Sometimes it stoops to gnaw Fujiyama, sometimes to slip its long and softly clasping tongue about the body of a sleeping child who smiles thinking its mother is lifting it.

2

Security, solidity—we laugh at them in our clique. It is tobacco to us, this side of her leg. We put it in our samovar and make tea of it. You see the stuff has possibilities. You think you are opposing the rich but the truth is you're turning toward authority yourself, to say nothing of religion. No, I do not say it means nothing. Why everything is nicely adjusted to our moods. But I would rather describe to you what I saw in the kitchen last night—overlook the girl a moment: there over the sink (1) this saucepan holds all, (2) this colander holds most, (3) this wire sieve lets most go and (4) this funnel holds nothing. You appreciate the progression. What need then to be always laughing? Quit phrase making—that is, not of course—but you will understand me or if not—why—come to breakfast sometime around evening on the fourth of January any year you please; always be punctual where eating is concerned.

———————

My little son's improvisations exceed mine: a round stone to him's a loaf of bread or "this hen could lay a dozen golden eggs." Birds fly about his bedstead; giants lean over him with hungry jaws; bears roam the farm by summer and are killed and quartered at a thought. There are interminable stories at eating time full of bizarre imagery, true grotesques, pigs that change to dogs in the telling, cows that sing, roosters that become mountains and oceans that fill a soup plate. There are groans and growls, dun clouds and sunshine mixed in a huge phantasmagoria that never rests, never ceases to unfold into—the day's poor little happenings. Not that alone. He has music which I have not. His tunes follow no scale, no rhythm—alone the mood in odd ramblings up and down, over and over with a rigor of invention that rises beyond the power to follow except in some more obvious flight. Never have I heard so crushing a critique as those desolate inventions, involved half-hymns, after his first visit to a Christian Sunday school.

3

This song is to Phyllis! By this deep snow I know it's springtime, not ring time! Good God no! The screaming brat's a sheep bleating, the rattling crib-side sheep shaking a bush. We are young! We are happy! says Colin. What's an icy room and the sun not up? This song is to Phyllis. Reproduction lets death in, says Joyce. Rot, say I. To Phyllis this song is!

That which is known has value only by virtue of the dark. This cannot be otherwise. A thing known passes out of the mind into the muscles, the will is quit of it, save only when set into vibration by the forces of darkness opposed to it.

XXIII

I

Baaaa! Ba-ha-ha-ha-ha-ha-ha-ha! *Bebe esa purga.* It is the goats of Santo Domingo talking. *Bebe esa purga!* Bebeesa-purga! And the answer is: *Yo no lo quiero beber!* Yonolo-quierobeber!

It is nearly pure luck that gets the mind turned inside out in a work of art. There is nothing more difficult than to write a poem. It is something of a matter of sleight of hand. The poets of the T'ang dynasty or of the golden age in Greece or even the Elizabethans: it's a kind of alchemy of form, a deft bottling of a fermenting language. Take Dante and his Tuscan dialect—It's a matter of position. The empty form drops from a cloud, like a gourd from a vine; into it the poet packs his phallus-like argument.

2

The red huckleberry bushes running miraculously along the ground among the trees everywhere, except where the land's tilled, these keep her from that tiredness the earth's touch lays up under the soles of feet. She runs beyond the wood follows the swiftest along the roads laughing among the birch clusters her face in the yellow leaves the curls before her eyes her mouth half open. This is a person in particular there where they have her—and I have only a wraith in the birch trees.

It is not the lusty bodies of the nearly naked girls in the shows about town, nor the blare of the popular tunes that make money for the manager. The girls can be procured

*rather more easily in other ways and the music is dirt cheap.
It is that this meat is savored with a strangeness which never
loses its fresh taste to generation after generation, either of
dancers or those who watch. It is beauty escaping, spinning
up over the heads, blown out at the overtaxed vents by
the electric fans.*

3

*In many poor and sentimental households it is a custom
to have cheap prints in glass frames upon the walls. These
are of all sorts and many sizes and may be found in any
room from the kitchen to the toilet. The drawing is always
of the worst and the colors, not gaudy but almost always
of faint indeterminate tints, are infirm. Yet a delicate ac-
curacy exists between these prints and the environment
which breeds them. But as if to intensify this relationship
words are added. There will be a "sentiment" as it is called,
a rhyme, which the picture illuminates. Many of these per-
tain to love. This is well enough when the bed is new and
the young couple spend the long winter nights there in de-
lightful seclusion. But childbirth follows in its time and a
motto still hangs above the bed. It is only then that the full
ironical meaning of these prints leaves the paper and the
frame and starting through the glass takes undisputed sway
over the household.*

XXIV

I

I like the boy. It's years back I began to draw him to me
—or he was pushed my way by the others. And what if
there's no sleep because the bed's burning; is that a reason to
send a chap to Greystone! Greystone! There's a name if
you've any tatter of mind left in you. It's the long back, nar-

rowing that way at the waist perhaps whets the chisel in me. How the flanks flutter and the heart races. Imagination! That's the worm in the apple. What if it run to paralyses and blind fires, here's sense loose in a world set on foundations. Blame buzzards for the eyes they have.

Buzzards, granted their disgusting habit in regard to meat, have eyes of a power equal to that of the eagles'.

2

Five miscarriages since January is a considerable record Emily dear—but hearken to me: The Pleiades—that small cluster of lights in the sky there—. You'd better go on in the house before you catch cold. Go on now!

Carelessness of heart is a virtue akin to the small lights of the stars. But it is sad to see virtues in those who have not the gift of the imagination to value them.

Damn me I feel sorry for them. Yet syphilis is no more than a wild pink in the rock's cleft. I know that. Radicals and capitalists doing a can-can tread the ground clean. Luck to the feet then. Bring a Russian to put a fringe to the rhythm. What's the odds? Commiseration cannot solve calculus. Calculus is a stone. Frost'll crack it. Till then, there's many a good backroad among the clean raked fields of hell where autumn flowers are blossoming.

Pathology literally speaking is a flower garden. Syphilis covers the body with salmon-red petals. The study of medicine is an inverted sort of horticulture. Over and above all this floats the philosophy of disease which is a stern dance.

One of its most delightful gestures is bringing flowers to
the sick.

3

For a choice? Go to bed at three in the afternoon with
your clothes on: dreams for you! Here's an old bonne-
femme in a pokebonnet staring into the rear of a locomo-
tive. Or if this prove too difficult take a horse-drag made
of green limbs, a kind of leaf cloth. Up the street with it!
Ha, how the tar clings. Here's glee for the children. All's
smeared. Green's black. Leap like a devil, clap hands and
cast around for more. Here's a pine wood driven head
down into a mud-flat to build a school on. Oh la, la! sand
pipers made mathematicians at the state's cost.

XXV

I

There's force to this cold sun, makes beard stubble stand
shinily. We look, we pretend great things to our glass—
rubbing our chin: This is a profound comedian who grim-
aces deeds into slothful breasts. This is a sleepy president,
without followers save oak leaves—but their coats are of
the wrong color. This is a farmer—plowed a field in his
dreams and since that time—goes stroking the weeds that
choke his furrows. This is a poet left his own country—

The simple expedient of a mirror has practical use for
arranging the hair, for observation of the set of a coat, etc.
But as an exercise for the mind the use of a mirror cannot
be too highly recommended. Nothing of a mechanical na-
ture could be more conducive to that elasticity of the atten-
tion which frees the mind for the enjoyment of its special
prerogatives.

2

A man can shoot his spirit up out of a wooden house, that is, through the roof—the roof's slate—but how far? It is of final importance to know that. To say the world turns under my feet and that I watch it passing with a smile is neither the truth nor my desire. But I would wish to stand—you've seen the kingfisher do it—where the largest town might be taken in my two hands, as high let us say as a man's head—some one man not too far above the clouds. What would I do then? Oh I'd hold my sleeve over the sun awhile to make church bells ring.

———————

It is obvious that if in flying an airplane one reached such an altitude that all sense of direction and every intelligible perception of the world were lost there would be nothing left to do but to come down to that point at which eyes regained their power.

Towels will stay in a heap—if the window's shut and oil in a bottle—if the cork's there. But if the meat's not cut to suit it's no use rising before sun up, you'll never sweep the dust from these floors. Hide smiles among the tall glasses in the cupboard, come back when you think the trick's done and you'll find only dead flies there. It's beyond hope. You were not born of a Monday.

———————

There are divergences of humor that cannot be reconciled. A young woman of much natural grace of manner and very apt at a certain color of lie is desirous of winning the good graces of one only slightly her elder but nothing comes of her exertions. Instead of yielding to a superficial advantage she finally gives up the task and continues in her own delicate bias of peculiar and beautiful design much to the secret delight of the onlooker who is thus regaled

*by the spectacle of two exquisite and divergent natures
playing one against the other.*

3

Hark! There's laughter! These fight and draw nearer,
we—fight and draw apart. They know the things they say
are true bothways, we miss the joke—try to—Oh, try to.
Let it go at that. There again! Real laughter. At least we
have each other in the ring of that music. "He saved a little
then had to go and die." But isn't it the same with all of
us? Not at all. Some laugh and laugh, with little grey eyes
looking out through the chinks—but not brown eyes rolled
up in a full roar. One can't have everything.

---

*Going along an illworn dirt road on the outskirts of a mill
town one Sunday afternoon two lovers who have quarreled
hear the loud cursing and shouts of drunken laborers and
their women, followed by loud laughter and wish that their
bodies were two fluids in the same vessel. Then they fall
to twitting each other on the many ways of laughing.*

XXVI

1

Doors have a back side also. And grass blades are double-
edged. It's no use trying to deceive me, leaves fall more by
the buds that push them off than by lack of greenness. Or
throw two shoes on the floor and see how they'll lie if
you think it's all one way.

2

There is no truth—sh!—but the honest truth and that is
that touch-me-nots mean nothing, that daisies at a distance

seem mushrooms and that—your Japanese silk today was not the sky's blue but your pajamas now as you lean over the crib's edge are   and day's in! Grassgreen the mosquito net caught over your head's butt for foliage. What else? except odors—an old hallway. Moresco. Salvago. —and a game of socker. I was too nervous and young to win— that day.

3

All that seem solid: melancholias, *idées fixes*, eight years at the academy, Mr. Locke, this year and the next and the next—one like another—whee!—they are April zephyrs, were one a Botticelli, between their chinks, pink anemones.

Often it happens that in a community of no great distinc- tion some fellow of superficial learning but great stupidity will seem to be rooted in the earth of the place the most solid figure imaginable   impossible to remove him.

XXVII

I

The particular thing, whether it be four pinches of four divers white powders cleverly compounded to cure surely, safely, pleasantly a painful twitching of the eyelids or say a pencil sharpened at one end, dwarfs the imagination, makes logic a butterfly, offers a finality that sends us spinning through space, a fixity the mind could climb forever, a re- volving mountain, a complexity with a surface of glass; the gist of poetry. *D. C. al fin.*

2

There is no thing that with a twist of the imagination cannot be something else. Porpoises risen in a green sea,

the wind at nightfall bending the rose-red grasses and you
—in your apron running to catch—say it seems to you to
be your son. How ridiculous! You will pass up into a cloud
and look back at me, not count the scribbling foolish that
puts wings to your heels, at your knees.

3

Sooner or later as with the leaves   forgotten the swing-
ing branch long since and summer: they scurry before a
wind on the frost-baked ground—have no place to rest—
somehow invoke a burst of warm days not of the past
nothing decayed: crisp summer!—neither a copse for resur-
rected frost eaters but a summer removed undestroyed
a summer of dried leaves scurrying with a screech, to and
fro in the half dark—twittering, chattering, scraping. Hagh!

———————————

*Seeing the leaves dropping from the high and low
branches the thought rises: this day of all others is the
one chosen, all other days fall away from it on either side
and only itself remains in perfect fullness. It is its own
summer, of its leaves as they scrape on the smooth ground
it must build its perfection. The gross summer of the year
is only a halting counterpart of those fiery days of secret
triumph which in reality themselves paint the year as if
upon a parchment, giving each season a mockery of the
warmth or frozenness which is within ourselves. The true
seasons blossom or wilt not in fixed order but so that many
of them may pass in a few weeks or hours whereas some-
times a whole life passes and the season remains of a piece
from one end to the other.*

Spring and All

To
Charles Demuth

Introduction

Spring and All

SPRING AND ALL is a fooling-around book that became a crucial book. It was printed in Dijon and first published in Paris in 1923 (around 300 copies) by Robert McAlmon's Contact Publishing Co. A devoted friend to Williams and experimental literature, McAlmon was also offering early books by Ernest Hemingway, Ezra Pound, Gertrude Stein and others. *Spring and All* is a beautiful, misshapen box that contains, among other things, William Carlos Williams's most impassioned pleas on behalf of the imagination, several of his greatest short poems, various indictments of contemporary civilization (at one point he imaginatively destroys all civilization west of the Carpathian Mountains), and several manifestos for modern poetry. Until now the book has not been reprinted in its entirety.

Speaking of *Spring and All* in *I Wanted to Write a Poem*, Williams tells us something about his method and emotions at the time:

"Nobody ever saw it—it had no circulation at all—but I had a lot of fun with it. It consists of poems interspersed with prose, the same idea as *Improvisations*. It was written when all the world was going crazy about typographical form and is really a travesty on the idea. Chapter headings are printed upside down on purpose, the chapters are numbered all out of order, sometimes with a Roman numeral, sometimes with an Arabic, anything that came in handy. The prose is a mixture of philosophy and nonsense. It made sense to me, at least to my disturbed mind—because it *was* disturbed at that time—but I doubt if it made any sense to anyone else.

"But the poems were kept pure—no typographical tricks

when they appear—set off in prose. They are numbered
consistently; none had titles though they were to have
titles later. . . ."

Spring and All took many turns Williams never antici-
pated as he wrote it. There is no point in trying to classify
the book. It is neither fiction, criticism, poetry nor fact.
It is all—or parts of all. Williams has been to winter and
hell in the *Improvisations* of *Kora in Hell*. Now he finds
spring. He embraces it and all that life implies.

The prose portions of the book seem as random as the
paragraphs of *Kora*. Sentences end in midair. Ideas that
might don't take flight. Mostly Williams is trying to clarify
and intensify his conception of where modern art, especially
poetry, should come from and what it should do. He re-
sponds to attacks on his rhyme-less, rhythm-less poetry
with a funny monologue: "You have robbed me. God, I
am naked. What shall I do?" He conceives of the imagina-
tion as a post-evolutionary force capable of repeating evolu-
tion: "Yes, the imagination, drunk with prohibitions, has
destroyed and recreated everything afresh in the likeness
of that which it was." He states his fundamental proposi-
tion that "the artist does exactly what every age must do
with life, fix the particular with the universal." Williams re-
quires that the artist see absolutely into things so that the
insight becomes the thing itself. He finds his predecessors
in Homer, Scheherazade, Whitman. He finds his contem-
poraries among painters because his poetry was becoming
a way of seeing as well as writing. If the prose and poetry
of *Spring and All* have been separated during the years
since first publication, that's a mistake. Williams begins
the book by addressing it to the imagination, his goddess.
He enunciates his literary principles in the prose. He dem-
onstrates them in the poetry.

The poems took Williams a giant step forward. In *Spring
and All* he once and for all abandoned the imagism and
Keatsian classism of his three first books of poems. Like
spring bursting along the road to the contagious hospital,

Williams himself "enters the new world naked." The poems take modern experiences—jazz musicians, a girl with one leg hanging over a balcony, the mind picture-snapping as his car moves, daydreams at a water faucet in June—and they give these experiences "a sense of completion." Gone from Williams's poems are the reflex-action rhetoric and symbols of the nineteenth century. He shows us (especially in "The Rose Is Obsolete") that some of the old symbols may have the means of making new associations—with the junkyards of the United States or the universe itself, depending on the imagination. The language is all ordinary. The rhythms are spoken. The familiar world, utterly anti-poetic and beyond the grasp of the rituals of literature, is rediscovered and infused with newness through the powers of the imagination. "The exaltation men feel before a work of art is the feeling of reality they draw from it," Williams says. He makes over the reality traditional literature lost as it adopted a fixed form and official subject matter.

Williams tells us about himself. About halfway through the book he says what *Kora in Hell* meant—salvation. He admits the price he pays for his art: "The better work men do is always done under stress and at great personal cost." And in an environment that feeds him poems about the emptiness of old age, lost young slatterns, and people with broken brains, Williams identifies with Poe. He "could not have written a word without the violence of expulsive emotion combined with the in-driving force of a crudely repressive environment. Between the two his imagination was forced into being. . . ."

Williams found his way in *Spring and All*. He would try to write his poetry differently—"in the realm of the imagination as plain as the sky is to a fisherman"—for the rest of his life.

w.s.

Spring and All

IF ANYTHING of moment results—so much the better. And so much the more likely will it be that no one will want to see it.

There is a constant barrier between the reader and his consciousness of immediate contact with the world. If there is an ocean it is here. Or rather, the whole world is between: Yesterday, tomorrow, Europe, Asia, Africa,—all things removed and impossible, the tower of the church at Seville, the Parthenon.

What do they mean when they say: "I do not like your poems; you have no faith whatever. You seem neither to have suffered nor, in fact, to have felt anything very deeply. There is nothing appealing in what you say but on the contrary the poems are positively repellent. They are heartless, cruel, they make fun of humanity. What in God's name do you mean? Are you a pagan? Have you no tolerance for human frailty? Rhyme you may perhaps take away but rhythm! why there is none in your work whatever. Is this what you call poetry? It is the very antithesis of poetry. It is antipoetry. It is the annihilation of life upon which you are bent. Poetry that used to go hand in hand with life, poetry that interpreted our deepest promptings, poetry that inspired, that led us forward to new discoveries, new depths of tolerance, new heights of exaltation. You moderns! it is the death of poetry that you are accomplishing. No. I cannot understand this work. You have not yet suffered a cruel blow from life. When you have suffered you will write differently?"

Perhaps this noble apostrophe means something terrible

fantasy is diff than
Imagination

for me, I am not certain, but for the moment I interpret it to say: "You have robbed me. God, I am naked. What shall I do?" —By it they mean that when I have suffered (provided I have not done so as yet) I too shall run for cover; that I too shall seek refuge in fantasy. And mind you, I do not say that I will not. To decorate my age.

But today it is different.

The reader knows himself as he was twenty years ago and he has also in mind a vision of what he would be, some day. Oh, some day! But the thing he never knows and never dares to know is what he is at the exact moment that he is. And this moment is the only thing in which I am at all interested. Ergo, who cares for anything I do? And what do I care?

I love my fellow creature. Jesus, how I love him: end-ways, sideways, frontways and all the other ways—but he doesn't exist! Neither does she. I do, in a bastardly sort of way.

To whom then am I addressed? To the imagination.

In fact to return upon my theme for the time nearly all writing, up to the present, if not all art, has been especially designed to keep up the barrier between sense and the vaporous fringe which distracts the attention from its ago-nized approaches to the moment. It has been always a search for "the beautiful illusion." Very well. I am not in search of "the beautiful illusion."

And if when I pompously announce that I am addressed —To the imagination—you believe that I thus divorce myself from life and so defeat my own end, I reply: To refine, to clarify, to intensify that eternal moment in which we alone live there is but a single force—the imagination. This is its book. I myself invite you to read and to see.

In the imagination, we are from henceforth (so long as you read) locked in a fraternal embrace, the classic caress of author and reader. We are one. Whenever I say, "I" I mean also, "you." And so, together, as one, we shall begin.

CHAPTER 19

o meager times, so fat in everything imaginable! imagine the
New World that rises to our windows from the sea on
Mondays and on Saturdays—and on every other day of
the week also. Imagine it in all its prismatic colorings, its
counterpart in our souls—our souls that are great pianos
whose strings, of honey and of steel, the divisions of the
rainbow set twanging, loosing on the air great novels of
adventure! Imagine the monster project of the moment:
Tomorrow we the people of the United States are going
to Europe armed to kill every man, woman and child in the
area west of the Carpathian Mountains (also east) sparing
none. Imagine the sensation it will cause. First we shall kill
them and then they, us. But we are careful to spare the
Spanish bulls, the birds, rabbits, small deer and of course—
the Russians. For the Russians we shall build a bridge from
edge to edge of the Atlantic—having first been at pains to
slaughter all Canadians and Mexicans on this side. Then, oh
then, the great feature will take place.

Never mind; the great event may not exist, so there is
no need to speak further of it. Kill! kill! the English, the
Irish, the French, the Germans, the Italians and the rest:
friends or enemies, it makes no difference, kill them all. The
bridge is to be blown up when all Russia is upon it. And
why?

Because we love them—all. That is the secret: a new
sort of murder. We make *leberwurst* of them. Bratwurst.
But why, since we are ourselves doomed to suffer the same
annihilation?

If I could say what is in my mind in Sanscrit or even
Latin I would do so. But I cannot. I speak for the integrity
of the soul and the greatness of life's inanity; the formality
of its boredom; the orthodoxy of its stupidity. Kill! kill!
let there be fresh meat. . . .

The imagination, intoxicated by prohibitions, rises to

drunken heights to destroy the world. Let it rage, let it kill. The imagination is supreme. To it all our works forever, from the remotest past to the farthest future, have been, are and will be dedicated. To it alone we show our wit by having raised in its honor as monument not the least pebble. To it now we come to dedicate our secret project: the annihilation of every human creature on the face of the earth. This is something never before attempted. None to remain; nothing but the lower vertebrates, the mollusks, insects and plants. Then at last will the world be made anew. Houses crumble to ruin, cities disappear giving place to mounds of soil blown thither by the winds, small bushes and grass give way to trees which grow old and are succeeded by other trees for countless generations. A marvellous serenity broken only by bird and wild beast calls reigns over the entire sphere. Order and peace abound.

This final and self inflicted holocaust has been all for love, for sweetest love, that together the human race, yellow, black, brown, red and white, agglutinated into one enormous soul may be gratified with the sight and retire to the heaven of heavens content to rest on its laurels. There, soul of souls, watching its own horrid unity, it boils and digests itself within the tissues of the great Being of Eternity that we shall then have become. With what magnificent explosions and odors will not the day be accomplished as we, the Great One among all creatures, shall go about contemplating our self-prohibited desires as we promenade them before the inward review of our own bowels— et cetera, et cetera, et cetera . . . and it is spring—both in Latin and Turkish, in English and Dutch, in Japanese and Italian; it is spring by Stinking River where a magnolia tree, without leaves, before what was once a farmhouse, now a ramshackle home for millworkers, raises its straggling branches of ivorywhite flowers.

CHAPTER XIII

Thus, weary of life, in view of the great consummation which awaits us—tomorrow, we rush among our friends congratulating ourselves upon the joy soon to be. Thoughtless of evil we crush out the marrow of those about us with our heavy cars as we go happily from place to place. It seems that there is not time enough in which to speak the full of our exaltation. Only a day is left, one miserable day, before the world comes into its own. Let us hurry! Why bother for this man or that? In the offices of the great newspapers a mad joy reigns as they prepare the final extras. Rushing about, men bump each other into the whirring presses. How funny it seems. All thought of misery has left us. Why should we care? Children laughingly fling themselves under the wheels of the street cars, airplanes crash gaily to the earth. Someone has written a poem.

Oh life, bizarre fowl, what color are your wings? Green, blue, red, yellow, purple, white, brown, orange, black, grey? In the imagination, flying above the wreck of ten thousand million souls, I see you departing sadly for the land of plants and insects, already far out to sea. (Thank you, I know well what I am plagiarizing) Your great wings flap as you disappear in the distance over the pre-Columbian acres of floating weed.

The new cathedral overlooking the park, looked down from its towers today, with great eyes, and saw by the decorative lake a group of people staring curiously at the corpse of a suicide: Peaceful, dead young man, the money they have put into the stones has been spent to teach men of life's austerity. You died and teach us the same lesson. You seem a cathedral, celebrant of the spring which shivers for me among the long black trees.

CHAPTER VI

Now, in the imagination, all flesh, all human flesh has been dead upon the earth for ten million, billion years. The bird has turned into a stone within whose heart an egg, unlaid, remained hidden.

It is spring! but miracle of miracles a miraculous miracle has gradually taken place during these seemingly wasted eons. Through the orderly sequences of unmentionable time EVOLUTION HAS REPEATED ITSELF FROM THE BEGINNING.

Good God!

Every step once taken in the first advance of the human race, from the amoeba to the highest type of intelligence, has been duplicated, every step exactly paralleling the one that preceded in the dead ages gone by. A perfect plagiarism results. Everything is and is new. Only the imagination is undeceived.

At this point the entire complicated and laborious process begins to near a new day. (More of this in Chapter XIX) But for the moment everything is fresh, perfect, recreated.

In fact now, for the first time, everything IS new. Now at last the perfect effect is being witlessly discovered. The terms "veracity," "actuality," "real," "natural," "sincere" are being discussed at length, every word in the discussion being evolved from an identical discussion which took place the day before yesterday.

Yes, the imagination, drunk with prohibitions, has destroyed and recreated everything afresh in the likeness of that which it was. Now indeed men look about in amazement at each other with a full realization of the meaning of "art."

CHAPTER 2

It is spring: life again begins to assume its normal ap-
pearance as of "today." Only the imagination is undeceived.
The volcanos are extinct. Coal is beginning to be dug again
where the fern forests stood last night. (If an error is noted
here, pay no attention to it.)

CHAPTER XIX

I realize that the chapters are rather quick in their se-
quence and that nothing much is contained in any one of
them but no one should be surprised at this today.

THE TRADITIONALISTS OF PLAGIARISM

It is spring. That is to say, it is approaching THE BE-
GINNING.

In that huge and microscopic career of time, as it were
a wild horse racing in an illimitable pampa under the stars,
describing immense and microscopic circles with his hoofs
on the solid turf, running without a stop for the millionth
part of a second until he is aged and worn to a heap of skin,
bones and ragged hoofs—In that majestic progress of life,
that gives the exact impression of Phidias's frieze, the men
and beasts of which, though they seem of the rigidity of
marble are not so but move, with blinding rapidity, though
we do not have the time to notice it, their legs advancing
a millionth part of an inch every fifty thousand years—In
that progress of life which seems stillness itself in the mass
of its movements—at last SPRING is approaching.

In that colossal surge toward the finite and the capable
life has now arrived for the second time at that exact mo-
ment when in the ages past the destruction of the species
Homo sapiens occurred.

*Ambiguity of this
Sentence - in the
destruction of Homo sapiens is
the beginning*

Now at last that process of miraculous verisimilitude, that great copying which evolution has followed, repeating move for move every move that it made in the past—is approaching the end.

Suddenly it is at an end. THE WORLD IS NEW.

I

By the road to the contagious hospital
under the surge of the blue
mottled clouds driven from the

northeast—a cold wind. Beyond, the
waste of broad, muddy fields
brown with dried weeds, standing and fallen

patches of standing water
the scattering of tall trees

All along the road the reddish
purplish, forked, upstanding, twiggy
stuff of bushes and small trees
with dead, brown leaves under them
leafless vines—

Lifeless in appearance, sluggish
dazed spring approaches—

They enter the new world naked,
cold, uncertain of all
save that they enter. All about them
the cold, familiar wind—

Now the grass, tomorrow
the stiff curl of wildcarrot leaf

One by one objects are defined—
It quickens: clarity, outline of leaf

But now the stark dignity of
entrance—Still, the profound change

has come upon them: rooted they
grip down and begin to awaken

II

Pink confused with white
flowers and flowers reversed
take and spill the shaded flame
darting it back
into the lamp's horn

petals aslant darkened with mauve

red where in whorls
petal lays its glow upon petal
round flamegreen throats

petals radiant with transpiercing light
contending
                    above

the leaves
reaching up their modest green
from the pot's rim

and there, wholly dark, the pot
gay with rough moss.

A terrific confusion has taken place. No man knows
whither to turn. There is nothing! Emptiness stares us once

more in the face. Whither? To what end? Each asks the other. Has life its tail in its mouth or its mouth in its tail? Why are we here? Dora Marsden's philosophic algebra. Everywhere men look into each other's faces and ask the old unanswerable question: Whither? How? What? Why?

At any rate, now at last spring is here!

The rock has split, the egg has hatched, the prismatically plumed bird of life has escaped from its cage. It spreads its wings and is perched now on the peak of the huge African mountain Kilimanjaro.

Strange recompense, in the depths of our despair at the unfathomable mist into which all mankind is plunging, a curious force awakens. It is HOPE long asleep, aroused once more. Wilson has taken an army of advisers and sailed for England. The ship has sunk. But the men are all good swimmers. They take the women on their shoulders and buoyed on by the inspiration of the moment they churn the free seas with their sinewy arms, like Ulysses, landing all along the European seaboard.

Yes, hope has awakened once more in men's hearts. It is NEW! Let us go forward!

The imagination, freed from the handcuffs of "art," takes the lead! Her feet are bare and not too delicate. In fact those who come behind her have much to think of. Hm. Let it pass.

CHAPTER I

SAMUEL BUTLER

The great English divine, Sam Butler, is shouting from a platform, warning us as we pass: There are two who can invent some extraordinary thing to one who can properly employ that which has been made use of before.

Enheartened by this thought THE TRADITIONAL-ISTS OF PLAGIARISM try to get hold of the mob. They seize those nearest them and shout into their ears: Tradition! The solidarity of life!

The fight is on: These men who have had the governing of the mob through all the repetitious years resent the new order. Who can answer them? One perhaps here and there but it is an impossible situation. If life were anything but a bird, if it were a man, a Greek or an Egyptian, but it is only a bird that has eyes and wings, a beak, talons and a cry that reaches to every rock's center, but without intelligence? —

The voice of the Delphic Oracle itself, what was it? A poisonous gas from a rock's cleft.

Those who led yesterday wish to hold their sway a while longer. It is not difficult to understand their mood. They have their great weapons to hand: "science," "philosophy" and most dangerous of all "art."

Meanwhile, SPRING, which has been approaching for several pages, is at last here.

—they ask us to return to the proven truths of tradition, even to the twice proven, the substantiality of which is known. Demuth and a few others do their best to point out the error, telling us that design is a function of the IMAGINATION, describing its movements, its colors—but it is a hard battle. I myself seek to enter the lists with these few notes jotted down in the midst of the action, under distracting circumstances—to remind myself (see p. 89, paragraph 2) of the truth.

III

The farmer in deep thought
is pacing through the rain
among his blank fields, with
hands in pockets,
in his head
98   the harvest already planted.

A cold wind ruffles the water
among the browned weeds.
On all sides
the world rolls coldly away:
black orchards
darkened by the March clouds—
leaving room for thought.
Down past the brushwood
bristling by
the rainsluiced wagonroad
looms the artist figure of
the farmer—composing
—antagonist

*there's that word
antagonist again*

IV

The Easter stars are shining
above lights that are flashing—
coronal of the black—
                              Nobody
to say it—
               Nobody to say: pinholes

Thither I would carry her
among the lights—
Burst it asunder
break through to the fifty words
necessary—

               a crown for her head with
castles upon it, skyscrapers
filled with nut-chocolates—

                    dovetame winds—
stars of tinsel

from the great end of a cornucopia
of glass

So long as the sky is recognized as an association
is recognized in its function of accessory to vague words
whose meaning it is impossible to rediscover
its value can be nothing but mathematical certain limits
of gravity and density of air
The farmer and the fisherman who read their own lives
there have a practical corrective for—
they rediscover or replace demoded meanings to the re-
ligious terms
Among them, without expansion of imagination, there is
the residual contact between life and the imagination which
is essential to freedom
The man of imagination who turns to art for release and
fulfilment of his baby promises contends with the sky
through layers of demoded words and shapes. Demoded, not
because the essential vitality which begot them is laid waste
—this cannot be so, a young man feels, since he feels it in
himself—but because meanings have been lost through lazi-
ness or changes in the form of existence which have let
words empty.
Bare handed the man contends with the sky, without ex-
perience of existence seeking to invent and design.
Crude symbolism is to associate emotions with natural
phenomena such as anger with lightning, flowers with love
it goes further and associates certain textures with
Such work is empty. It is very typical of almost all that
is done by the writers who fill the pages every month of
such a paper as. Everything that I have done in the past—
except those parts which may be called excellent—by
chance, have that quality about them.

It is typified by use of the word "like" or that "evocation" of the "image" which served us for a time. Its abuse is apparent. The insignificant "image" may be "evoked" never so ably and still mean nothing.

With all his faults Alfred Kreymborg never did this. That is why his work—escaping a common fault—still has value and will tomorrow have more.

Sandburg, when uninspired by intimacies of the eye and ear, runs into this empty symbolism. Such poets of promise as ruin themselves with it, though many have major sentimental faults besides.

Marianne Moore escapes. The incomprehensibility of her poems is witness to at what cost (she cleaves herself away) as it is also to the distance which the most are from a comprehension of the purpose of composition.

The better work men do is always done under stress and at great personal cost.

It is no different from the aristocratic compositions of the earlier times, The Homeric inventions

but

these occurred in different times, to this extent, that life had not yet sieved through its own multiformity. That aside, the work the two-thousand-year-old poet did and that we do are one piece. That is the vitality of the classics.

So then—Nothing is put down in the present book—except through weakness of the imagination—which is not intended as of a piece with the "nature" which Shakespeare mentions and which Hartley speaks of so completely in his *Adventures:* it is the common thing which is anonymously about us.

Composition is in no essential an escape from life. In fact if it is so it is negligible to the point of insignificance. Whatever "life" the artist may be forced to lead has no relation to the vitality of his compositions. Such names as Homer, the blind; Scheherazade, who lived under threat—Their compositions have as their excellence an identity with life since they are as actual, as sappy as the leaf of the tree which never moves from one spot.

101

What I put down of value will have this value: an escape from crude symbolism, the annihilation of strained associations, complicated ritualistic forms designed to separate the work from "reality"—such as rhyme, meter as meter and not as the essential of the work, one of its words.

But this smacks too much of the nature of—This is all negative and appears to be boastful. It is not intended to be so. Rather the opposite.

The work will be in the realm of the imagination as plain as the sky is to a fisherman—A very clouded sentence. The word must be put down for itself, not as a symbol of nature but a part, cognizant of the whole—aware—civilized.

V

Black winds from the north
enter black hearts. Barred from
seclusion in lilies they strike
to destroy—

Beastly humanity
where the wind breaks it—

                              strident voices, heat
quickened, built of waves

Drunk with goats or pavements

Hate is of the night and the day
of flowers and rocks. Nothing
is gained by saying the night breeds
murder—It is the classical mistake

The day

All that enters in another person
all grass, all blackbirds flying

all azalea trees in flower
salt winds—

Sold to them men knock blindly together
splitting their heads open

That is why boxing matches and
Chinese poems are the same—That is why
Hartley praises Miss Wirt

There is nothing in the twist
of the wind but—dashes of cold rain

It is one with submarine vistas
purple and black fish turning
among undulant seaweed—

Black wind, I have poured my heart out
to you until I am sick of it—

Now I run my hand over you feeling
the play of your body—the quiver
of its strength—

The grief of the bowmen of Shu
moves nearer—There is
an approach with difficulty from
the dead—the winter casing of grief

How easy to slip
into the old mode, how hard to
cling firmly to the advance—

VI

No that is not it
nothing that I have done

nothing
I have done

is made up of
nothing
and the diphthong

ae

together with
the first person
singular
indicative

of the auxiliary
verb
to have

everything
I have done
is the same

if to do

is capable
of an
infinity of
combinations

involving the
moral
physical
and religious

codes

for everything
and nothing

are synonymous
when

energy in vacuo
has the power
of confusion

which only to
have done nothing
can make
perfect

The inevitable flux of the seeing eye toward measuring itself by the world it inhabits can only result in himself crushing humiliation unless the individual raise to some approximate co-extension with the universe. This is possible by aid of the imagination. Only through the agency of this force can a man feel himself moved largely with sympathetic pulses at work—

A work of the imagination which fails to release the senses in accordance with this major requisite—the sympathies, the intelligence in its selective world, fails at the elucidation, the alleviation which is—

In the composition, the artist does exactly what every eye must do with life, fix the particular with the universality of his own personality—Taught by the largeness of his imagination to feel every form which he sees moving within himself, he must prove the truth of this by expression.

The contraction which is felt.

All this being anterior to technique, that can have only a sequent value; but since all that appears to the senses on a work of art does so through

fixation by the imagination of the external as well internal means of expression the essential nature of technique or transcription. **105**

Only when (this position) is reached can life proper be said to begin since only then can a value be affixed to the forms and activities of which it consists.

Only then can the sense of frustration which ends. All composition defeated.

Only through the imagination is the advance of intelligence possible, to keep beside growing understanding.

Complete lack of imagination would be the same at the cost of intelligence, complete.

Even the most robust constitution has its limits, though the Roman feast with its reliance upon regurgitation to prolong it shows an active ingenuity, yet the powers of a man are so pitifully small, with the ocean to swallow—that at the end of the feast nothing would be left but suicide.

That or the imagination which in this case takes the form of humor, is known in that form—the release from physical necessity. Having eaten to the full we must acknowledge our insufficiency since we have not annihilated all food nor even the quantity of a good sized steer. However we have annihilated all eating: quite plainly we have no more appetite. This is to say that the imagination has removed us from the banal necessity of bursting ourselves—by acknowledging a new situation. We must acknowledge that the ocean we would drink is too vast—but at the same time we realize that extension in our case is not confined to the intestine only. The stomach is full, the ocean no fuller, both have the same quality of fullness. In that, then, one is equal to the other. Having eaten, the man has released his mind.

THIS catalogue might be increased to larger proportions without stimulating the sense.

In works of the imagination that which is taken for great good sense, so that it seems as if an accurate precept were discovered, is in reality not so, but vigor and accuracy of the imagination alone. In work such as Shakespeare's—

This leads to the discovery that has been made today— old catalogues aside—full of meat—

"the divine illusion has about it that inaccuracy which re-
veals that which I mean."

There is only "illusion" in art where ignorance of the
bystander confuses imagination and its works with cruder
processes. Truly men feel an enlargement before great or
good work, an expansion but this is not, as so many believe
today a "lie," a stupefaction, a kind of mesmerism, a thing
to block out "life," bitter to the individual, by a "vision of
beauty." It is a work of the imagination. It gives the feeling
of completion by revealing the oneness of experience; it
rouses rather than stupefies the intelligence by demonstrat-
ing the importance of personality, by showing the indi-
vidual, depressed before it, that his life is valuable—when
completed by the imagination. And then only. Such work
elucidates—

Such a realization shows us the falseness of attempting to
"copy" nature. The thing is equally silly when we try to
"make" pictures—

But such a picture as that of Juan Gris, though I have not
seen it in color, is important as marking more clearly than
any I have seen what the modern trend is: the attempt is
being made to separate things of the imagination from life,
and obviously, by using the forms common to experience so
as not to frighten the onlooker away but to invite him,

The rose is obsolete
but each petal ends in
an edge, the double facet
cementing the grooved
columns of air—The edge
cuts without cutting
meets—nothing—renews
itself in metal or porcelain—

whither? It ends—

But if it ends
the start is begun
so that to engage roses
becomes a geometry—

Sharper, neater, more cutting
figured in majolica—
the broken plate
glazed with a rose

Somewhere the sense
makes copper roses
steel roses—

The rose carried weight of love
but love is at an end—of roses

If is at the edge of the
petal that love waits

Crisp, worked to defeat
laboredness—fragile
plucked, moist, half-raised
cold, precise, touching

What

The place between the petal's
edge and the

From the petal's edge a line starts
that being of steel
infinitely fine, infinitely
rigid penetrates
the Milky Way
without contact—lifting

from it—neither hanging
nor pushing—

The fragility of the flower
unbruised
penetrates spaces˙

VIII

The sunlight in a
yellow plaque upon the
varnished floor

is full of a song
inflated to
fifty pounds pressure

at the faucet of
June that rings
the triangle of the air

pulling at the
anemones in
Persephone's cow pasture—

When from among
the steel rocks leaps
J. P. M.

who enjoyed
extraordinary privileges
among virginity

to solve the core
of whirling flywheels
by cutting

the Gordian knot
with a Veronese or
perhaps a Rubens—

whose cars are about
the finest on
the market today—

And so it comes
to motor cars—
which is the son

leaving off the g
of sunlight and grass—
Impossible

to say, impossible
to underestimate—
wind, earthquakes in

Manchuria, a
partridge
from dry leaves

    Things with which he is familiar, simple things—at the
same time to detach them from ordinary experience to the
imagination. Thus they are still "real" they are the same
things they would be if photographed or painted by Monet,
they are recognizable as the things touched by the hands
during the day, but in this painting they are seen to be in
some peculiar way—detached
    Here is a shutter, a bunch of grapes, a sheet of music, a
picture of sea and mountains (particularly fine) which the
onlooker is not for a moment permitted to witness as an
"illusion." One thing laps over on the other, the cloud laps
over on the shutter, the bunch of grapes is part of the

handle of the guitar, the mountain and sea are obviously not "the mountain and sea," but a picture of the mountain and the sea. All drawn with admirable simplicity and excellent design—all a unity—

This was not necessary where the subject of art was not "reality" but related to the "gods"—by force or otherwise. There was no need of the "illusion" in such a case since there was none possible where a picture or a work represented simply the imaginative reality which existed in the mind of the onlooker. No special effort was necessary to cleave where the cleavage already existed.

I don't know what the Spanish see in their Velázquez and Goya but

Today where everything is being brought into sight the realism of art has bewildered us, confused us and forced us to re-invent in order to retain that which the older generations had without that effort.

Cézanne—

The only realism in art is of the imagination. It is only thus that the work escapes plagiarism after nature and becomes a creation

Invention of new forms to embody this reality of art, the one thing which art is, must occupy all serious minds concerned.

From the time of Poe in the U. S.—the first American poet had to be a man of great separation—with close identity with life. Poe could not have written a word without the violence of expulsive emotion combined with the in-driving force of a crudely repressive environment. Between the two his imagination was forced into being to keep him to that reality, completeness, sense of escape which is felt in his work—his topics. Typically American—accurately, even inevitably set in his time.

So, after this tedious diversion—whatever of dull you find among my work, put it down to criticism, not to poetry. You will not be mistaken—Who am I but my own critic? Surely in isolation one becomes a god—At least one becomes something of everything, which is not wholly god-like, yet a little so—in many things.

It is not necessary to count every flake of the truth that falls; it is necessary to dwell in the imagination if the truth is to be numbered. It is necessary to speak from the imagination—

The great furor about perspective in Holbein's day had as a consequence much fine drawing, it made coins defy gravity, standing on the table as if in the act of falling. To say this was lifelike must have been satisfying to the master, it gave depth, pungency.

But all the while the picture escaped notice—partly because of the perspective. Or if noticed it was for the most part because one could see "the birds pecking at the grapes" in it.

Meanwhile the birds were pecking at the grapes outside the window and in the next street Bauermeister Kummel was letting a gold coin slip from his fingers to the counting table.

The representation was perfect, it "said something one was used to hearing" but with verve, cleverly.

Thus perspective and clever drawing kept the picture continually under cover of the "beautiful illusion" until today, when even Anatole France trips, saying: "Art—all lies!"—today when we are beginning to discover the truth that in great works of the imagination A CREATIVE FORCE IS SHOWN AT WORK MAKING OBJECTS WHICH ALONE COMPLETE SCIENCE AND ALLOW INTELLIGENCE TO SURVIVE—his picture lives anew. It lives as pictures only can: by their power TO ESCAPE ILLUSION and stand between man and nature as saints once stood between man and the sky—their reality in such work, say, as that of Juan Gris

No man could suffer the fragmentary nature of his understanding of his own life—

Whitman's proposals are of the same piece with the modern trend toward imaginative understanding of life. The

largeness which he interprets as his identity with the least
and the greatest about him, his "democracy" represents the
vigor of his imaginative life.

IX

What about all this writing?

O "Kiki"
O Miss Margaret Jarvis
The backhandspring

I: clean
   clean
   clean: yes . . . New-York

Wrigley's, appendicitis, John Marin:
skyscraper soup—

Either that or a bullet!

Once
anything might have happened
You lay relaxed on my knees—
the starry night
spread out warm and blind
above the hospital—

Pah!

It is unclean
which is not straight to the mark—

In my life the furniture eats me

the chairs, the floor
the walls

which heard your sobs
drank up my emotion—
they which alone know everything

and snitched on us in the morning—

What to want?

Drunk we go forward surely
Not I

beds, beds, beds
elevators, fruit, night-tables
breasts to see, white and blue—
to hold in the hand, to nozzle

It is not onion soup
Your sobs soaked through the walls
breaking the hospital to pieces

Everything
—windows, chairs
obscenely drunk, spinning—
white, blue, orange
—hot with our passion

wild tears, desperate rejoinders
my legs, turning slowly
end over end in the air!

But what would you have?

All I said was:
there, you see, it is broken

stockings, shoes, hairpins
your bed, I wrapped myself round you—

I watched

You sobbed, you beat your pillow
you tore your hair
you dug your nails into your sides

I was your nightgown
                    I   watched!

Clean is he alone
after whom stream
the broken pieces of the city—
flying apart at his approaches

but I merely
caress you curiously

fifteen years ago and you still
go about the city, they say
patching up sick school children

Understood in a practical way, without calling upon
mystic agencies, of this or that order, it is that life becomes
actual only when it is identified with ourselves. When we
name it, life exists. To repeat physical experiences has no—
    The only means he has to give value to life is to recognize
it with the imagination and name it; this is so. To repeat
and repeat the thing without naming it is only to dull the
sense and results in frustration.
this makes the artist the prey of life. He is easy of attack.
    I think often of my earlier work and what it has cost me
not to have been clear. I acknowledge I have moved cha-
otically about refusing or rejecting most things, seldom ac-
cepting values or acknowledging anything.
                        because I early recognized the futility of
acquisitive understanding and at the same time rejected re-
ligious dogmatism. My whole life has been spent (so far) in   **115**

seeking to place a value upon experience and the objects of experience that would satisfy my sense of inclusiveness without redundancy—completeness, lack of frustration with the liberty of choice; the things which the pursuit of "art" offers—

But though I have felt "free" only in the presence of works of the imagination, knowing the quickening of the sense which came of it, and though this experience has held me firm at such times, yet being of a slow but accurate understanding, I have not always been able to complete the intellectual steps which would make me firm in the position.

So most of my life has been lived in hell—a hell of repression lit by flashes of inspiration, when a poem such as this or that would appear

What would have happened in a world similarly lit by the imagination

Oh yes, you are a writer! a phrase that has often damned me, to myself. I rejected it with heat but the stigma remained. Not a man, not an understanding but a WRITER. I was unable to recognize.

I do not forget with what heat too I condemned some poems of some contemporary praised because of their loveliness—

I find that I was somewhat mistaken—ungenerous

Life's processes are very simple. One or two moves are made and that is the end. The rest is repetitious.

The *Improvisations*—coming at a time when I was trying to remain firm at great cost—I had recourse to the expedient of letting life go completely in order to live in the world of my choice.

I let the imagination have its own way to see if it could save itself. Something very definite came of it. I found myself alleviated but most important I began there and then to revalue experience, to understand what I was at—

The virtue of the improvisations is their placement in a world of new values—

their fault is their dislocation of sense, often complete. But it is the best I could do under the circumstances. It was the best I could do and retain any value to experience at all.

Now I have come to a different condition. I find that the values there discovered can be extended. I find myself extending the understanding to the work of others and other things—

I find that there is work to be done in the creation of new forms, new names for experience

and that "beauty" is related not to "loveliness" but to a state in which reality plays a part

Such painting as that of Juan Gris, coming after the impressionists, the expressionists, Cézanne—and dealing severe strokes as well to the expressionists as to the impressionists group—points forward to what will prove the greatest painting yet produced.

—the illusion once dispensed with, painting has this problem before it: to replace not the forms but the reality of experience with its own—

up to now shapes and meanings but always the illusion relying on composition to give likeness to "nature"

now works of art cannot be left in this category of France's "lie," they must be real, not "realism" but reality itself—

they must give not the sense of frustration but a sense of completion, of actuality—It is not a matter of "representation"—which may be represented actually, but of separate existence.

enlargement—revivification of values,

X

The universality of things
draws me toward the candy
with melon flowers that open

about the edge of refuse
proclaiming without accent
the quality of the farmer's

shoulders and his daughter's
accidental skin, so sweet
with clover and the small

yellow cinquefoil in the
parched places. It is
this that engages the favorable

distortion of eyeglasses
that see everything and remain
related to mathematics—

in the most practical frame of
brown celluloid made to
represent tortoiseshell—

A letter from the man who
wants to start a new magazine
made of linen

and he owns a typewriter—
July 1, 1922
All this is for eyeglasses

to discover. But
they lie there with the gold
earpieces folded down

tranquilly Titicaca—

XI

In passing with my mind
on nothing in the world

but the right of way
I enjoy on the road by

virtue of the law   —
I saw

an elderly man who
smiled and looked away

to the north past a house—
a woman in blue

who was laughing and
leaning forward to look up

into the man's half
averted face

and a boy of eight who was
looking at the middle of

the man's belly
at a watchchain—

The supreme importance
of this nameless spectacle

sped me by them
without a word—

Why bother where I went?
for I went spinning on the

four wheels of my car
along the wet road until

I saw a girl with one leg
over the rail of a balcony

When in the condition of imaginative suspense only will
the writing have reality, as explained partially in what pre-
cedes—Not to attempt, at that time, to set values on the
word being used, according to presupposed measures, but to
write down that which happens at that time—

To perfect the ability to record at the moment when the
consciousness is enlarged by the sympathies and the unity
of understanding which the imagination gives, to practice
skill in recording the force moving, then to know it, in the
largeness of its proportions—

It is the presence of a

This is not "fit" but a unification of experience

That is, the imagination is an actual force comparable to
electricity or steam, it is not a plaything but a power that
has been used from the first to raise the understanding of—
it is, not necessary to resort to mysticism—In fact it is this
which has kept back the knowledge I seek—

The value of the imagination to the writer consists in its
ability to make words. Its unique power is to give created
forms reality, actual existence

This separates

Writing is not a searching about in the daily experience
for apt similes and pretty thoughts and images. I have ex-
perienced that to my sorrow. It is not a conscious recording
of the day's experiences "freshly and with the appearance
of reality"—This sort of thing is seriously to the develop-
ment of any ability in a man, it fastens him down, makes
him a—It destroys, makes nature an accessory to the par-
ticular theory he is following, it blinds him to his world,—

120   The writer of imagination would find himself released

[handwritten margin note: writing as recording the moving force of our imagination — the imag. is an actual force which raises the understanding]

from observing things for the purpose of writing them down later. He would be there to enjoy, to taste, to engage the free world, not a world which he carries like a bag of food, always fearful lest he drop something or someone get more than he,

A world detached from the necessity of recording it, sufficient to itself, removed from him (as it most certainly. is) with which he has bitter and delicious relations and from which he is independent—moving at will from one thing to another—as he pleases, unbound—complete

and the unique proof of this is the work of the imagination not "like" anything but transfused with the same forces which transfuse the earth—at least one small part of them.

Nature is the hint to composition not because it is familiar to us and therefore the terms we apply to it have a least common denominator quality which gives them currency—but because it possesses the quality of independent existence, of reality which we feel in ourselves. It is opposed to art but apposed to it.

the use
of analogy

I suppose Shakespeare's familiar aphorism about holding the mirror up to nature has done more harm in stabilizing the copyist tendency of the arts among us than—

the mistake in it (though we forget that it is not S. speaking but an imaginative character of his) is to have believed that the reflection of nature is nature. It is not. It is only a sham nature, a "lie."

Of course S. is the most conspicuous example desirable of the falseness of this very thing.

He holds no mirror up to nature but with his imagination rivals nature's composition with his own.

He himself become "nature"—continuing "its" marvels —if you will

I am often diverted with a recital which I have made for myself concerning Shakespeare: he was a comparatively uninformed man, quite according to the orthodox tradition, who lived from first to last a life of amusing regularity and simplicity, a house and wife in the suburbs, delightful children, a girl at court (whom he really never confused with his writing) and a café life which gave him with the freshness of discovery, the information upon which his imagination fed. London was full of the concentrates of science and adventure. He saw at "The Mermaid" everything he knew. He was not conspicuous there except for his spirits.

His form was presented to him by Marlow, his stories were the common talk of his associates or else some compiler set them before him. His types were particularly quickened with life about him.

Feeling the force of life, in his peculiar intelligence, the great dome of his head, he had no need of anything but writing material to relieve himself of his thoughts. His very lack of scientific training loosened his power. He was unencumbered.

For S. to pretend to knowledge would have been ridiculous—no escape there—but that he possessed knowledge, and extraordinary knowledge, of the affairs which concerned him, as they concerned the others about him, was self-apparent to him. It was not apparent to the others.

His actual power was PURELY of the imagination. Not permitted to speak as W.S., in fact peculiarly barred from speaking so because of his lack of information, learning, not being able to rival his fellows in scientific training or adventure and at the same time being keen enough, imaginative enough, to know that there is no escape except in perfection, in excellence, in technical excellence—his buoyancy of imagination raised him NOT TO COPY them, not to holding the mirror up to them but to equal, to surpass them as a creator of knowledge, as a vigorous, living force above their heads.

His escape was not simulated but real. Hamlet no doubt was written about at the middle of his life.

He speaks authoritatively through invention, through characters, through design. The objects of his world were real to him because he could use them and use them with understanding to make his inventions—

The imagination is a—

The vermiculations of modern criticism of S. particularly amuse when the attempt is made to force the role of a Solon upon the creator of Richard 3d.

So I come again to my present day gyrations.

So it is with the other classics: their meaning and worth can only be studied and understood in the imagination— that which begot them only can give them life again, re-enkindle their perfection—

unless to study by rote or scientific research—Useful for certain understanding to corroborate the imagination—

Yes, Anatole was a fool when he said: It is a lie. —That is it. If the actor simulates life it *is* a lie. But—but why continue without an audience?

The reason people marvel at works of art and say: How in Christ's name did he do it?—is that they know nothing of the physiology of the nervous system and have never in their experience witnessed the larger processes of the imagination.

It is a step over from the profitless engagements of the arithmetical.

XII

The red paper box
hinged with cloth

is lined
inside and out
with imitation
leather

It is the sun
the table
with dinner
on it for
these are the same—

Its twoinch trays
have engineers
that convey glue
to airplanes

or for old ladies
that darn socks
paper clips
and red elastics—

What is the end
to insects
that suck gummed
labels?

for this is eternity
through its
dial we discover
transparent tissue
on a spool

But the stars
are round
cardboard
with a tin edge

and a ring
to fasten them
to a trunk
for the vacation—

XIII

Crustaceous
wedge

of sweaty kitchens
on rock
overtopping
thrusts of the sea

Waves of steel
from
swarming backstreets
shell
of coral
inventing
electricity—

Lights
speckle
El Greco
lakes
in renaissance
twilight
with triphammers

which pulverize
nitrogen
of old pastures
to dodge
motorcars
with arms and legs—

The aggregate
is untamed
encapsulating
irritants
but
of agonized spires
knits
peace

125

where bridge stanchions
rest
certainly
piercing
left ventricles
with long
sunburnt fingers

XIV

of death
the barber
the barber
talked to me

cutting my
life with
sleep to trim
my hair—

It's just
a moment
he said, we die
every night—

And of
the newest
ways to grow
hair on

bald death—
I told him
of the quartz
lamp

and of old men
with third
sets of teeth
to the cue

of an old man
who said
at the door—
Sunshine today!

for which
death shaves
him twice
a week

XV

The decay of cathedrals
is efflorescent
through the phenomenal
growth of movie houses

whose catholicity is
progress since
destruction and creation
are simultaneous

without sacrifice
of even the smallest
detail even to the
volcanic organ whose

woe is translatable
to joy if light becomes
darkness and darkness
light, as it will—

But schism which seems
adamant is diverted
from the perpendicular
by simply rotating the object

cleaving away the root of
disaster which it
seemed to foster. Thus
the movies are a moral force

Nightly the crowds
with the closeness and
universality of sand
witness the selfspittle

which used to be drowned
in incense and intoned
over by the supple jointed
imagination of inoffensiveness

backed by biblical
rigidity made into passion plays
upon the altar to
attract the dynamic mob

whose female relative
sweeping grass Tolstoi
saw injected into
the Russian nobility

It is rarely understood how such plays as Shakespeare's
were written—or in fact how any work of value has been
written, the practical bearing of which is that only as the
work was produced, in that way alone can it be understood
    Fruitless for the academic tapeworm to hoard its ex-
crementa in books. The cage—

The most of all writing has not even begun in the province from which alone it can draw sustenance.

There is not life in the stuff because it tries to be "like" life.

First must come the transposition of the faculties to the only world of reality that men know: the world of the imagination, wholly our own. From this world alone does the work gain power, its soil the only one whose chemistry is perfect to the purpose.

The exaltation men feel before a work of art is the feeling of reality they draw from it. It sets them up, places a value upon experience—(said that half a dozen times already)

XVI

O tongue
licking
the sore on
her netherlip

O toppled belly

O passionate cotton
stuck with
matted hair

Elysian slobber
from her mouth
upon
the folded handkerchief

I can't die

—moaned the old
jaundiced woman

rolling her
saffron eyeballs

I can't die
I can't die

XVII

Our orchestra
is the cat's nuts—

Banjo jazz
with a nickelplated

amplifier to
soothe

the savage beast—
Get the rhythm

That sheet stuff
's a lot a cheese.

Man
gimme the key

and lemme loose—
I make 'em crazy

with my harmonies—
Shoot it Jimmy

Nobody
Nobody else

but me—
They can't copy it

XVIII

The pure products of America
go crazy—
mountain folk from Kentucky

or the ribbed north end of
Jersey
with its isolate lakes and

valleys, its deaf-mutes, thieves
old names
and promiscuity between

devil-may-care men who have taken
to railroading
out of sheer lust of adventure—

and young slatterns, bathed
in filth
from Monday to Saturday

to be tricked out that night
with gauds
from imaginations which have no   *post-colonialism in place
                                        of peasant traditions*

peasant traditions to give them
character
but flutter and flaunt

sheer rags—succumbing without
emotion
save numbed terror   **131**

under some hedge of choke-cherry
or viburnum—
which they cannot express—

Unless it be that marriage
perhaps
with a dash of Indian blood

will throw up a girl so desolate
so hemmed round
with disease or murder

that she'll be rescued by an
agent—
reared by the state and

sent out at fifteen to work in
some hard pressed
house in the suburbs—

some doctor's family, some Elsie—
voluptuous water
expressing with broken

brain the truth about us—
her great
ungainly hips and flopping breasts

addressed to cheap
jewelry
and rich young men with fine eyes

as if the earth under our feet
were
an excrement of some sky

and we degraded prisoners
destined
to hunger until we eat filth

while the imagination strains
after deer
going by fields of goldenrod in

the stifling heat of September
Somehow
it seems to destroy us

It is only in isolate flecks that
something
is given off

No one
to witness
and adjust, no one to drive the car

Or better: prose has to do with the fact of an emo-
tion; poetry has to do with the dynamization of emotion
into a separate form. This is the force of imagination.
prose: statement of facts concerning emotions, intellectual
states, data of all sorts—technical expositions, jargon, of all
sorts—fictional and other—
poetry: new form dealt with as a reality in itself.
The form of prose is the accuracy of its subject matter—
how best to expose the multiform phases of its material
    the form of poetry is related to the movements of the
imagination revealed in words—or whatever it may be—
the cleavage is complete
    Why should I go further than I am able? Is it not enough
for you that I am perfect?
    The cleavage goes through all the phases of experience.
It is the jump from prose to the process of imagination that

is the next great leap of the intelligence—from the simulations of present experience to the facts of the imagination—

the greatest characteristic of the present age is that it is stale—stale as literature—

To enter a new world, and have there freedom of movement and newness.

I mean that there will always be prose painting, representative work, clever as may be in revealing new phases of emotional research presented on the surface.

But the jump from that to Cézanne or back to certain of the primitives is the impossible.

The primitives are not back in some remote age—they are not BEHIND experience. Work which bridges the gap between the rigidities of vulgar experience and the imagination is rare. It is new, immediate—It is so because it is actual, always real. It is experience dynamized into reality.

Time does not move. Only ignorance and stupidity move. Intelligence (force, power) stands still with time and forces change about itself—sifting the world for permanence, in the drift of nonentity.

Pío Baroja interested me once—

Baroja leaving the medical profession, some not important inspector's work in the north of Spain, opened a bakery in Madrid.

The isolation he speaks of, as a member of the so called intellectual class, influenced him to abandon his position and engage himself, as far as possible, in the intricacies of the design patterned by the social class—He sees no interest in isolation—

These gestures are the effort for self preservation or the preservation of some quality held in high esteem—

Here it seems to be that a man, starved in imagination, changes his milieu so that his food may be richer—The social class, without the power of expression, lives upon imaginative values.

I mean only to emphasize the split that goes down

through the abstractions of art to the everyday exercises of the most primitive types—

there is a sharp division—the energizing force of imagi- nation on one side—and the acquisitive—PROGRESSIVE force of the lump on the other

The social class with its religion, its faith, sincerity and all the other imaginative values is positive (yes)

the merchant, hibernating, unmagnetized—tends to drop away into the isolate, inactive particles—Religion is con- tinued then as a form, art as a convention—

To the social, energized class—ebullient now in Russia the particles adhere because of the force of the imagina- tion energizing them—

Anyhow the change of Baroja interested me

Among artists, or as they are sometimes called "men of imagination" "creators," etc. this force is recognized in a pure state—All this can be used to show the relationships between genius, hand labor, religion—etc. and the lack of feeling between artists and the middle class type—

The jump between fact and the imaginative reality

The study of all human activity is the delineation of the cresence and ebb of this force, shifting from class to class and location to location—rhythm: the wave rhythm of Shakespeare watching clowns and kings sliding into nothing

XIX

This is the time of year
when boys fifteen and seventeen
wear two horned lilac blossoms
in their caps—or over one ear

What is it that does this?

It is a certain sort—
drivers for grocers or taxidrivers
white and colored—

fellows that let their hair grow long
in a curve over one eye—

Horned purple

Dirty satyrs, it is
vulgarity raised to the last power

They have stolen them
broken the bushes apart
with a curse for the owner—

Lilacs—

They stand in the doorways
on the business streets with a sneer
on their faces

adorned with blossoms

Out of their sweet heads
dark kisses—rough faces

XX

The sea that encloses her young body
ula lu la lu
is the sea of many arms—

The blazing secrecy of noon is undone
and and and
the broken sand is the sound of love—

The flesh is firm that turns in the sea
O la la
the sea that is cold with dead men's tears—

Deeply the wooing that penetrated
to the edge of the sea
returns in the plash of the waves—

a wink over the shoulder
large as the ocean—
with wave following wave to the edge

coom barrooom—

It is the cold of the sea
broken upon the sand by the force
of the moon—

In the sea the young flesh playing
floats with the cries of far off men
who rise in the sea

with green arms
to homage again the fields over there
where the night is deep—

la lu la lu
but lips too few
assume the new—marrruu

Underneath the sea where it is dark
there is no edge
so two—

XXI

one day in Paradise
a Gipsy

smiled
to see the blandness

of the leaves—
so many

so lascivious
and still

XXII

so much depends
upon

a red wheel
barrow

glazed with rain
water

beside the white
chickens

The fixed categories into which life is divided must always hold. These things are normal—essential to every activity. But they exist—but not as dead dissections.

The curriculum of knowledge cannot but be divided into the sciences, the thousand and one groups of data, scientific, philosophic or whatnot—as many as there exist in Shakespeare—things that make him appear the university of all ages.

But this is not the thing. In the galvanic category of— The same things exist, but in a different condition when energized by the imagination.

The whole field of education is affected—There is no end of detail that is without significane.

Education would begin by placing in the mind of the student the nature of knowledge—in the dead state and the nature of the force which may energize it.

This would clarify his field at once—He would then see the use of data

But at present knowledge is placed before a man as if it were a stair at the top of which a DEGREE is obtained which is superlative.

nothing could be more ridiculous. To data there is no end. There is proficiency in dissection and a knowledge of parts but in the use of knowledge—

It is the imagination that—

That is: life is absolutely simple. In any civilized society everyone should know EVERYTHING there is to know about life at once and always. There should never be permitted, confusion—

There are difficulties to life, under conditions there are impasses, life may prove impossible—But it must never be lost—as it is today—

I remember so distinctly the young Pole in Leipzig going with hushed breath to hear Wundt lecture—In this mass of intricate pholsophic data what one of the listeners was able to maintain himself for the winking of an eyelash. Not one. The inundation of the intelligence by masses of complicated fact is not knowledge. There is no end—

And what is the fourth dimension? It is the endlessness of knowledge—

It is the imagination on which reality rides—It is the imagination—It is a cleavage through everything by a force that does not exist in the mass and therefore can never be discovered by its anatomization.

It is for this reason that I have always placed art first and esteemed it over science—in spite of everything.

Art is the pure effect of the force upon which science depends for its reality—Poetry

The effect of this realization upon life will be the emplacement of knowledge into a living current—which it has always sought—

In other times—men counted it a tragedy to be dislocated from sense—Today boys are sent with dullest faith to technical schools of all sorts—broken, bruised

few escape whole—slaughter. This is not civilization but stupidity—Before entering knowledge the integrity of the imagination—

The effect will be to give importance to the sub-divisions of experience—which today are absolutely lost—There exists simply nothing.

Prose—When values are important, such—For example there is no use denying that prose and poetry are not by any means the same IN INTENTION. But then what is prose? There is no need for it to approach poetry except to be weakened.

With decent knowledge to hand we can tell what things are for

I expect to see values blossom. I expect to see prose be prose. Prose, relieved of extraneous, unrelated values must return to its only purpose; to clarity to enlighten the understanding. There is no form to prose but that which depends on clarity. If prose is not accurately adjusted to the exposition of facts it does not exist—Its form is that alone. To penetrate everywhere with enlightenment—

Poetry is something quite different. Poetry has to do with the crystallization of the imagination—the perfection of new forms as additions to nature—Prose may follow to enlighten but poetry—

Is what I have written prose? The only answer is that form in prose ends with the end of that which is being communicated—If the power to go on falters in the middle of a sentence—that is the end of the sentence—Or if a new phase enters at that point it is only stupidity to go on.

140   There is no confusion—only difficulties.

XXIII

The veritable night
of wires and stars

the moon is in
the oak tree's crotch

and sleepers in
the windows cough

athwart the round
and pointed leaves

and insects sting
while on the grass

the whitish moonlight
tearfully

assumes the attitudes
of afternoon—

But it is real
where peaches hang

recalling death's
long promised symphony

whose tuneful wood
and stringish undergrowth

are ghosts existing
without being

save to come with juice
and pulp to assuage

the hungers which
the night reveals

so that now at last
the truth's aglow

with devilish peace
forestalling day

which dawns tomorrow
with dreadful reds

the heart to predicate
with mists that loved

the ocean and the fields—
Thus moonlight

is the perfect
human touch

XXIV

The leaves embrace
in the trees

it is a wordless
world

without personality
I do not

seek a path
I am still with

Gipsy lips pressed
to my own—

It is the kiss
of leaves

without being
poison ivy

or nettle, the kiss
of oak leaves—

He who has kissed
a leaf

need look no further—
I ascend

through
a canopy of leaves

and at the same time
I descend

for I do nothing
unusual—

I ride in my car
I think about

prehistoric caves
in the Pyrenees—

the cave of
Les Trois Frères

    The nature of the difference between what is termed
prose on the one hand and verse on the other is not to be

discovered by a study of the metrical characteristics of the words as they occur in juxtaposition. It is ridiculous to say that verse grades off into prose as the rhythm becomes less and less pronounced, in fact, that verse differs from prose in that the meter is more pronounced, that the movement is more impassioned and that rhythmical prose, so called, occupies a middle place between prose and verse.

It is true that verse is likely to be more strongly stressed than what is termed prose, but to say that this is in any way indicative of the difference in nature of the two is surely to make the mistake of arguing from the particular to the general, to the effect that since an object has a certain character that therefore the force which gave it form will always reveal itself in that character.

Of course there is nothing to do but to differentiate prose from verse by the only effective means at hand, the external, surface appearance. But a counter proposal may be made, to wit: that verse is of such a nature that it may appear without metrical stress of any sort and that prose may be strongly stressed—in short that meter has nothing to do with the question whatever.

Of course it may be said that if the difference is felt and is not discoverable to the eye and ear then what about it anyway? Or it may be argued, that since there is according to my proposal no discoverable difference between prose and verse that in all probability none exists and that both are phases of the same thing.

Yet, quite plainly, there is a very marked difference between the two which may arise in the fact of a separate origin for each, each using similar modes for dis-similar purposes; verse falling most commonly into meter but not always, and prose going forward most often without meter but not always.

This at least serves to explain some of the best work I see today and explains some of the most noteworthy failures which I discover. I search for "something" in the writing which moves me in a certain way—It offers a sugges-

Prose + Poetry are to be distinguished by their separate purposes

tion as to why some work of Whitman's is bad poetry and some, in the same meter is prose.

The practical point would be to discover when a work is to be taken as coming from this source and when from that. When discovering a work it would be—If it is poetry it means this and only this—and if it is prose it means that and only that. Anything else is a confusion, silly and bad practice.

I believe this is possible as I believe in the main that Marianne Moore is of all American writers most constantly a poet—not because her lines are invariably full of imagery they are not, they are often diagramatically informative, and not because she clips her work into certain shapes—her pieces are without meter most often—but I believe she is most constantly a poet in her work because the purpose of her work is invariably from the source from which poetry starts—that it is constantly from the purpose of poetry. And that it actually possesses this characteristic, as of that origin, to a more distinguishable degree when it eschews verse rhythms than when it does not. It has the purpose of poetry written into and therefore it is poetry.

I believe it possible, even essential, that when poetry fails it does not become prose but bad poetry. The test of Marianne Moore would be that she writes sometimes good and sometimes bad poetry but always—with a single purpose out of a single fountain which is of the sort—

The practical point would be to discover—

I can go no further than to say that poetry feeds the imagination and prose the emotions, poetry liberates the words from their emotional implications, prose confirms them in it. Both move centrifugally or centripetally toward the intelligence.

Of course it must be understood that writing deals with words and words only and that all discussions of it deal with single words and their association in groups.

As far as I can discover there is no way but the one I have marked out which will satisfactorily deal with certain lines such as occur in some play of Shakespeare or in a poem of Marianne Moore's, let us say: Tomorrow will be the first of April—

Certainly there is an emotional content in this for anyone living in the northern temperate zone, but whether it is prose or poetry—taken by itself—who is going to say unless some mark is put on it by the intent conveyed by the words which surround it—

Either to write or to comprehend poetry the words must be recognized to be moving in a direction separate from the jostling or lack of it which occurs within the piece.

Marianne's words remain separate, each unwilling to group with the others except as they move in the one direction. This is even an important—or amusing—character of Miss Moore's work.

Her work puzzles me. It is not easy to quote convincingly.

XXV

Somebody dies every four minutes
in New York State—

To hell with you and your poetry—
You will rot and be blown
through the next solar system
with the rest of the gases—

What the hell do you know about it?

AXIOMS

Do not get killed

Careful Crossing Campaign
Cross Crossings Cautiously

THE HORSES   black
                &
PRANCED   white

What's the use of sweating over
this sort of thing, Carl; here
it is all set up—

Outings in New York City

Ho for the open country

Don't stay shut up in hot rooms
Go to one of the Great Parks
Pelham Bay for example

It's on Long Island Sound
with bathing, boating
tennis, baseball, golf, etc.

Acres and acres of green grass
wonderful shade trees, rippling brooks

    Take the Pelham Bay Park Branch
    of the Lexington Ave. (East Side)
    Line and you are there in a few
    minutes

Interborough Rapid Transit Co.

XXVI

The crowd at the ball game
is moved uniformly

by a spirit of uselessness
which delights them—

147

all the exciting detail
of the chase

and the escape, the error
the flash of genius—

all to no end save beauty
the eternal—

So in detail they, the crowd,
are beautiful

for this
to be warned against

saluted and defied—
It is alive, venemous

it smiles grimly
its words cut—

The flashy female with her
mother, gets it—

The Jew gets it straight—it
is deadly, terrifying—

It is the Inquisition, the
Revolution

It is beauty itself
that lives

day by day in them
idly—

This is
the power of their faces

It is summer, it is the solstice
the crowd is

cheering, the crowd is laughing
in detail

permanently, seriously
without thought

The imagination uses the phraseology of science. It attacks, stirs, animates, is radio-active in all that can be touched by action. Words occur in liberation by virtue of its processes.

In description words adhere to certain objects. and have the effect on the sense of oysters, or barnacles.

But the imagination is wrongly understood when it is supposed to be a removal from reality in the sense of John of Gaunt's speech in Richard the Second: to imagine possession of that which is lost. It is rightly understood when John of Gaunt's words are related not to their sense as objects adherent to his son's welfare or otherwise but as a dance over the body of his condition accurately accompanying it. By this means of the understanding, the play written to be understood as a play, the author and reader are liberated to pirouette with the words which have sprung from the old facts of history, reunited in present passion.

To understand the words as so liberated is to understand poetry. That they move independently when set free is the mark of their value

Imagination is not to avoid reality, nor is it description nor an evocation of objects or situations, it is to say that poetry does not tamper with the world but moves it—It affirms reality most powerfully and therefore, since reality needs no personal support but exists free from human action, as proven by science in the indestructibility of matter and of force, it creates a new object, a play, a dance which is not a mirror up to nature but—

As birds' wings beat the solid air without which none could fly so words freed by the imagination affirm reality by their flight

Writing is likened to music. The object would be it seems to make poetry a pure art, like music. Painting too. Writing, as with certain of the modern Russians whose work I have seen, would use unoriented sounds in place of conventional words. The poem then would be completely liberated when there is identity of sound with something—perhaps the emotion.

I do not believe that writing is music. I do not believe writing would gain in quality or force by seeking to attain to the conditions of music.

I think the conditions of music are objects for the action of the writer's imagination just as a table or—

According to my present theme the writer of imagination would attain closest to the conditions of music not when his words are disassociated from natural objects and specified meanings but when they are liberated from the usual quality of that meaning by transposition into another medium, the imagination.

Sometimes I speak of imagination as a force, an electricity or a medium, a place. It is immaterial which: for whether it is the condition of a place or a dynamization its effect is the same: to free the world of fact from the impositions of "art" (see Hartley's last chapter) and to liberate the man to act in whatever direction his disposition leads.

The word is not liberated, therefore able to communicate release from the fixities which destroy it until it is accurately tuned to the fact which giving it reality, by its own reality establishes its own freedom from the necessity of a word, thus freeing it and dynamizing it at the same time.

XXVII

Black eyed susan
rich orange
round the purple core

the white daisy
is not
enough

Crowds are white
as farmers
who live poorly

But you
are rich
in savagery—

Arab
Indian
dark woman

The Great American Novel

Introduction

The Great American Novel

WILLIAM CARLOS WILLIAMS'S first extended work of prose, *The Great American Novel* was published in 1923 in Paris in an edition of 300 copies. Thirty-five years later Williams recalled it in *I Wanted to Write a Poem* as "a travesty on what I considered conventional American writing. People were always talking about the Great American Novel so I thought I'd write it. The heroine is a little Ford car—she was very passionate—a hot little baby." In his *Autobiography* Williams calls the book "a satire on the novel form in which a little (female) Ford car falls more or less in love with a Mack truck."

Williams was remembering only partly right. A couple of paragraphs do deal with automotive eroticism. The book strikes a few glancing blows of satire. But for the most part it really is an attempt to write a serious novel. It's a commentary on the impossibility of doing that within established conventions. It's also a prolonged examination of contemporary American life as Williams was experiencing it and as he perceived its sources from his understanding of history.

The Great American Novel was one of the first anti-novels written in the U.S.—plotless, hostile to the tradition of the novel, hung up on problems of language and time, indifferent to the attention span of its readers, capricious in selection of materials, hiding treasures of description and narration in fogs of aesthetic argument. It requires functional devotion to Williams to read the book once. Read twice it becomes a delight. One develops a taste for Williams's arbitrariness because it has purpose.

155

After starting with himself, Williams gradually turns *The Great American Novel* into a discovery of the United States of his time. He sweats over the lack of an indigenous American culture: "Tell me, wet streets, what are we coming to, we in this country? Are we doomed? Must we be another Europe or another Japan with our coats copied from China, another bastard country in a world of bastards?" He picks up pieces of book reviews, bills, advertisements for women's clothing, public announcements, letters from would-be readers. Fragments from his domestic life, episodes from his medical practice (a child is delivered, a hysterectomy is performed), accounts of his comings and goings make the book more journal than novel. As a kind of personally received social history, the book holds a sustained fascination. Not only is the America Williams describes banal, crude, crass and brutalized, it seems to have no cultural funds that can be converted into the Great American Novel every innocent young writer dreams of creating. To find anything worth building on, Williams has to go back to the *Nuevo Mundo* of Christopher Columbus or the religious lunacies of frontier folk. Williams is bombarded by the irrelevancies of existence in the modern United States and he fires them back at us with a reportorial coldness. He fools around with lyrical themes, but they can't go anywhere in this environment. He announces to his wife that he has discovered the means of becoming a truly great writer; she replies, "What did you say, dear, I have been asleep?"

Even the language available to Williams is debased, an import with all the juice drained out. It becomes alive only when Williams captures objects with it or hears mountain folk speak of flowers and trees. Altogether it's a crummy life Williams sees in the United States. The inhabitants of his wasteland breathe hydrochloric acid, handle mercury, and fabricate reprocessed wool sheets. Nobody with any sense would try to write a Great American Novel about such a life with a parachuted language. Or else he would write exactly this kind of a non-Great American non-Novel.

What to do about it? Take flight via the imagination. Kick the permanence habit. It's "a great army with its tail in antiquity." Join vulgarity and reality, as Williams does, in a grotesque celebration of everything, flat or sharp, that life brings. Adorn and exaggerate life through the power of the mind to fantasize, to capture random associations, to turn the grimmest facts of America into the richest texture.

"Do you mean that you are attempting to set down the American background?" one of Williams's nameless characters asks. "You will go mad."

No, he did not go mad. He learned how not to. The imagination.

w.s.

The Great American Novel

I

THE FOG

IF THERE is progress then there is a novel. Without progress
there is nothing. Everything exists from the beginning. I
existed in the beginning. I was a slobbering infant. Today
I saw nameless grasses—I tapped the earth with my knuckle.
It sounded hollow. It was dry as rubber. Eons of drought.
No rain for fifteen days. No rain. It has never rained. It
will never rain. Heat and no wind all day long better say
hot September. The year has progressed. Up one street
down another. It is still September. Down one street, up
another. Still September. Yesterday was the twenty-second.
Today is the twenty-first. Impossible. Not if it was last
year. But then it wouldn't be yesterday. A year is not as
yesterday in his eyes. Besides last year it rained in the early
part of the month. That makes a difference. It rained on
the white goldenrod. Today being misplaced as against last
year makes it seem better to have white—Such is progress.
Yet if there is to be a novel one must begin somewhere.

Words are not permanent unless the graphite be scraped
up and put in a tube or the ink lifted. Words progress into
the ground. One must begin with words if one is to write.
But what then of smell? What then of the hair on the trees
or the golden brown cherries under the black cliffs. What
of the weakness of smiles that leaves dimples as much as to
say: forgive me—I am slipping, slipping, slipping into noth-
ing at all. Now I am not what I was when the word was
forming to say what I am. I sit so on my bicycle and look
at you greyly, dimpling because it is September and I am
older than I was. I have nothing to say this minute. I shall
never have anything to do unless there is progress, unless

you write a novel. But if you take me in your arms—why the bicycle will fall and it will not be what it is now to smile greyly and a dimple is so deep—you might fall in and never, never remember to write a word to say good-bye to your cherries. For it is September. Begin with September.

To progress from word to word is to suck a nipple. Imagine saying: My dear, I am thirsty, will you let me have a little milk—This to love at first sight. But who do you think I am, says white goldenrod? Of course there is progress. Of course there are words. But I am thirsty, one might add. Yes but I love you and besides I have no milk. Oh yes, that is right. I forgot that we were speaking of words. Yet you cannot deny that to have a novel one must have milk. Not at the beginning. Granted, but at the end at least. Yes, yes, at the end. Progress from the mere form to the substance. Yes, yes, in other words: milk. Milk is the answer.

But how have milk out of white goldenrod? Why, that was what the Indians said. The bosom of the earth sprays up a girl balancing, balancing on a bicycle. Rapidly she passes through the first—the second eight years. Progress, you note. But September was rainy last year and how can it ever be dry again unless one go back to the year before that. There are no words. It cannot be any otherwise than as this is built the bosom of the earth shrinks back; phosphates. Yet to have a novel—Oh catch up a dozen good smelly names and find some reason for murder, it will do. But can you not see, can you not taste, can you not smell, can you not hear, can you not touch—words? It is words that must progress. Words, white goldenrod, it is words you are made out of—THAT is why you want what you haven't got.

Progress is to get. But how can words get. —Let them get drunk. Bah. Words are words. Fog of words. The car runs through it. The words take up the smell of the car. Petrol. Face powder, arm pits, food-grease in the hair, foul breath, clean musk. Words. Words cannot progress. There cannot be a novel. Break the words. Words are indivisible crystals. One cannot break them—Awu tsst grang splith gra pragh og bm—Yes, one can break them. One can make words. Progress? If I make a word I make myself into a word. Such is progress. I shall make myself into a word. One big word. One big union. Such is progress. It is a novel. I begin small and make myself into a big splurging word: I take life and make it into one big blurb. I begin at my childhood. I begin at the beginning and make one big—Bah.

What difference is it whether I make the words or take the words. It makes no difference whatever.

There cannot be a novel. There can only be pyramids, pyramids of words, tombs. Their warm breasts heave up and down calling for a head to progress toward them, to fly onward, upon a word that was a pumpkin, now a fairy chariot, and all the time the thing was rolling backward to the time when one believed. Hans Anderson didn't believe. He had to pretend to believe. It is a conspiracy against childhood. It runs backward. Words are the reverse motion. Words are the flesh of yesterday. Words roll, spin, flare up, rumble, trickle, foam—Slowly they lose momentum. Slowly they cease to stir. At last they break up into their letters—Out of them jumps the worm that was—His hairy feet tremble upon them.

Leaving the meeting room where the Mosquito Extermination Commission had been holding an important fall conference they walked out on to the portico of the County Court House Annex where for a moment they remained in the shadow cast by the moon. A fog had arisen in which the egg-shaped white moon was fixed—so it seemed. They walked around the side of the old-fashioned wooden building—constructed in the style of the fine residences of sixty years ago and coming to the car he said: Go around that side as I will have to get in here by the wheel. The seat was wet with dew and cold—after the exceptionally hot day. They sat on it nevertheless. The windshield was opaque with the water in minute droplets on it—through which the moon shone with its inadequate light. That is, our eyes being used to the sun the moon's light is inadequate for us to see by. But certain bats and owls find it even too strong, preferring the starlight. The stars also were out.

Turning into the exit of the parking space he stopped the car and began to wipe the wind-shield with his hand. Take this rag said the other, with one hand already in his trouser pocket. So the glass was wiped on both sides, the top and the bottom pane and the cloth—which looked a good deal like a handkerchief—was returned to the owner —who put it back where it came from not seeming to mind that it was wet and dirty. But of course the man is a mechanic in a certain sense and doesn't care.

On the highway they began to encounter fog. It seemed in the rush of the car to come and meet them. It came suddenly, with a rush and in a moment nothing could be seen but the white billows of water crossed in front by the flares of the headlights. And so it went all the way home, sometimes clearer, sometimes so thick he had to stop, nearly —ending in his own bed-room with his wife's head on the pillow in the perfectly clear electric light. The light shone brightest on the corner of her right eye, which was nearest it, also on the prominences of her face.

Her right arm was under her head. She had been reading. The magazine Vanity Fair, which he had bought thinking of her, lay open on the coverlet. He looked at her and she at him. He smiled and she, from long practice, began to read to him, progressing rapidly until she said: You can't fool me.

He became very angry but understood at once that she had penetrated his mystery, that she saw he was stealing in order to write words. She smiled again knowingly. He became furious.

II

I'm new, said she, I don't think you'll find my card here.
You're new; how interesting. Can you read the letters on
that chart? Open your mouth. Breathe. Do you have head-
aches? No. Ah, yes, you are new. I'm new, said the oval
moon at the bottom of the mist funnel, brightening and
paling. I don't think you'll find my card there. Open your
mouth—Breathe—A crater big enough to hold the land
from New York to Philadelphia. New! I'm new, said the
quartz crystal on the parlor table—like glass—Mr. Tiffany
bought a car load of them. Like water or white rock candy
—I'm new, said the mist rising from the duck pond, rising,
curling, turning under the moon—Unknown grasses asleep
in the level mists, pieces of the fog. Last night it was an
ocean. Tonight trees. Already it is yesterday. Turned into
the wrong street seeking to pass the power house from
which the hum, hmmmmmmmmmmmmm—sprang. Elec-
tricity has been discovered for ever. I'm new, says the great
dynamo. I am progress. I make a word. Listen! UMMMM-
MMMMMMMM—

Ummmmmmmmmmm—Turned into the wrong street at
three A.M. lost in the fog, listening, searching—Waaaa! said
the baby. I'm new. A boy! A what? Boy. Shit, said the
father of two other sons. Listen here. This is no place to
talk that way. What a word to use. I'm new, said the sudden
word.

The fog lay in deep masses on the roads at three A.M.
Into the wrong street turned the car seeking the high
pitched singing tone of the dynamos endlessly spinning in
the high banquet hall, filling the house and the room where
the bed of pain stood with progress. Ow, ow! Oh help me
somebody! said she. UMMMMMM sang the dynamo in the
next street, UMMMM. With a terrible scream she drowned
out its sound. He went to the window to see if his car
was still there, pulled the curtain aside, green—Yes it was
still there under the light where it would not be so likely

to be struck by other cars coming in the fog. There it was as still as if it were asleep. Still as could be. Not a wheel moved. No sound came from the engine. It stood there under the purple arc-light, partly hidden by a pole which cast a shadow toward him in the masses of floating vapor. He could see the redtaillight still burning brightly with the electricity that came from the battery under the floor boards. No one had stolen the spare tire. It was very late. —Well, said he, dropping the shade and thinking that maybe when he was busy someone might easily come up from the meadows and take the spare tire—Well, I suppose I had better see how things have progressed.

And so he backed out into the main street and turned up another block. And there he saw. The great doors were open to full view of the world. A great amphitheatre of mist lighted from the interior of the power house. In rows sat the great black machines saying vrummmmmmmmmmmmmm. Stately in the great hall they sat and generated electricity to light the cellar stairs with. To warm the pad on Mrs. Voorman's belly. To cook supper by and iron Abie's pyjamas. Here was democracy. Here is progress—here is the substance of words—ummmmm: that is to say meat or linen or belly ache. —Three A.M. To be exact twenty-eight minutes past three.

And all this was yesterday—Yesterday and there at her window I saw her, the lady of my dreams. her long and sallow face, held heavily near the glass, overlooking the street where the decayed-meat wagon passes and the ice-cream cart rumbles with its great power and the complicated affairs of the town twitter toward the open sewer in the meadows by the Button Factory. Orange peel, tomato peel floating in a whitish, soapy flow—Her face without expression, the lady I am dying for, her right shoulder as high as her ear, the line of the shoulder sloping down acutely to the neck, her left shoulder also raised so that her head seemed to lie loose in a kind of saddle.

Supreme in stupidity and a fog of waste, profit in what

is left. Oh what delectable morsel is left. Blessed hunchback, scum of loves weekly praying in all churches—which by the way take up the very best sites in the town. There she sat, her body low down below the window frame, only her face showing, and looked at me dully, looked because I looked—and my heart leaped up to her in passionate appeal that she should be my queen and run with me over the foggy land—Forward—Onward and upward forever.

So saying the day had progressed toward the afternoon and under the poplars the dried leaves had begun to collect. It had been unbearably hot. September is a hot month. The leaves had fallen one by one. No wind. One by one pushed off by the buds which swollen by the heat had thought that winter was over. Off with you. You stand in the way of progress, say the young leaves. Sitting on his chair he seemed like any other man but to get to the bed he suddenly descended to the floor. On his long arms—he Apollo, and using the stumps of his legs, apelike on all fours and talking quietly he swung himself up over the edge of the bed and lay down.

Over the field—for the fog had left the grasses in the early morning when the sun came up with majestic progression, haughtily leaving the dropping city under him—over the field—for it was late in the afternoon and the sunlight shone in with his poor broken legs, crippled as he was—the sun shone in from the west. The car had turned in to the wrong street and he had gone into the store where the paralyzed Scotchman whom he had never seen before put him on the way—climbing into his bed sent his rays almost level over a patch of red grass hot and blinding. Over the field the heat rose and in it even from a distance due to the blur of light on their wings a great swarm of gnats could be seen turning, twisting in the air, rising falling—over the grass, fringed with the progressing sun.

But with great sweeps and sudden turns a dozen dragon flies seeming twice as large as they really were, from the sun blurring their transparent wings, darted back and forth over the field catching and eating the gnats. Swiftly the gnats progressed into the dragon flies, swiftly coalescing—and from time to time a droplet of stuff fell from the vent of a feeding dragon fly,—and the little sound of this stuff striking the earth could not be heard with its true poetic force. Lost. Lost in a complicated world. Except in the eyes of God. But a word, a word rang true. Shit, said the father. With this name I thee christen: he added under his breath.

And yet—one must begin somewhere.

Deeply religious, he walked into the back yard and watching lest the children see him and want what they shouldn't have he approached the grape vines. Selecting a bunch of Delawares he picked it with some difficulty spilling a few of the fruit. Then he walked to the other side and found some blue ones. These too he ate. Then some white which he ate also one by one swallowing the pulp and the seeds and spitting out the skins. He continued to eat but no word came to satisfy.

Somehow a word must be found. He felt rather a weight in his belly from eating so many grapes. He, himself that must die someday, he the deeply religious friend of great men and women in incipience, he couldn't find a word. Only words and words. He ate another bunch of the grapes. More words. And never THE word.

A novel must progress toward a word. Any word that— Any word. There is an idea.

His brother was ill. He must go home. The sun will soon be on the Pacific coast. To bed, to bed—take off the clothes beginning on the outside and working in. How would it be to take off the underwear first, then the shirt—

Progress is damn foolishness—It is a game. Either I have or—a thieves' game. Hold me close, closer, close as you can. I can't hold you any closer. I have been stealing. I should never touch anything. I should never think of anything but you. I love another. It is a word. I have left you alone to run wild with a girl. I would be tame. Lies flicker in the sun. Visions beset noonday. Through the back win-

dow of the shoe-shine parlor a mass of golden glow flashes
in the heat. Come into my heart while I am running—jump-
ing from airplane to plane in midair. I cannot stop: the
word I am seeking is in your mouth—I cannot stop. Hold
me against—

You are wrong, wrong Alva N. Turner. It is deeper than
you imagine. I perceive that it may be permissible for a
poet to write about a poetic sweetheart but never about a
wife—should have said possible. It is not possible. All men
do the same. Dante be damned. Knew nothing at all. Lied to
himself all his life. Profited by his luck and never said
thanks. God pulled the lady up by the roots. Never even
said thank you. Quite wrong. Look what he produced.
Page after page. Helped the world to bread. Have another
slice of bread Mr. Helseth. No thank you—Not hungry to-
night? Something on his mind.

The word. Who.

Liberate the words. You tie them. Poetic sweet-heart.
Ugh. Poetic sweetheart. My dear Miss Word let me hold
your W. I love you. Of all the girls in school you alone are
the one—

Dramatize myself make it sing together as if the world
were a bird who married to the same mate five years under-
stood in the end transmigration of souls.

Nonsense. I am a writer and will never be anything else.
In which case it is impossible to find the word. But to have
a novel one must progress with the words. The words must
become real, they must take the place of wife and sweet-
heart. They must be church—Wife. It must be your wife.
It must be a thing adamant with the texture of wind. Wife.

Am I a word? Words, words, words—

And approaching the end of the novel in his mind as he
sat there with his wife sleeping alone in the next room he
could feel that something unusual had happened. Something
had grown up in his life dearer than—It, as the end. The
words from long practice had come to be leaves, trees, the
corners of his house—such was the end. He had progressed

leaving the others far behind him. Alone in that air with the words of his brain he had breathed again the pure mountain air of joy—there night after night in his poor room. And now he must leave her. She the—He had written the last word and getting up he understood the fog as it billowed before the lights.

That which had been impossible for him at first had become possible. Everything had been removed that other men had tied to the words to secure them to themselves. Clean, clean he had taken each word and made it new for himself so that at last it was new, free from the world for himself—never to touch it—dreams of his babyhood—poetic sweet-heart. No. He went in to his wife with exalted mind, his breath coming in pleasant surges. I come to tell you that the book is finished.

I have added a new chapter to the art of writing. I feel sincerely that all they say of me is true, that I am truly a great man and a great poet.

What did you say, dear, I have been asleep?

III

It is Joyce with a difference. The difference being greater opacity, less erudition, reduced power of perception —Si la sol fa mi re do. Aside from that simple, rather stupid derivation, forced to a ridiculous extreme. No excuse for this sort of thing. Amounts to a total occlusion of intelligence. Substitution of something else. What? Well, nonsense. Since you drive me to it.

Take the improvisations: What the French reader would say is: *Oui, ça; j'ai déjà vu ça; ça c'est de Rimbaud*. Finis.

Representative American verse will be that which will appear new to the French . . . . prose the same.

Infertile Joyce laments the failure of his sterile pen. Siegfried Wagner runs to his Mama crying: Mutti, Mutti, listen, I have just composed a beautiful Cantata on a theme I discovered in one of father's operas.

In other words it comes after Joyce, therefore it is no good, of no use but a secondary local usefulness like the Madison Square Garden tower copied from Seville—It is of no absolute good. It is not NEW. It is not an invention.

Invention, I want to buy you some clothes. Now what would you really like to have? Let us pretend we have no intelligence whatever, that we have read ALL there is to read and that Rimbaud has taught us nothing, that Joyce has passed in a cloud, that, in short, we find nothing to do but begin with Macaulay or King James, that all writing is forbidden us save that which we recognize to be inadequate. NOW show your originality, *mon ami*. NOW let me see what you can do with your vaunted pen.

Nothing could be easier.

My invention this time, my dear, is that literature is a pure matter of words. The moon making a false star of the weather vane on the steeple makes also a word. You do not know the fine hairs on a hickory leaf? Try one in the woods some time. You will grasp at once what I mean.

But Joyce. He is misjudged, misunderstood. His vaunted invention is a fragile fog. His method escapes him. He has not the slightest notion what he is about. He is a priest, a roysterer of the spirit. He is an epicurean of romance. His true genius flickers and fails: there's the peak, there in the trees—For God's sake can't you see it! Not that tree but the mass of rocks, that reddish mass of rocks, granite, with the sun on it between that oak and the maple. —That is not an oak. Hell take it what's the use of arguing with a botanist.

But I will not have my toothpicks made of anything but maple. Mr. Joyce will you see to it that my toothpicks are not made of anything but maple? Irish maple. Damn it, it's for Ireland. Pick your teeth, God knows you need to. The trouble with writing of the old style is that the teeth don't fit. They were made for Irishmen—as a class.

Tell me now, of what in your opinion does Mr. Joyce's art consist, since you have gone so far as to criticize the teeth he makes? —Why, my dear, his art consists of words.

What then is his failure, O God.—His failure is when he mistakes his art to be something else.

What then does he mistake his art to be, Rosinante?—He mistakes it to be several things in more or less certain rotation from botany—Oh well it's a kind of botany you know —from botany to—to—litany. Do you know his poetry?

But you must not mistake his real, if hidden, service. He. has in some measure liberated words, freed them for their proper uses. He has to be a great measure destroyed what is known as "literature." For me as an American it is his only important service.

It would be a pity if the French failed to discover him for a decade or so. Now wouldn't it? Think how literature would suffer. Yes think—think how LITERATURE would suffer.

At that the car jumped forward like a live thing. Up the steep board incline into the garage it leaped—as well as a thing on four wheels could leap—But with great dexterity he threw out the clutch with a slight pressure of his left foot, just as the fore end of the car was about to careen against a mass of old window screens at the garage end. Then pressing with his right foot and grasping the hand-brake he brought the machine to a halt—just in time— though it was no trick to him, he having done it so often for the past ten years.

It seemed glad to be at home in its own little house, the trusty mechanism. The lights continued to flare intimately against the wooden wall as much to say:

> And what is good poetry made of
> And what is good poetry made of
> Of rats and snails and puppy-dog's tails
> And that is what good poetry is made of
>
> And what is bad poetry made of
> And what is bad poetry made of
> Of sugar and spice and everything nice
> That is what bad poetry is made of

Here I am back again. The engine sighed and stopped at the
twist of the key governing the electric switch. Out went
the lights with another twist of the wrist. The owner
groped his way to the little door at the back and emerged
into the moonlight, into the fog, leaving his idle car behind
him to its own thoughts. There it must remain all night, re-
quiring no food, no water to drink, nothing while he, being
a man, must live. His wife was at the window holding the
shade aside.

A rebours: Huysman puts it. My dear let us free our-
selves from this enslavement. We do not know how thor-
oughly we are bound. It must be a new definition, it must
cut us off from the rest. It is in a different line. Good morn-
ing Boss said the old colored man working on the railroad
and started to sing: Jesus, Jesus I love you. It was Sunday,
he was working on the railroad on Sunday and had to put
up some barrier. It is an end to art temporarily. That upstart
Luther. My God don't talk to me of Luther, never changed
his bed clothes for a year. Well, my dear, IT's COMING just
the same. To hell with art. To hell with literature. The old
renaissance priests guarded art in their cloisters for three
hundred years or more. Sunk their teeth in it. The ONE solid
thing. Don't blame me if it went down with them. DOWN,
you understand. First through the middle of the rose win-
dow. You are horror struck. One word: Bing! One accurate
word and a shower of colored glass following it. Is it MY
fault? Ask the French if that is literature.

Do you mean to say that art—O ha, ha. Do you mean to
say that art—O ha ha. Well spit it out. Do you mean to say
that art is SERIOUS?—Yes. Do you mean to say that art does
any WORK?—Yes. Do you mean—? Revolution. Russia.
Kropotkin. Farm, Factory and Field. —CRRRRRRASH. —
Down comes the world. There you are gentlemen, I am an
artist.

What then would you say of the usual interpretation of
the word "literature"?—Permanence. A great army with its
tail in antiquity. Cliché of the soul: beauty.

But can you have literature without beauty? It all depends on what you mean by beauty.

There is beauty in the bellow of the BLAST, etc. from all previous significance. —To me beauty is purity. To me it is discovery, a race on the ground.

And for this you are willing to smash—

Yes, everything. —To go down into hell. —Well let's look.

IV

That's all very fine about *le mot juste* but first the word must be free. —But is there not some other way? It must come about gradually. Why go down into hell when— Because words are not men, they have no adjustments that need to be made. They are words. They can not be anything but free or bound. Go about it any way you chose.

The word is the thing. If it is smeared with colors from right and left what can it amount to?

I'd hate to have to live up there, she said with a frown. It was the soul that spoke. In her words could be read the whole of democracy, the entire life of the planet. It fell by chance on his ear but he was ready, he was alert.

And the little dusty car: There drawn up at the gutter was a great truck painted green and red. Close to it passed the little runabout while conscious desire surged in its breast. Yes there he was the great powerful mechanism, all in his new paint against the gutter while she rolled by and saw—The Polish woman in the clinic, yellow hair slicked back. Neck, arms, breast, waist, hips, etc. This is THE thing—The small mechanism went swiftly by the great truck with fluttering heart in the hope, the secret hope that perhaps, somehow he would notice—HE, the great truck in his massiveness and paint, that somehow he would come to her. Oh I wouldn't like to live up there!

FOG HOLDS UP LINERS say the head lines. It is a blackness,

a choking smother of dirty water in suspension. —You should have been here this morning. You could look out and see nothing but a sea of cloud below us. Right at our feet the fog began and stretched off as far as the eye could perceive.

Up out of the trees with a whirr started the sparrows. With a loud clatter the grouse got up at his feet. The ground was full of mushrooms. Everything, no matter what it is must be re-valuated.

The red grass will soon open into feathers.

Peter Broom, yes sah, my grandfather sah, the greatest man in Prince George County. He had three hundred children.

So many things, so many things: heat.

What then are you trying to say in THIS chapter? And what of your quest of THE word? What of A.N.T. ant?

Why someone has offended Wells. He has retorted with NEO-ACADEMICIAN: And: No new form of the novel required. Lack of substance always takes the form of novelty mongering. Empire must be saved! Saved for the proletariat.

On the side of the great machine it read: Standard Motor Gasoline, in capital letters. A great green tank was built upon the red chassis, FULL of gas. The little car looked and her heart leaped with shy wonder.

Save the words. Save the words from themselves. They are like children. Young Men's Hebrew Association. Save them while they're still young. Words must not be allowed to say, to do—Geld them. They are not REALLY words they are geldings. Save the words. Yes, I repeat SAVE THE WORDS. When Voronoff would have had words to transplant, interstitial words—he said save the words.

And what has anything Wells says to do with serious writing. FIRST let the words be free. The words are men, therefore they are not men. They cannot, must not, will not be mustered of the people, by the people, for the people. They are words. They will have their way.

Puh, puh, puh, puh! said the little car going up hill. But the great green and red truck said nothing but continued to discharge its gasoline into a tank buried in the ground near the gutter.

And the fog had coalesced into rain. Rain to soak the firewood the boys had left beside their old fire, like good scouts, for those to come after and the great car continued to discharge.

V

What then is a novel? *Un novello*, pretty, pretty Baby. It is a thing of fixed form. It is pure English. Yes, she is of Massachusetts stock. Her great grandfather was thrown out of the Quaker church for joining the Continental army. Hates the English. Her life is a novel—almost too sensational.

The story of Miss Li—so well told.

Qu'avez-vous vu? Or they that write much and see little. Not much use to us.

Speak of old Sun Bow pacing his mesa instead of Felipe Segundo in the barren halls of El Escorial—or asleep in his hard bed at one corner of the griddle.

My mother would have a little Negro boy come with a brush and sit at her feet and brush her legs by the hour.

Expressionism is to express skilfully the seething reactions of the contemporary European consciousness. Cornucopia. In at the small end and—blui! Kandinsky.

But it's a fine thing. It is THE thing for the moment—in Europe. The same sort of thing, reversed, in America has a water attachment to be released with a button. That IS art. Everyone agrees that that IS art. Just as one uses a handkerchief.

It is the apotheosis of relief. Dadaism in one of its prettiest modes: *rien, rien, rien.* —But wait a bit. Maybe Dadaism is not so weak as one might imagine. —One takes it for granted almost without a thought that expressionism is the release of SOMETHING. Now then Aemilius, what is European consciousness composed of? —Tell me in one word. —*Rien, rien, rien!* It is at least very complicated. Oh very.

You damned jackass. What do you know about Europe? Yes, what in Christ's name do you know? Your mouth is a sewer, a cloaca.

Complicated consciousness quite aside from a possible re-valuation. It has no value for ME. It is all very interesting and God knows we have enough to learn. The swarming European consciousness. But there it is much simpler—No good to us.

Swarming European consciousness: Kreisler and Ysaye were the only ones with any value. They had a few pennies over and above expenses. They swarm here now for something to eat. But the funniest are the ones from Russia; each excoriates the playing of the other and calls the other a Sheeny. Wow!

Really you are too naive. They are merely reacting to the American atmosphere—It is their work that counts. And besides a virtuoso is not really creative in any serious sense. Would a great artist, say Kandinsky—? In any case it all seems to preoccupy you so, and in a book about America, really—

Take their work. I resent it all. I hate every symphony, every opera as much as a Negro should hate *Il Trovatore*. Not perhaps hate it in a purely aesthetic sense but from under. It is an impertinence. Where in God's name is our Alexander to cut, cut, cut, through this knot.

Europe is nothing to us. Simply nothing. Their music is death to us. We are starving—not dying—not dying mind you—but lean-bellied for words. God I would like to see some man, some one of the singers step out in the midst of some one of Aida's songs and scream like a puma.

But you poor fellow, you use such inept figures. Aida has been dead artistically in Munich for fifty years.

Wagner then—Strauss. It is no difference to me. Tear it

all apart. Start with one note. One word. Chant it over and over forty different ways.

But it would be stupid—

It would, if it were what I mean—it would be accurate. It would articulate with something. It would signify relief. Release I mean. It would be the beginning.

Do not imagine I do not see the necessity of learning from Europe—or China but we will learn what we will, and never what they would teach us. America is a mass of pulp, a jelly, a sensitive plate ready to take whatever print you want to put on it—We have no art, no manners, no intellect—we have nothing. We water at the eyes at our own stupidity. We have only mass movement like a sea. But we are not a sea—

Europe we must—We have no words. Every word we get must be broken off from the European mass. Every word we get placed over again by some delicate hand. Piece by piece we must loosen what we want. What we will have. Will they let it go? Hugh.

I touch the words and they baffle me. I turn them over in my mind and look at them but they mean little that is clean. They are plastered with muck out of the cities.—

We must imitate the motivation and shun the result.

We are very few to your many—

But what is all this but waste energy.

No it is not. It is as near as I can come for the present to the word. What good to talk to me of Santayana and your later critics. I brush them aside. They do not apply. They do not reach me any more than a baby's hand reaches the moon. I am far under them. I am less, far less if you will. I am a beginner. I am an American. A United Stateser. Yes it's ugly, there is no word to say it better. I do not believe in ugliness. I do not want to call myself a United Stateser but what in—but what else am I? Ugliness is a horror to me but it is less abhorrent than to be like you even in the most remote, the most minute particular. For the moment I hate you, I hate your orchestras, your librar-

ies, your sciences, your yearly salons, your finely tuned
intelligences of all sorts. My intelligence is as finely tuned
as yours but it lives in hell, it is doomed to eternal—per-
haps eternal—shiftings after what? Oh to hell with Masters
and the rest of them. To hell with everything I have myself
ever written.

Here's a man wants me to revise, to put in order. My
God what I am doing means just the opposite from that.
There is no revision, there can be no revision—

Down came the rain with a crash. For five days it had
been pending. With a loud splash it seemed to strike the
earth as if it were body meeting body. The poplar leaves
swirled and swirled. The gutters were wedged with water.

Oh you fool you are thicker than rain drops.

Give me to Musorgski. I am tired. Take me to the opera
tonight and let me see Nijinsky dance his *Till Eulenspiegel*
for I am tired to death with looking for sense among Amer-
ican poets. Igor will retrieve my courage. I could sit and
listen in his lap for ever. Were not the American Indians
Mongols? Or they must have been. Why could they not
have been Chinese? Why could not the early Emperors
have discovered America? Tell me, wet streets, what we
are coming to, we in this country? Are we doomed? Must
we be another Europe or another Japan with our coats
copied from China, another bastard country in a world of
bastards? Is this our doom or will we ever amount to
anything?

Drown me in pictures like Marsden, make me a radical
artist in the conventional sense. Give me the intelligence
of a Wells. God, Ford is so far beyond him that what
Wells says really sounds sensible.

Must it be a civilization of fatigued spirits? Then give
me Ford. My God it is too disgusting.

Great men of America! O very great men of America
please lend me a penny so I won't have to go to the opera.

Why not capitalize Barnum—?

Bravo, bravo mon vieux! A noble apostrophe to your

country but don't you realize that it is not a matter of country but the time—The time.

For God's sake Charlie bring a lemon pie.

So they lay in the little brook and let the cold water run up their bare bellies.

VI

In spite of the moon in mid sky and the plaster of dully shining leaves on the macadam and all the other signs of the approach of fine weather there rang in his head: Such a cuddle muddle: Is that modern German poetry? I never saw such a lot of things mixed together under one title. These are modern times, Pa, airships and automobiles; you cover space—

And that's all right—

O America! Turn your head a little to the left please. So. Now are you ready? Watch my hand. Now: *Lohengrin* in ITALIAN, SUNG AT MANHATTAN—San Carlo Company Revives Wagner Opera, with Anna Fitziu as Elsa.

Sweet kisses that come in the night—O Argyrol!

Rain, rain, for three days and three nights.

In the night a caesura. Suddenly the fire bell begins to ring. I wake with a start and hear the small boy calling from the next room. Eight thousand people wake and count the strokes of the black bells. It is not our signal. Someone has been set afire. The engines pass with a crash and roar of the exhausts. Their siren whistles shriek with a fortissimo rise and fall. In a thousand beds men of forty, women of thirty-eight, girls in their teens, boys tired from football practice and little boys and girls down to babyhood wake and think the same thoughts. They listen and count the number of strokes, and sink back saying to themselves: Fire! Presently all but the few who are immediately affected are again asleep. The fire has burnt itself out. Slowly the sun has been crossing Europe and will soon appear fresh from the sea with his benison. The tie of that black thought in the night will be broken. The opportunity will be lost forever. Each will rise and dress and go out into the rain on whatever errand the day has chosen for him.

Rain all day long. The sun does not appear. The heat is suffocating. The rattle of the torrent fills the ears. Water is everywhere.

In the night a wind wakens. It comes from the southwest about midnight and takes the trees by their heavy leaves twisting them until they crack. With a roar the wind batters at the houses, shaking them as if it were a heavy hand. And again for the second night running eight thousand men and women and boys and girls wake and listen or get up to close windows and to look out at the trees leaning with snapping branches, tossing and seething with a sound of escaping steam. It has grown cold. Pull up the covers. It has grown cold. Sixteen thousand hands have drawn the covers closer about the bodies. The wind is cold.

The sun has come back. The air is washed clean. Leaves lie plastered upon the streets, against the tree trunks, upon the very house sides. The bird bath is filled to overflowing. A lame man is hurrying for the train.

They had talked for hours. The new project was beginning to take form. It was the evening of the second day. There stood the train puffing out great volumes of dense smoke which no sooner arose than it was caught in the wind and sent flying out ahead of the train. I wish to God I were on that train wherever it might be going. Oh well, remarked the younger man and said good-bye, which is what it is to be a man.

He was too old, remarked the voice in the room next to the one in which the woman was lying, he never should have gone out in that rain. Too cold! At times it seems possible, even now. She took the hair between her thumb and index finger of the right hand and using her left hand swiftly stroked the little hair strands back toward the head to make it stand out. Ratting it, I told her. It ruins the hair. Oh well I haven't much left, it might as well be broken.

She wore blue stockings under a very quiet dress but the world has not beheld a more maddening spectacle. Devoted to the art of writing, he read with his mind watching her and his mind in the sky seeking, seeking some earth to stand on when the boys were tearing up the soggy turf with their cleats. What to do? There it is. The wind hesitated whether or not to impregnate her. So many things were to be considered. In the years since his passage over Ponce de Leon's soldiers on the beach—the wind footloose, gnawing the leaves, had witnessed flying footballs that it had blown out of bounds. He had not a word to stand on, yet he stood, not knowing why. Fear clutched his heart. Visions of uprooted trees passed over his heart as he shook her heavy skirt about her knees. But she, oblivious to it all, walked with downcast eyes—looking at her feet or smiling pleasantly at one here and there in the crowd that was shouting and pressing to see the players.

In the night all nature was asleep as she lay with her young cheek pressed against her pillow and slept. The boys tossed and turned from the stiffness in their joints and from the bruises received in the game. But she lay quiet and asleep, the breath coming slowly in regular flow from her hollow nostrils moving them slightly back and forth.

Under the covers her young form could be made out, the left shoulder, the hips and the legs and feet, the left knee slightly bent and fallen to the mattress before the other. Not a sound in the room for a million years. Still she lay there asleep. —The wind has turned into hail.

Spring flowers are blossoming in the wind. There is the tulip, the jonquil and the violet—for it is September and no man shall know his defeat. So there are spring flowers that grew up through the ice that will be present later. It is of ice that they have made the flowers.

Yet sometimes it seems that it would still be possible. And this is romance: to believe that which is unbelievable.

This is faith: to desire that which is never to be obtained, to ride like a swallow on the wind—apparently for the pleasure of flight.

The swallow's bill is constructed in such a way that in flying with his mouth open tiny insects that enter are ensnared in hair-like gills so that he is fed.

Here are a pretty pair of legs in blue stockings, feed. Yet without the thought of a possible achievement that would make it possible to command the achievement of certain— The boys kick the ball and pay no attention. The boys kick the ball up into the wind and the wind hurriedly writes a love note upon it: Meet me tonight. Say you are going to the Library and I will have my car at the corner of Fern Street. I have something to tell you. There is one word you must hear: You.

There is one word you must hear. It will come out at my lips and enter in at your ears. It might be written with letters on white paper but it is a word that I want you to have out of the lips into your ear. And she answers: I will be there. So he does not keep his appointment. Off he goes in search of a word.

But she goes home and weeps her eyes out. Her pillow is wet with her tears—

What do you think! He has left his wife, and a child in the high school has been ill a week, weeping her eyes out and murmuring his name. Is it not terrible?

It is the wind! The wind is in the poplars twiddling the fading leaves between his fingers idly and thinking, thinking of the words he will make, new words to be written on white paper but never to be spoken by the lips to pass into her ear.

Quietly he goes home to his wife and taking her by the shoulder wakes her: Here I am.

VII

Nuevo Mundo! shouted the sailors. The sea was rippling like the bottom of a woven grassrope chair. A new world! Taking out their finest satins and putting on new armor the commanders of the little party ordered boats to be made ready and the royal standards of Aragon and Castile to be taken into them. The men meanwhile feeling the balmy air and seeing green and a shore for the first time in two months were greedily talking of fresh fruit—after their monotonous and meager diet of meat—of milk, of a chance to walk free in the air, to escape their commanders, and of women. Yes perhaps there would be women, beautiful savages of manifold charms. But most of all they were filled with the wild joy of release from torment of the mind. For not one among them but expected to be eaten by a god or a monster long since or to have been boiled alive by a hypertropical sea. Excitedly they went down the ladders and took their places at the words of the boatswain spoken in the Castilian tongue.

Of Columbus' small talk on that occasion nothing remains but it could not have been of Eric the Discoverer. Nor of the parties of Asiatics and Islanders—Pacific Islanders who had in other ages peopled the continents from the east. No matter: *Nuevo Mundo!* had shouted the sailors and *Nuevo Mundo* it was sure enough as they found out as soon as they had set foot on it and Columbus had kneeled and said prayers and the priest had spoken his rigmarole in the name of Christ and the land was finally declared taken over for Ferdinand and Isabella the far distant king and queen.

Yes it was indeed a new world. They the product of an age-long civilization beginning in India, it is said, and growing through conquest and struggle of all imaginable sorts through periods of success and decline, through ages of walkings to and fro in the fields and woods and the streets of cities that were without walls and had walls and burst their walls and became ruins again; through the changes of speech: Sanscrit, Greek, Latin growing crooked in the mouths of peasants who would rise and impose their speech on their masters, and on divisions in the state and savage colonial influences, words accurate to the country, Italian, French and Spanish itself not to speak of Portuguese. Words! Yes this party of sailors, men of the sea, brothers of a most ancient guild, ambassadors of all the ages that had gone before them, had indeed found a new world, a world, that is, that knew nothing about them, on which the foot of a white man had never made a mark such as theirs were then making on the white sand under the palms. *Nuevo Mundo!*

The children released from school lay in the gutter and covered themselves with the fallen poplar leaves.—A new world! All summer the leaves had been thick on the branches but now after the heat and the rain and the wind the branches were beginning to be bare. More sky appeared to their eyes than ever before. With what relief the children had pranced in the wind! Now they lay half covered in the leaves and enjoying the warmth looked out on the new world.

And he was passing and saw them. And wondered if it were too late to be Eric. What a new world they had made of it with their Cortezes, their Pizarros yes and their Lord Howes, their Washingtons even. The Declaration of Independence. I wonder, he said, whether it could be possible that the influence of the climate—I wonder if the seed, the sperm of that, existed in Columbus. Was it authentic? Is there a word to be found there? Could it be that in those men who had crossed, in the Norse as well as the Mongols, something spontaneous could not have been implanted out of the air? Or was the declaration to be put to the credit of that German George? Was it only the result of local conditions?

"A new declaration of independence, signed by Columbus, found in Porto Rico."

Indians in any case, pale yellow and with lank black hair came to the edge of the bushes and stared: The Yaquis territory lay north of the river Fuertes. To the south was Carrancista territory. The valley was fertile, the Indians wanted it.

During the week of November 13th, 17th, 1916—word reached Los Mochis that Gen. Banderas and the Villistas from Chihuahua had been defeated by the Carrancistas near Fuertes and were in retreat. During this week two Indians were captured by Los Mochis police and hung on willow trees below the Jaula.

On Saturday November 13th, Col. Escobar and his Carrancistas of the Fifth regiment of Sinaloa were withdrawn from Los Mochis and Aguila and concentrated in San Blas. Banderas and his Villistas meanwhile had come down the Fuertes, effected a junction with Bacomo and his Mayo Indians, and Monday night crossed the river above Los Tastos, tore out the telephone at the pumps and started for Los Mochis. All gate keepers encountered on the road were killed as were their families. Mr. Wilcox estimated the combined forces participating in the raid and on the other side of the river at 6,000.

The first intimation of the raid was at one o'clock in the morning of Tuesday when with a *"Villa! Vive Villa! Vive Villa!"* the raiders swarmed into Los Mochis from three sides, shooting cursing as they galloped into town. From all over the town came the sound of smashing doors and windows, shots, yells and screams.

When I came here the Indians all used bows and arrows. Conscripted during the many revolutions they had deserted with their rifles until at last, after 800 of them, in a body, went over they used the rifle extensively. Wilcox lived at the pumps with his wife and daughter. A cocky Englishman, he poopooed the danger. He had been in the habit of telephoning into the town, seven miles, whenever a raid was coming. It was agreed we Americans were to keep to our houses, take our animals off the roads and wait with

more or less excitement until it was over. We never notified
the Mexicans. Had we done so once we should not have
escaped the next raid. This time the Villistas were with the
Indians. As you saw the first thing they did was to rip out
the wires. Washington had just accepted Carranza as the
power in authority and the Villistas were angry.

Wilcox and his wife and daughter were locked in a room
all the first night while Banderas and Bacomo argued over
their fate. Banderas was for killing Wilcox and taking over
his wife and daughter for camp women. But the Indian
stood out against him. It seems Wilcox had at one time
given the Indians some sacks of beans when they were
hard up for food. They remembered this. It was a good
thing for the three.

At a previous raid an American engineer living near
Wilcox was found dead. He was supposed to have run.
Looked just like a pin-cushion, with the feathered arrows
that were in him. Funniest thing you ever saw in your life.
There were four bullets in him also.

The Americans were too scattered to resist. It was de-
cided to save the few guns by hiding them. Bacomo rode
up to the house with his escort,—ordered to give up all
guns and cartridges. At the last moment he turned back
from the stairs, entered Mrs. Johnson's room where the
ladies were sitting on the beds and ordered them to get up.
Under the mattress a miscellaneous collection of riot guns,
rifles, shot guns, automatics, pistols and cartridges were
found. When all the guns and cartridges to the last shell
had been loaded on the horses behind the drunken soldiers
Bacomo refused C.'s request for one of the riot guns and
with a polite bow and a *"Con permiso, senores,"* he rode
off.

In Mr. Johnson's cellar they had found all sorts of bottles
from Scotch to German *Scheisswasser* and had drunk it all
indiscriminately.

Cattle had eaten the standing rice. The pigs had got loose
and over-run everything. Returning there were corpses on

all sides. About one of these a triple battle raged. The pigs were ranged on one side, the dogs on another and from a third a flock of vultures crept up from time to time. The pigs and dogs would make a united rush at the birds who would fly a few feet into the air and settle a yard or so away.

These pictures are of Bacomo taken a year later just as he was being taken from the train by his captors. He was a physical wreck at the time but at the time of the raid he was a magnificent specimen of a man. It seemed there was some silver buried near Los Mochis which they wanted. He would not disclose its whereabouts unless they freed him and they would not free him unless he spoke first.

The end is shown in this picture. Here he is with the pick and spade at his feet surrounded by the Carrancista soldiers. He dug his grave and was shot and they buried him there.

The Indians have made a local saint of him and every night you will see candles burning on the spot and little plates of rice and other food placed there for his spirit.—

For a moment Columbus stood as if spell-bound by the fact of this new country. Soon however he regained his self-possession and with Alonso Pinzón ordered the trunks of trifles to be opened which, being opened, the Indians drew near in wonder and began to try to communicate with these gods.

It was indeed a new world.

VIII

No man can tell the truth and survive—save through prestige. And no child either. Aristocracy is license to tell the truth. And to hear it. Witness the man William in Henry Fifth, the camp incident. Fear clutched at his heart.

Agh-ha-ha! Shouted the *vaqueros* plunging their spurs into the bronchos' sides. Up with the heels. Buck, buck,

buck. Agh-ha-ha! *Fortissimo.* The wild and unexpected cry out of the Mexican Indian country rang through the quiet house so that the pup leaped up and rushed to the door.

Someone had taken the apple. Both denied they had had a hand in it. Each accused the other. The truth did not appear. For an hour the man tried his best to arrive at a just decision. Joseph Smith shook where he stood and fell frothing at the mouth. He was of Vermont mountain stock. His birth among the poor white trash there had not even been thought worth recording. Yet a vision came to him of the marriage in Cana. Christ drank the wine and Martha and Mary her sister became his wives—so to speak. It is the truth. The world shall be saved anew, said Joseph Smith in the mountains of Vermont—where the mushrooms are so plentiful among the fir trees.

Who had given the boy the apple against the father's express orders? Had he taken it himself—which he denied or had the girl gone into the store room—as he asserted but which she denied—and selected it herself? Where was the truth?

In Illinois Brigham Young was recruited. Off they set with fifty oxen for the Promised Land away over the prairies and deserts—through the Sioux country, in search of Zion. The whole world they would leave behind and for the truth's sake they would live in that far country—to be discovered, to which the Lord would lead them.

Go upstairs sir and take your clothes off. You shall go to bed for this lie—I'll say I took the apple Daddy, said the boy sobbing violently, but she gave it to me. In minute detail he repeated the story of how the apple was picked out of the basket by the girl and handed to him to eat.

Lions of the Lord. The boy would not give up his bride to Brigham and was *altered,* as a rebel. She went mad. In '49 a party of gold seekers came by accident into the valley they had found. They were gently received. A warning was given of hostile Indians and a special guard was appointed to conduct them safely on their way. But Brigham had

had a dream. Men must not wander into the valley of Zion to disturb the ways of God's holy ones. A blood sacrifice had been demanded of Brigham by the Lord. John D. Lee was selected as he who must lend himself to the Almighty will of God for the good of the church and state. Slowly the party of gold seekers departed for California. At the narrow defile at Mountain Meadow the treacherous business was performed. All but a child were killed and Brigham and the Lord were revenged. Later John D. Lee was convicted of murder by government authorities and shot. A poor ignorant tool in the hands of that most mighty Lion of the Lord.

And you my girl. You have lied to me before this. Did you or did you not take the apple? No one will be punished but I must have the truth. Tomorrow is Sunday. You shall go to church, and up to the minister you shall march, and he will ask you what I am asking you now. In the face of God you shall say to him that you did not take that apple, then I shall know. Did you or did you not take that apple? I will have the truth. And you my young sir, I shall not punish you but I must have the truth. You shall stay in bed all day tomorrow, all next week as long as it takes for one of you to change your story. I will have the truth.

The mountains are savage about the valley. The lake is bitter, scalding with the salt. They knew they had found the Dead Sea. At last the child confessed, with bitter and hard tears that he had taken the fruit himself. It was the truth.

Clear and cold the moon shone in the partly denuded poplars. It was midnight and the little fellow to whom he had determined to teach the meaning of the truth was snug in his bed. Years before that Utah had been admitted to the Union as a state and polygamy had been more or less abandoned. The young folk were beginning to be ashamed of the narrowness of their cult and the bones of the fathers were rotten.

The glassy half moon in the dark leaves cast a dull light over the world upon which a calm had descended. Suddenly the Pleiades could be heard talking together in Phœnician. Their words were clear as dropping water: What things they do in this new world: they said. Let us from now on swear to each other that we will give up every thought of wisdom and seek no further for the truth— which is, after all a veritable moon. —At this the moon was overcast for a moment by a falling leaf. The answer that came from that clear but broken ball rose slowly toward the stars: The child is asleep. Let us warn him of the folly of words. Let us bless him only with words that change often and never stiffen nor remain to form sentences of seven parts. To him I send a message of words like running water. —At this the stars smiled for they were married to one—

Elena, yo soy un wonder, she would say. *Vu par le jury*. And who is the jury but myself. The boy had struck her with a stone. Come we shall go and apologize, said Brigham Young. Into the neighbour's kitchen they walked. An older sister was cleaning the gas range. Where is your sister? But the truth is that all the while he had been hoping that just what had happened would happen. His eye ran up and down the girl's form. Secretly he was happy to have found her alone. I'm sorry, I will never do it again, Never again. Never again. Oh never, never again.

And how can I, now that it is all over, and I am old? But at first I tell you I cried my eyes out. I had just been admitted to the Beaux Arts. All was as near perfect as could well be. I had the friendship of La Baronne d'Orsay and then the stars withdrew their aid. I had to go back to Porto Rico. I had to leave everything behind to go back to that country where there was nothing.

There life ended. But it is over now. I was just beginning to do things. I tell you I cried my eyes out. But I am old now. I wanted you to see these drawings, to show you it was not a bluff.

The Indians are gone. It is late now. It is cold. September
is over. October is cold. Words should be—Words should
be—I am tired to death.

But two enormous women, middle aged, dignified, with
still broad backs came down the street just as the very dirty
little boy was crossing over. The three arrived at the en-
trance to the path at the same moment. The women looked
hard at the filthy little boy whose face was stickly from
apple-juice and black, with a great circle of dirt around
the mouth. The women looked and the little boy hung
his head and stumbled off into the long grass, almost falling
into the abandoned foundation.

And so the little company went on foot 20,000 miles along
what later became known as Emigration Trail, overcoming
incredible obstacles, eating the draught oxen, through sav-
age mountains on, on to the Mountain Meadow Massacre.
For they would worship the Lord their God in peace and
in their own way. At last the Mayflower was in the harbor
and the Pilgrims had landed and dispersed.

Yes, it was a New World.

But they have prospered and today the Mormon Church
is all for goodness and it is powerful and rich.

A favorite trick of the Mayo Indians is, if they meet a
man with good clothes, to take what they want and let him
go on in his drawers.

So it was with infinite satisfaction that on looking up the
little boy saw those two terrible viragos suddenly as low
as he. *Nuevo Mundo.*

IX

Calang-glang! Calang-glang! went the bells of the little
Episcopal Church at Allendale. It was eight o'clock in the
evening. A row of cars stood along the curb, each with its
headlights lit, but dimmed so as not to make too much of
a glare on the road, at the same time to save the battery
while complying with the law!

On sped the little family all crowded into one seat, the two children sleeping.

In the Dutch church on the old Paramus Road Aaron Burr was married to Mrs. Prevost, Jataqua! It is near Ho-ho-kus, cleft-in-the-rocks, where the Leni Lenapes of the Delaware nation had their village from time immemorial. Aaron, my darling, life begins anew! It is a new start. Let us look forward staunchly together—

The long, palm-like leaves of the ailanthus trees moved slowly up and down in the little wind, up and down.

And along this road came the British. Aaron, the youth from Princeton, gathered his command together and drove them back. Mother I cannot sleep in this bed, it is full of *British soldiers.* Why so it is! How horrid.

And he too, on his memorable retreat, that excellent judge of horseflesh, George Washington, he too had passed over this road; and these trees, the oldest of them, had witnessed him. And now the wind has torn the finest of them in half.

Nothing more wonderful than to see the pears attached by their stems to the trees. Earth, trunk, branch, twig and the fruit: a circle soon to be completed when the pear falls. They had left at eleven and soon they would be home. The little car purred pleasantly to itself at the thought of the long night. Oh, to be a woman, thought the speeding mechanism. For they had wrapped something or other in a piece of newspaper and placed it under the seat and there were pictures there of girls—or grown women it might be, in very short skirts. Steadily the wheels spun while on the paper were printed these words:

The Perfection of Pisek-designed Personality Modes: A distinctly forward move in the realm of fashion is suggested by the new personality modes, designed by Pisek . . . modes that are genuine inspirations of individual styling, created for meeting the personal preferences of a fastidiously fashionable clientèle, the woman and the miss who seek personality in dress in keeping with their charms, characteristics and station . . . Thus you can expect at Pisek's only those *tailleurs,* gowns, wraps and frocks that bear the unmistakable stamp of individuality—styles that encourage and inspire admiration for their splendid simplicity and differentness . . . come to Pisek's . . . (the more the better) . . . see the new ideas in fashions . . . You'll not be disappointed . . .

What chit of a girl could have appreciated you, my darling boy, as I do. A man of your personality, so fresh in wit, so brimming with vigor and new ideas. Aaron my dear, dear boy, life has not yet begun. All is new and untouched in the world waiting, like the pear on the tree, for you to pluck it. Everyone loves you and will wait on you. For you everything is possible. Bing! and Hamilton lies dead.

As old Mr. Goss, who lost his hearing from an explosion of fireworks in Philadelphia after Lee's defeat, has said in his high nasal twang: Quite right, quite right, I've seen the country saved 8 times in the last fifty years.

At any rate it was a new world to them; they two together would conquer and use, life had smiled upon them. *Nuevo Mundo.*

Along the road the Dutch settlers came out from their attractive brown stone houses as the happy and distinguished couple went by. It was a great day for the little colony of New Jersey. There over the misty meadows the lights of Weehawken were beginning to glimmer as the little car and its precious freight drew near the end of the journey. The pear fell to the earth and was eaten by the pigs.

I wonder if he'll recognize me in my Greenwich Village honkie-tonk bobbed hair. The hairdresser said: Don't you do it, when I said I'd like mine bobbed too. So many of the girls had theirs done a year ago and now it's just at that impossible stage where you can't do a thing with it. Better go to Europe or California until it grows again. There's a reason for travel: As the hair progresses the days grow fewer.

But is South Africa after all the country of the future?

Over the great spaces of New Jersey, Pennsylvania, Ohio, Indiana he sped in the Pullman car. City after city swept up to him, paused awhile at his elbow and plunged away to the rear with the motion of a wheel whose hub was hidden in infinity. And such indeed was exactly the case. He was being ground between two wheels, one on either side of the car and it was their turning that thrust him forward at such speed. The wheat was up in the fields but a fellow passenger assured him that in Kansas, only two days before, he had seen wheat twice as high—which explains the cause of so many abandoned farms in Vermont, he remembered, and settled back to another hour of idle staring. A new country he kept saying to himself. On a siding were cars loaded with emigrants from Holland booked through to San Francisco.

Into the elevator stepped the young man in a petty officer's uniform. His Spanish was exquisite to hear. The first battleship since the Spanish-American war was anchored in New York harbor. How well he bears himself. The Spanish are the only people in Europe whom civilization has not ruined. Savage men, big bearded chins—but shaved clean. They know how to treat their women—better than the French for the French—after all are *blagueurs* to a man. The Spanish stand still. What an ass a man will make of himself in a strange country! In armor De Soto wandering haphazard over Alabama. The Seminoles for guides. Buried him in the Mississippi. It is my river, he said. Roll Jordan roll. It is *my* river for I discovered it and into it let my body, in full armor, be put to rest. The cat-fish ate it. So roll Jordan roll. Diada Daughter of Discord: read it.

In Illinois, far in the west, over that trackless waste of forest and mountain and river and lake they came at last to a valley that pleased them and there they determined to build. So they fell to hewing trees and building their houses, work to which they had been bred and trained for two generations since Plymouth and Salem days. Cornwallis had been beaten fifty years before and Pitt had rushed to see the King crying: All is lost. A new world had been born. Here in the primeval forest the little colony of New Englanders hoped to realize success and plenty.

In Bonnie, Illinois, the Presbyterian minister is a very good man. He is as good a preacher as Bonnie can afford and if anybody said that Bonnie is made up of mad-men— He would be shot. *Nuevo Mundo*, shouted the sailors. But their cry was by now almost extinct.

In polite stories the world had been made acquainted with the picturesque lives of these commonplace but worthy people. In detail their story had been told. Over the precipice in Yosemite the Bridal Veil Falls had been launching its water for a thousand years and ignorance was fattening his belly apace.

Bonnie, Ill., October 22. Dear Bill: Am up to my ears in painting, and am preparing to go to Alton, Ill., to work in the State Hospital, if I get a call, so am too busy now to read your book but think I'm going to like it and will devour it later. Sincerely. A. N. Turner.

And the little boy crept into the great chest like Peppo into the Cardinal's tomb and began to pick up the mothballs that had been left there when the winter things were removed.

An Indian would sense the facts as he wished. A tree would speak to him with a definite identity. It would not at least seem endowed with human characteristics: a voice, that would be all.

X

Arnold, this wind is, the wise and sagacious captain. Henchman of the wind. The wind is a lion with hooked

teeth. The saber-toothed tiger inhabited the region west of
the Alleghenies throughout the Pleistocene age. With a
snarl it wrenches the limbs of the trees from their places
and tosses them to earth where they lie with the leaves
still fluttering.

Vacuous; full of wind. Her whole pelvis is full of intes-
tine but aside from the ptosis I find nothing really wrong.
The uterus appears to be normal. The bleeding may come
from a cyst. At least there is no good reason for removing
—for a hysterectomy. There it is. It. Like some tropical
fruit color of the skunk cabbage flower. There it is, that
mystical pear, glistening with the peritoneum. Here the
caverns. Alpha if not omega. Talk politely and obey the
law. But do not remove it.

Oh my country. Shall it be a hysterectomy? Arnold there
is a wind with a knife's edge.

And Remy says the spring of curiosity is broken at thirty.
Nothing left at fifty but the facts of bed and table. He has
the lilt of Heine at his best and in places quite equals the
work of the author of Danny Deever. The catgut had
slipped out of the needle. The young interne held the point
of the suture between his fingers and the nurse approached
the needle as accurately as she could. But the man's hand
trembled slightly. For a moment they tried to complete
the connection but failing in their attempt the nurse took
the end in her other hand and soon had the needle threaded.
The young doctor looked up as much as to say thank you.

Such a wind. At fifteen they seem noble, desirable be-
yond dreams. In the winter the trees at least remain stems
of wood that resist with a will, whose branches rebound
against the impact of sleet. At thirty they are what they
are. The boy rebels and she with her hair in distressed tan-
gles about the disorderly boudoir cap, at mid-day, whines
and snatches at him as he jerks and defies her. It is beyond
her strength to control a boy of nine. Clutching her dressing
sack—oh slobbery morsel—about her breastless form with
one hand she rushes as far as she dares to the porch edge,

glancing furtively about for chance gentlemen or neighbors and tries to overtake the youngster. No, the young man has really escaped. He goes to school filthy again and what will they think of his mother.

At fifteen they are slender and coquettish and they cry if you are rough with them. Great burly fellow, she seemed to him all that he was not, the quintessence of Ibsenism, the wind among the reeds. Or perhaps the reed in the wind. Something to love, to take into the arms, to protect— If you can find any reason for doing a hysterectomy doctor, do it. Her husband is good for nothing at all. She at least is a power in her family. She is not like the native American women of her class, she is a Polock. You never saw such courage.

The schooner left Southampton bound for New York with a cargo of rails—steel rails. But the English emigrants were not like these modern messes. Those round, expressionless peasant faces of today. See that one there with the little boy at her side. Castle Garden. At last we are to be in America, where gold is in the streets. Look at that face. That is the kind of immigration we want. Look at the power in that jaw. Look at that nose. She is one who will give two for every stroke she has to take. Look at the intensity of her gaze. Well, she's English, that's the reason. Nowadays they have no more of that sort. These Jews and Polocks, Sicilians and Greeks. Good-bye America!

The head nurse's legs under her practical short skirt were like mighty columns. They held the seriousness of her looks, her steady, able hands. A fine woman.

XI

The American background is America. If there is to be a new world Europe must not invade us. It is not a matter of changing the y to i as in Chile. They are bound.

The background of America is not Europe but America.

Eh bien mon vieux coco, this stuff that you have been
writing today, do you mean that you are attempting to
set down the American background? You will go mad.
Why? Because you are trying to do nothing at all. The
American background? It is Europe. It can be nothing else.
Your very method proves what I say. You have no notion
what you are going to write from one word to the other.
It is madness. You call this the background of American
life? Madness?

As far as I have gone it is accurate.

It is painting the wind.

Ah, that would be something.

Mais ça, are you a plain imbecile? That is a game for chil-
dren. Why do you not do as so many of your good writers
do? Your Edgar Lee Masters, your Winesburg, Ohio. Have
you not seen the photographs of men and women on your
walls? They are a type, as distinct as a Frenchman or a Ger-
man. Study these men, know their lives. You have a real
work to do, you have the talent, the opportunity even. This
is your work in life. You Americans, you are wasteful,
mad—

Our background.

You would paint the wind. Well, it has been tried—
many times, and do you know where that leads?

I know where it has led.

But do you know? Have you seen, felt, heard what they
have seen, felt, heard, our Villons—

Apollo was out of breath but the nymph was more tired
than he. The chase must soon have ended when she falling
to her knees half from the will to be there half from fatigue
besought her mistress Diana to save her from the God's
desire. And she was changed into a laurel bush.

All about the hills where they stood the hard waxen
leaves of the laurel glistened above the dead leaves of the
hardwood trees, the beech, the maple, the oak.

You imagine I am French because I attack you from the
continental viewpoint. You are wrong. I am from the coun-

try of your friends Musorgski, Dostoevski, Chekhov. At least if you will not yield me the point that America cannot be new, cannot do anything unless she takes the great heritage which men of all nations and ages have left to the human race.

You mean that I should not be an American but—Turgenev, enjoy you more if, well, if you were more comprehensible, a little more particular, *vous comprenez?* You sweep out your arms, you—I see no faces, no details of the life, no new shape—

The druggist's boy cannot be distinguished from his master when he says, Hello, over the phone—Is that what you mean?

Well, you are very much children, you Americans.

It is not to be avoided as far as I can see.

Let us have now a beginning of composition. We have had enough of your improvisations.

I am consumed by my lusts. No American can imagine the hunger I have.

It is the itch, monsieur. It is neurasthenia. Desire is not a thing to speak of as if it were a matter of filling the stomach. It is wind, gas. You are empty my friend. Eat. Then and then only.

Like all men save perhaps the Chinese you are most transparent when you imagine yourself most protected.

Her bosom reached almost to her knees. That morning in the October garden she had picked a violet for him and placed it in his coat. Watching the feet of men and women as they touched the pavement a strong odor of violets crossed his path.

He turned and saw the massive Jewess waddling by. It had been good perfume too.

These Polocks. Their heads have no occiput. They are flat behind. It is why when they put on their American hats the things slip down about their ears. The Negro's head isn't that way. You know how the bump goes out behind in so many of them. The club sandwich on her plate kept sliding apart, the top slice of bread would slip. Then she took the pieces in her fingers and poked the lettuce in under the sheet. On her breast was a black pin. It formed a circle. She looked up with her mouth full of food and resting both elbows on the table chewed America thoughtfully while she held the state of Maryland in her firm fingers. The ends of each finger were stubby, the nails cut short and as clean as well manicured nails could well be. Clatter, clatter, clatter. He could see himself in the plate glass behind her. He was conscious of his hat which he had not removed. He was at this table with these five women—one of them young, ready—and he had not removed his hat. There was in fact no place to put it.

I am begging, frankly. Ten cents a ticket. I have to raise fifty dollars by the end of next week. We want to fit up a room in our hall where the colored working girls can come and rest. On Thursdays we serve tea. Then they go back to the office. When the impact is over the man must think. I tell you I do not contemplate with relish seeing my children bred out of all these girls. Is it wrong? Well, I thought you said you had an appetite. Impregnate eighty of them, right and left as you see them here in this room. It would not be impossible. I cannot think of my children running about in the environment in which these have to live. My dear sir, you are a fool. You are lying to yourself —As to the girls, I frankly desire them. I desire many, many, many.

There she sat on the bench of the subway car looking idly about, being rushed under the river at great speed to the kitchen of her mother's flat. Malodorous mother. Or wrinkled hard-put-to-it mother. Savior of the movies. After the impact his great heart had expanded so as to include the whole city, every woman young and old there having impregnated with sons and daughters. For everyone loved him. And he knew how to look into their eyes with both passion and understanding. Each had taken him to

her soul of souls where the walls were papered with edi-
torials from the Journal and there he had made himself
father to her future child. As they went upstairs he saw
her heels were worn—Who will understand the hugeness
of my passion?

But he had understood. The truth lay under the surface.
Why then not—No two can remain together without train-
ing. Who better than that one who is practiced. The faith-
ful husband of the clothing store madam is used to her.
They functionate well together. He puts his hat in the
right place. His money in the right bank. His arm fitted
in just the posture best suited to their mutual height and
width. All their practices were mated.

But he was an outsider. He was new to all. Her shoes
are stitched up the back.

Card-index minds, the judges have. Socialism, immorality
and lunacy are about synonyms to the judge. Property is
sacred and human liberty is bitter, bitter, bitter to their
tongues.

Walk up the stairs there little girl. But she is naked!
These are all doctors. So the little tot struggled up the very
high clinic steps, naked as she was, and all the doctors
looked at her. She had some spots on her body that had
been there a year. Had I been her father I would know
why I am a fool.

Naked and free, free to be damned in to hell by a chance
vagrant to whom she had taken a fancy. Her father did
not know her. Did not even know that she existed. Cared
less. We will look after her said the head doctor.

XII

That cat is funny. I think she'd be a good one for the
circus. When she's hungry she bites your legs. Then she
jumps at you as much as to say: *Caramba*, give me some-
thing.

America needs the flamboyant to save her soul—said Vachel Lindsay to the indifferent mountains.

He might have added that America tries to satisfy this need in strange and often uncatalogued ways. America, living an exemplary three-meals-a-day-and-bed-time life in a wall-papered home, goes now and then *en masse*, by Gosh, to the circus to see men, women and animals perform exquisite and impossible feats of daring. What could be more flamboyant than the trapeze-performer hurtling through the air, the tiger leaping through man-made hoops, or the elephant poising his mighty bulk on his two forelegs lifted to the top of bottles? What more flamboyant than the painted clown, timeless type of the race, laughing that he may not weep, grinning through a thousand tragic jests while little human beings perform their miraculous tricks around him?

Jazz, the Follies, the flapper in orange and green gown and war-paint of rouge—impossible frenzies of color in a world that refuses to be drab. Even the movies, devoid as they are of color in the physical sense, are gaudy in the imaginations of the people who watch them; gaudy with exaggerated romance, exaggerated comedy, exaggerated splendor of grotesqueness or passion. Human souls who are not living impassioned lives, not creating romance and splendor and grotesqueness—phases of beauty's infinite variety—such people wistfully try to find these things outside themselves; a futile, often a destructive quest.

The imagination will not down. If it is not a dance, a song, it becomes an outcry, a protest. If it is not flamboyance it becomes deformity; if it is not art, it becomes crime. Men and women cannot be content, any more than children, with the mere facts of a humdrum life—the imagination must adorn and exaggerate life, must give it splendor and grotesqueness, beauty and infinite depth. And the mere acceptance of these things from without is not enough—it is not enough to agree and assert when the imagination demands for satisfaction creative energy. Flamboyance expresses faith in that energy—it is a shout of delight, a declaration of richness. It is at least the beginning of art.

All right go ahead: A TEXAS PRIZE CONTEST—The Southern Methodist University at Dallas, Texas, recently emerged from a prize contest which had a strange *dénouement*—

Look here young man, after this you examine those girls in the cold weather.

Who is Warner Fabian? *Flaming Youth* is the story of the super-flapper, of her affairs at country clubs and cozy home-dances with all the accompaniments of prohibition stimulants. Warner Fabian believes that the youth of this country feeds on excitement and rushes to knowledge "heeled" by way of petting parties and the elemental stimulus of jazz. The barriers of convention are down. Youth makes its own standards and innocence, according to the author, has been superseded by omniscience.

It doesn't matter that Warner Fabian is a *nom de plume* which conceals the identity of one of the ablest scientists of this country who has dared to look facts in the face, facts physical, moral and emotional. He has written the truth about youth, the youth of today as he sees it.

FLAMING YOUTH by Warner Fabian is the writing on the wall. It is the *Quo Vadis?* of the present moment.

Those who are following in the *Metropolitan* magazine the fortunes of Pat, the most sophisticated and yet at the same time one of the most deliciously lovely heroines of recent novels, and the fortunes of her two sisters, may protest that Mr. Fabian's portrayal of youth in this novel is outscotting Fitzgerald and overdancing in the Dark. We feel however that this story of three girls and their many men is one which may sufficiently frighten mothers and electrify fathers and hit the younger set hard enough between the eyes to help America's youth to, at least, a gradual return to sanity.

And so the beginning of art ends in a gradual return to sanity.

To-day modern scientific research has provided the most

efficient agent for the treatment of local inflammation: DIONAL applied locally over the affected areas acts promptly with prolonged effect. Drugless. Non-irritant. Non-toxic. Indicated in Mastitis, Burns, Boil, Tonsilitis, Mastoiditis, Sprain, Abcess, Bronchitis, Mumps, Contusion, Ulcers, Pneumonia.

If a man died on a stretcher he simply said: Dump it out. And ordered us back for another load.

Intended to stop at the school but his mind waylaid him. Down the hill came the ash-cart—on the wrong side of the street. He, up the hill, perforce went wrong also and with great headway. Just as he was about to pass the cart another car swung out from behind it, headed down hill at full speed. It was too late for any of the three to stop. In three seconds there would be death for someone. Angels would be waiting for mother's little boy. Without the minutest loss of time, in time with the Boston Symphony Orchestra at its best he swung far to the left, up over the curb, between two trees, onto the sidewalk—by luck no one was passing—and going fifty feet came back between two trees, over the curb to the roadway and continued his empty progress, rather hot in the face, it must be confessed. He felt happy and proud.

But he had missed his street.

Well let it go. Far away in front of him a locomotive stood indifferently at the avenue end, emitting great clouds of smoke. It was autumn, clear and cold.

But you Scandinavians, said the Frenchman, it is impossible to live in this way. Why France, which is ten times as rich as your countries, could not do it. You do not know what money is for. You throw it away like a sickness. To drink champagne like this is madness, and it is every night, everywhere, in Christiania, Copenhagen, everywhere.

And there she sits staring out, not at the sea, but over Long Island Sound. Dreaming of her sons—and of the money she will make next year by renting the better of her two little shacks.

When you have paid up the twenty shares you may, if you like, retain them as paid up shares in which case you will receive the 5% interest, or, if you feel that you would like to do so, you may increase your holding to thirty shares and receive the 6%. Of course everyone is not able to do that. Do not worry about it, we will notify you in plenty of time when your book is balanced at the end of the six months.

Let's see. What is the number of your house? Four eighty? I'll see that they send it right up.

You know last Sunday was my birthday. Seventy-three years old. I had a party, a surprise party—my relatives came from all sides. But I couldn't get her downstairs. She's afraid. We had a banister put on the stairs, cost me nine dollars but she will not do it. She's so fat you know, she's afraid of falling.

Re Commissions due—Amount $1.00. Dear Sir:—You will please take notice that unless we receive payment in full of your account within FIVE DAYS after receipt of this letter, we shall draw upon you for the amount due.

A collection agency draft notifies the banks—those great institutions of finance—that there is serious doubt regarding the way you pay your honest obligations. The bank will take note of it. From there the information quietly passes to the various Mercantile Agencies, Dun's, Bradstreet's, Martindale's. And this is ONLY ONE cog in the wheel of ARROW SERVICE. Our reports cover the whole field of credit reporting.

Your continued indifference to our requests for payment has forced us to consider this action. The draft, with a full history of the debt leaves our office in five days unless your check is received in the meantime.

Let your better judgment guide you, and pay this account without any more trouble or expense. Yours very truly—MEMBERS: Retail Credit Men's National Association. Commercial Law League of America. Rotary International. O Rotary International!

At this, De Soto, sick, after all the months of travel, stopped out of breath and looked about him. Hundreds of miles he had travelled through morass after morass, where the trees were so thick that one could scarcely get between them, over mountain and river but never did he come to the other side. The best he had done was to locate a river running across his path, the greatest he had ever seen or heard of, greater than the Nile, greater than the Euphrates, no less indeed than any. Here he had confronted the New World in all its mighty significance and something had penetrated his soul so that in the hour of need he had turned to this Mighty River rather than to do any other thing. Should it come to the worst he had decided what to do. Out of the tangle around him, out of the mess of his own past the river alone could give him rest. Should he die his body should be given to this last resting place. Into it Europe should pass as into a new world.

Near the shore he saw a school of small fish which seemed to look at him, rippling the water as they moved out in unison. Raising his heavy head De Soto gave the order to proceed. Four of the men lifted him on an improvised stretcher and the party, headed by the Indians, started again north along the bank.

The whole country was strange to them. But there at the edge of that mighty river he had seen those little fish who would soon be eating him, he, De Soto the mighty explorer—He smiled quietly to himself with a curious satisfaction.

XIII

It was a shock to discover that she, that most well built girl, so discreet, so comely, so able a thing in appearance, should be so stupid. There are things that she cannot learn. She will never finish school. Positively stupid. Why her little brother, no bigger than Hop o' my Thumb has caught

up to her and will soon outstrip her. Her older brother is
the brightest boy in the High School. She will I suppose
breed stupid children. Plant wizards choose the best out of
lots running into the millions. Choose here there every-
where for hybrids. A ten-pound white leghorn cockerel,
hens that lay eggs big enough to spoil the career of any
actor. She might though have bright children. What a pity
that one so likely should be so stupid. Easier to work with
but I should hate a child of mine to be that way. Excuses—
Try first. Argue after. Excuses. Do not dare.

There sat the seven boys—nine years old and there-abouts
—planning dire tortures for any that should seduce or touch
in any way their sisters. Each strove to exceed the other.
Tying his antagonist to a tree Apollo took out his knife
and flayed him. For sweet as the flute had been yet no man
can play the flute and sing at the same time. But the God
had first played his harp and then sung to his own accom-
paniment—a thing manifestly unfair. No doubt, his sense of
being in the wrong whetted his lust for the other's hide. In
any case he got what he was after. He was the winner and
that was all there was about it.

Each boy would think with a secret glow of a new tor-
ture: I would dip his hands in boiling lead—they often
melted old pieces of lead in a plumber's pot over a field fire
to make slugs for their bean shooters—then I would tie a
rope to his feet and drag him on cinders etc. . . . each in-
venting a worse torture than that pictured before. And all
for their sisters' virtue. So there under the east wall of the
Episcopal Church they sat in a group on the grass and
talked together for an hour.

The real empire builders of our colonial period were not
statesmen, the men of wealth, the great planters but the
unknown pioneers who fought single-handed and at once
both the primeval wilderness and the lurking savage. The
hand crooked to the ploughtail was shaped to the trigger.

The Mesa Verde cliff dwellers—a much advanced race—
formed a partnership with nature in the science of home

building. Masterpieces of architecture, the survivals of the cliff dwellings tell the story of the ages.

On the top of a point high above the steep cliffs stood Sun Temple, so called, scene of the great ceremonial dramas of the clan. The building is in the form of the letter D and many of the stones which make up the thousand-odd feet of walls are highly decorated.

The corner stone of the building contains a fossil leaf of a palm tree. Influenced by anything which even in shape resembled the sun, the primitive people walled in the leaf on three sides and made a shrine.

The word *bayeta* is merely Spanish for *baize*. Great quantities of this were made in England for the Spanish and Mexican trade, the major part of which was of a brilliant red color. In this way English *baize* became Spanish *bayeta* to the Indians of the American Southwest. Familiar with the art of weaving, these Indians unraveled the *bayeta*, retwisted it into one, two or three strands, and then rewove it into their blankets, which are now almost priceless. This old blanket was picked up by the author in a New Mexican corral, for the purpose of wiping his buggy axle. It was covered with filth and mud. A number of washings revealed this glorious specimen of the weaver's art.

Accepted by a cultured and talented belle, Lincoln, according to his law partner, had already been refused by Sarah Rickard, an obscure miss of sixteen, of whom apparently nothing further is known.

It was twelve feet from the rock into the water. As he stood looking down it seemed twenty. His eyes being five feet from his heels made it seem by that much higher than it was. He had never dived from such a height in his life. He had climbed up there to dive and he must dive or yield. What would he yield? At least it was something he did not intend to yield. He tried his best to imitate the others, he stood on the edge and plunged. It seemed to him that he plunged. As a matter of fact he dropped over the edge with his body bent almost double so that his thighs hit the water with a stinging impact, also the lower part of his belly, also the top of his head. He did not feel certain of himself for a moment or two after rising to the surface. That was about enough. Memory began to fill the blank of his mind.

There it was still, the men around Mrs. Chain's table on Locust St.: $3.50 a week. A week? Yes, three-fifty a week. And that place in Leipzig where they had only half cooked fresh pork. *Schwein schlachterei!* Bah. One week was enough there. Fräulein Dachs, *Pflaumensuppe*. That purple and sweet soup. The white cakes they sold on the station platform near Malaga, what were they called? It seemed to be some native bake peculiar to the place. The devil fish in a black sauce in Seville. Big lumps of dough, big as snowballs, *Sauerbraten*. But Mrs. Chain's prunes were the most wonderful. Watery tidbits. It was prunes or applesauce. Her daughter was simple I guess. Did her best to land one of the students, kept it up for twenty years. At that table I met one of my dearest friends. Will you have some bread? Yes. That look. It was enough. Youth is so rich. It needs no stage setting. Out went my heart to that face. There was something soft there, a reticence, a welcome, a loneliness that called to me. And he, he must have seen it in me too. We looked, two young men, and at once the tie was cemented. It was gaged accurately at once and sealed for all time. The other faces are so many prunes.

Have you ever seen a dish of small birds all lying on their backs on the dish and with feet in the air, all roasted stiff but brown and savory? Rice birds I think they called them. Or snails or baked eggs?

The old man raked slowly. It took him all day to finish the small lawn. But it was autumn and the leaves had fallen thickly. The bird bath was full of leaves. It was a sentimental picture. But after all why? The leaves must fall into every corner. If they fall into the bird bath that is all there is to it. Still it calls many things to the mind that are not evoked by the twingling of waves on a lake shore in August.

Clark had taken a job as clerk at Pocono, and she was a

Quakeress. They got to know each other very, very well.
And this girl in the steamer chair, it was the cattle men who
attracted her. Let her go then, he said tying the cord with
a piece of gauze twisted into a rope. When you bathe the
baby for the first time do not put him into a tub but sponge
him off carefully before the fire with castile soap and warm
water. Be careful not to get the soap into his eyes. Is it
nitrate of silver they use for a baby's eyes?

I could not tell whether it was a baby or a doll the little
girl was coddling. The Italians' babies are often so very
small. They dress them up so grotesquely too. It must be a
rigid custom with them.

Nothing at all. All at once it seemed that every ill word
he had ever spoken struck his ear at the same moment.
What a horrible roar it made. But there were other things,
too many to record. Corners of rooms sacred to so many
deeds. Here he had said so and so, done so and so. On that
picnic he had dared to be happy. All the older women had
watched him. With one girl under each arm he had let his
spirit go. They had been closer than anything he could
now imagine.

XIV

Particles of falling stars, coming to nothing. The air pits
them, eating out the softer parts. Sometimes one strikes the
earth or falls flaming into Lake Michigan with a great hiss
and roar. And if the lawless mob that rules Ireland with its
orderly courts and still more orderly minds will not desist
it must be crushed by England. So that to realize the futility
of American men intent upon that virtue to be found in
literature, literature, that is, of the traditional sort as known
in France and Prussia—to realize how each serious Ameri-
can writer in turn flares up for a moment and fizzles out,
burnt out by the air leaving no literary monument, no *Arc
de Triomphe* behind him, no India subdued—To realize

this it is necessary to go back to the T'ang dynasty where responsibility rested solely on the heads of the poets—etc. . . . etc. . . . Or better still why not seek in Aleppo or Jerusalem for the strain to save us.

America is lost. Ah Christ, Ah Christ that night should come so soon.

And the reason is that no American poet, no American man of letters has taken the responsibility upon his own person. The responsibility for what? There is the fire. Rush into it. What is literature anyway but suffering recorded in palpitating syllables? It is the quiet after the attack. Picking a sliver of bone from his mangled and severed leg he dipped it in his own gore and wrote an immortal lyric. Richard Coeur de Lion shot through the chest with an iron bolt wrote the first English—no, French, poem of importance. What of democratic Chaucer? He was only a poet but Richard was a man, an adventurer, a king. The half mad women rushed to impregnate themselves against him. And this is literature. This is the great desirable. Soaked in passion, baba au rhum, the sheer proof of the spirit will do the trick and America will be King. Up America. Up Coeur de Lion. Up Countess Wynienski the queen of Ireland.

Polyphemus took first one shape then another but Odysseus, the wise and crafty, held firm. He did not let go but Polyphemus did. In fact the God could not exist without Odysseus to oppose him.

Why man, Europe is YEARNING to see something new come out of America.

In a soup of passion they would see a little clam. Let us smile. This is—

The danger is in forgetting that the good of the past is the same good of the present. That the power that lived then lives today. That we too possess it. That true novelty is in good work and that no matter how good work comes it is good when it possesses power over itself. Europe's enemy is the past. Our enemy is Europe, a thing unrelated to us in any way. Our lie that we must fight to the last breath is that it is related to us.

We are deceived when they cry that Negro music is the only true American creation. It is the only true from the European point of view. Everything is judged from this point of view. But to us it is only new when we consider it from a traditional vantage. To us it means a thousand things it can never mean to a European. To us only can it be said to be alive. With us it integrates with our lives. That is what it teaches us. What in hell does it matter to us whether it is new or not when it is to us. It exists. It is good solely because it is a part of us. It is good THEREFORE and therefore only is it new. Everything that is done in Europe is a repetition of the past with a difference. Everything we do must be a repetition of the past with a difference. I mean that if Negro music is new in an absolute sense—which it is not by any means, if we are to consider the Ethiopian—the probable Ethiopian influence in Egypt—then it is new to Europe as it is to us.

It is not necessary for us to learn from anyone but ourselves—at least it would be a relief to discover a critic who looked at American work from the American viewpoint.

We are a young nation and have not had time or opportunity to catch up with nations that had ten centuries start of us. We still labor under the handicap of our Puritan lineage. . . .

We shall not be able to plead childhood any longer.

Eric the Red landed in Providence, Long Island, and was put in a cage so everyone could see him.

This sort of stupidity we have to combat. I am not talking of the mass of plumbers and carpenters. I am talking of the one thing that is permanent. Spirits. I am saying that America will screw whom it will screw and when and how it will screw. And that it will refrain from screwing when it will and that no amount of infiltration tactics from "superior civilizations" can possibly make us anything but bastards.

We are only children when we acknowledge ourselves to be children. Weight of culture, weight of learning, weight of everything such as abandon in any sense has nothing to do with it. We must first isolate ourselves. Free ourselves even more than we have. Let us learn the essentials of the American situation.

We who despise the blackguards in the old sense. We too are free. Free! We too, with paddles instead of turbines will discover the new world. We are able. We are kings in our own right.

We care nothing at all for the complacent Concordites? We can look at that imitative phase with its erudite Holmeses, Thoreaus, and Emersons. With one word we can damn it: England.

In Patagonia they kick up the skulls of the river men out of the dust after a flood. In Peru, in Machu Picchu the cyclopean wall on the top of the Andes remains to rival the pyramids which after all may have been built of blocks of some plaster stuff of which we have lost the combination.

I know not a land except ours that has not to some small extent made its title clear. Translate this into ancient Greek and offer it to Harvard engraved on copper to be hung in the watercloscts which freshmen use.

And why do they come to naught? these falling stars, etc.

It has been generally supposed that among the peoples of the earth the age of maturity comes earliest in the tropics and increases gradually as one goes northward. But in North America this rule has one striking exception. It is not rare among Esquimau women that they have their first child at 12 and children born before the mothers were 11 have been recorded. Point Barrow Alaska 300 miles north of the Arctic circle.

But the early maturity of the Esquimau girls is strictly in accord with the supposition that the hotter the environment the earlier the maturity. To all intents and purposes the typical Esquimau lives under tropical or subtropical conditions. The temperature of the Esquimau house indoors frequently rises to 90°. When they go out the cold air does not have a chance to come in contact with the body, except for a limited area of the face. When an Esquimau is well dressed his two layers of fur clothing imprison the body heat so effectively that the air in actual contact with his skin is always at the temperature of a tropical summer. He carries the climate about with him inside his clothes.

When an Esquimau comes inside such a house as the one I have been speaking of he strips off all clothing, immediately on entering, except his knee breeches, and sits naked from the waist up and from the knees down. Great streams of perspiration run down the face and body and are being continually mopped up with handfuls of moss.

The effect of the overheated houses is more direct upon the women than the men for they remain indoors a large part of the winter.

Otherwise in North America among the Indians as one goes north from Mexico toward the Arctic Ocean the colder the average temperature of the air that is in contact with the body through the year, the later the maturity of the girls. The most northerly of the Atabasca Indians appear to suffer a great deal from the cold.

The Dog Rib and Yellow Knife Indians are often so poorly clad that they have to be continually moving, for if they stop for even half an hour at a time their hands become completely numb.

In the evenings their wigwams are cheerful with a roaring fire but while one's face is almost scorched with the heat of the roaring flames one's back has hoar-frost forming upon it. At night the Indians go to sleep under their blankets covering up their heads and shivering all night. The average age of maturity of the girls of these tribes is as high or higher than that of north European whites.

But from the Slavey and Dog Rib Indians to the Esquimau country the conditions suddenly change. One comes in contact with a people that has a system of living almost perfectly adapted to a cold climate, while the northern Indians have a system almost unbelievably ill adapted to the conditions in which they live.

In Puritan New England they wrapped the lover and his lass in one blanket and left them before the dying hearth after the family retired. There was a name for it which I have forgotten.

XV

It was another day ended. Another day added to the days that had gone before. Merest superstition. The eternal moment remained twining in its hair the flowers of yesterday and tomorrow. The newer street lights sparked in the dark. The uphill street which that morning had been filled at its far end with the enormous medal-with-rays of the sun was now flecked with sparkles. It was Carlstadt, established as a free thinker's corporation by Carl Weiss of Berne from which all churches had been excluded. Another day—any day—.

There lay that great frame of a man with his heavy features relaxed his loose jowls rising and falling with each breath while the busy surgeons tinkered at his elbow. Soon they struck gold and out spurted the red. Martha, who had not gone downstairs for over an hour caught it in a white porcelain bowl, an ounce, two ounces—she thought—estimating the amount swiftly. Then four ounces, eight. He was a large man. When will they check it! His breathing had grown easier. He was benefited. A pint! He was white. In an hour men on horseback were riding north and south. Washington was dead. It was another day. Any day.

Davy Crockett had a literary style. Rather than blow his squirrel to bits he'd strike the tree just under its belly so that the concussion would stun it. Such was the country with the element of time subtracted. What is time but an impertinence?

Homesteading in the far Western states was a struggle. Every child born there had a mother who is thrice a heroine. A woman in such a country approached motherhood at a time when her husband had to be away from home. Up to the day of her confinement she had to milk, churn, care for the chickens, work in the garden and carry water to the house from a well three hundred yards away. . . . The day of her confinement she did a large washing then walked two miles to the home of a neighbor.

For that the brat seized her by the lug with his little sharp teeth and drew blood. We'll have to put him on the bottle.

Nothing, save for the moment! In the moment exists all the past and the future! Evolution—! Anti-peristalsis. Eighty-seven years ago I was born in a little village in the outskirts of Birmingham. The past is for those that lived in the past, the present is for today. Or—today! The little thing lay at the foot of the bed while the midwife—It was in England 1833. And now by the sea a new world death has come and left his chewing gum in an artery of her brain. But I'll pay you for this, she said as they were sliding her into the ambulance, I'll pay you for this. You young people think you are awfully smart, don't you. I don't want to see them again, those fuzzy things, what are they, trees?

Good gracious, do you call this making me comfortable? The two boys had her on the stretcher on the floor. Yes, stay here a week then I can do what I please but you want to do what you please first. I wonder how much she planned.

XVI

Another day, going evening foremost this time. Leaning above her baby in the carriage was Nettie Vogelman, grown heavier since we knew her in the sixth grade twenty-five years before and balancing great masses of prehistoric knowledge on her head in the shape of a purple ostrich-plume hat.

But where is romance in all this—with the great-coat she was wearing hanging from the bulge of her paps to the sidewalk? Romance! When knighthood was in flower. Rome. Elagabalus in a skirt married his man servant.

We struggle to comprehend an obscure evolution—opposed by the true and static church—when the compensatory involution so plainly marked escapes our notice. Living we fail to live but insist on impaling ourselves on fossil horns. But the church balanced like a glass ball where the jets of evolution and involution meet has always, in its prosperous periods, patronized the arts. What else could it do? Religion is the shell of beauty.

The fad of evolution is swept aside. It was only mildly interesting at the best. I'll give you a dollar my son for each of these books you read: *Descent of Man* and *Origin of Species*, reprinted by Dombie and Sons, Noodle Lane, Ken. W. London, England 1890.

Who will write the natural history of involution beginning with the stone razor age in Cornwall to the stone razor age in Papua? Oh China, China teach us! Ottoman, Magyar, Moor, teach us. Norse Eric the Discoverer teach us. Coeur de Lion, teach us. Great Catherine teach us. Phryne, Thaïs, Cleopatra, Brünnhilde, Lucretia Borgia teach us. What was it, Demosthenes, that she said to you? Come again?

Borne on the foamy crest of involution, like Venus on her wave, stript as she but of all consequence—since it is the return: See they return! From savages in quest of a bear we are come upon rifles, cannon. From Chaldeans solving the stars we have fallen into the bellies of the telescopes. From great runners we have evolved into speeches sent over a wire.

But our spirits, our spirits have prospered! Boom, boom. Oh yes, our spirits have grown—

The corrosive of pity, Baroja says, giving up medicine to be a baker.

Marriage is of the church because it is the intersection of *loci* by which alone there is place for a church to stand. Beauty is an arrow. Diana launched her shaft into the air and where the deer and the arrow met a church was founded and there beauty had died.

So youth and youth meet and die and there the church sets up its ceremony.

Who will write the natural history of involution?

I have forgotten something important that I wanted to say. Thus having forgotten and remembered that it was important the folly of all thought is revealed.

The deer lay panting on the leaves while Diana leaned over it to stab it in the neck with her dagger.

I have forgotten what I wanted to say.

Venus and Adonis.

The second time I saw her it was in a room of a hotel in the city.

XVII

As the Southern mountains are not like other mountains, so the mountaineers are not like others. For all their beauty these mountains are treacherous and alien, and the people who must wring a livelihood from the sawmills or from the tiny perpendicular farms high up under the sky come to be wary and secret like their woodlands.

The Cumberland mountain mother, by nature sharp and sane, has studied the moods of the mountains and of the animals. Illiterate though she be, she is full of ripe wisdom. Many, superior to the mountain woman in, say, sanitation might learn from sitting on cabin doorsteps that they are most often inferior to her in sanity.

Yet, frankly, it is often better to sit on the cabin doorstep than to go inside. The mountain mother struggles bravely against dirt, but if you live in a lonely two-room cabin, if you are the sole caretaker of six children under ten, and two cows and a large stony garden, and must help in the cornfield besides, you are excusable if in the end you "quit struggling." The mountain mother does not make herself and her husband and her children slaves to the housekeeping arts.

A mountain woman dips snuff—surreptitiously if she is young, frankly if she is old.

We settle down on the doorstep probably on straight chairs with seats of cornhusks twisted into a rope and then interwoven. There is a sound to which the mountains have accustomed me—the sharp jolting thud when a mother, if she possesses neither cradle nor rocker, puts her baby to sleep by jerking forward and backward on two legs of a straight chair. There is usually some two-year-old lying fast asleep on the bed just inside the door; or on the porch floor, plump and brown as a bun and studded with flies thick as currants.

Mountain children are as vigorous as baby oaks until they reach their teens, and then over-work begins to tell on growing bodies. A reedy boy of thirteen, just beginning to stretch to the length of spine and limb that characterizes the mountain air, often gets a stoop that he never afterward conquers. In the more remote lumber districts I have seen boys of ten and twelve work all day loading cars. There too, slim mountain girls of twelve and fourteen stand all day in the icy spray of the flume to stack bark on the cars.

Here where isolation makes people fiercely individualistic public opinion is as slow to deny a man's right to marry at the age he wishes as it is to deny his right to turn his corn into whisky. At the age when boys and girls first awake to the fact of sex they marry and the parents, although regretfully, let them.

The unmarried mother is most rare. A boy of sixteen sets himself to all the duties of fatherhood. A fourteen-year-old mother, with an ageless wisdom, enters without faltering on her future of a dozen children.

But here is Lory. But again a disgression—: In any account of the mountains one must remember that there are three distinct types: the people of the little villages, almost all remote from railroads; the itinerant lumber workers, wood-choppers and mill-hands who follow the fortunes of the portable sawmill as it exhausts first one remote cove then another; and the permanent farmers who have inherited their dwindling acres for generations. Yet at bottom the mountain mother is always the same.

Lory lives in a one-room lumber shack, and moves about once in three months. The walls are of planks with inch-wide cracks between them. There are two tiny windows with sliding wooden shutters and a door. All three must be closed when it is very cold. For better protection the walls are plastered over with newspapers, always peeling off and gnawed by woodrats. The plank floor does not prevent the red clay from oozing up. The shack is some fifteen feet square. It contains two stoves, two beds, two trunks, a table and two or three chairs. In it live six souls: two brothers, their wives and a baby apiece.

Lory is part Indian, one surmises from the straight hair dropping over her eyes and her slow squawlike movements. Her face is stolid except when it flashes into a smile of pure fun. Dark though she is her breast, bared from her dark purple dress, is statue white. She looks down on her first baby with a madonna's love and her words have in them a madonna's awe before a holy thing: "I ain't never a-goin' to whip him. He ain't never a-goin' to need it, for he won't get no meanness if I don't learn him none."

The setting is fairyland. Mountain folk go far toward living on beauty. The women may become too careless and inert even to scrape away the underbrush and plant a few sweet potatoes and cabbages. They may sit through lazy hours mumbling their snuff sticks, as does Mrs. Cole, while children and dogs and chickens swarm about them: but even Mrs. Cole can be roused by the call of beauty.

"My husband he's choppin' at the first clearin' two miles from here, and he's been plumb crazy over the yaller lady slippers up that-a-way. He's been sayin' I must take the two least kids, what ain't never seen sech, and go up there and see 'em 'fore they was gone. So yesterday we went. It sure was some climb over them old logs, but Gawd them lady slippers was worth it."

I shall never understand the mystery of a mountain woman's hair. No matter how old, how worn or ill she may be, her hair is always a wonder of color and abundance.

Ma Duncan at fifty-five is straight and sure-footed as an Indian; tall and slim and dark as a gypsy, with a gypsy's passionate love of out-of-doors. Her neighbors send for Ma Duncan from far and near in time of need. Going forth from her big farm boarding-house on errands of mercy. Up wild ravines to tiny cabins that seem to bud out like lichens from grey boulders wet with mountain streams, over foot logs that sway crazily over rock creeks, through waist-high undergrowth Ma Duncan goes with her stout stick.

As we reach a little grassy clearing Ma Duncan drops down to stretch out happily: So as I can hear what the old earth has to say me. . . . Reckon it says, "Quit your fussin' you old fool. Ain't God kept your gang a young uns all straight so fur? He ain't a-going back on you now, just because they're growd."

Presently Ma Duncan sits up, her hands about her knees, her hat fallen from her wealth of hair, her gun on the ground beside her—often she carries a gun in the hope of getting a gray squirrel to be done in inimitable brown cream gravy for breakfast.

She looks out sadly over much worn woodland, with the great stumps remaining:

"I wish you could have seen the great old trees that used to be here. If folks wasn't so mad for money they might be here and a preachin' the gospel of beauty. But folks is all for money and all for self. Some-day when they've cut off all the beauty that God planted to point us to him, folks will look round and wonder what us human bein's is here fur—"

The mountain woman lives untouched by all modern life. In two centuries mountain people have changed so little that they are in many ways the typical Americans.

"The Lord sent me back" former pastor tells men in session at the church. With tears in his eyes, he enters meeting, escorted by two sons. Dramatic scene follows as he asks forgiveness for mistake he has made. Was in Canada and Buffalo. His explanation of absence is satisfactory to family and members he met last night.

Miss Hannen in seclusion at home. Her family declines to give statement.

Dominie Cornelius Densel, forty-eight years old, former pastor, etc. . . . who left his wife and eight children etc. came home last night.

Miss T. Hannen, twenty-six years old, etc. . . . who disappeared from her home, etc. . . . on the same afternoon that the dominie was numbered among the missing also came to her home the same evening.

Pictures of the missing dominie and member of his church who are home again.

XVIII

Commodius renamed the tenth month Amazonius. But he died a violent death and the old name was returned.

I had five cents in my pocket and a piece of apple pie in my hand, said Prof. M. I. Pupin, of Columbia University, describing the circumstances of his arrival in America in the steerage of the steamship Westphalia from Hamburg half a century ago.

Today that American scholar of Serbian birth holds the chair in electro-mechanics at Columbia University.

Prof. Pupin is merely one of a host of former immigrants whose names are linked with the great strides in science, commerce, finance and industry and whose careers furnish living proof that America, besides breeding great men, imports them.

Claude Monet was born in Columbia, Ohio.

In industry and commerce the stories of many of the successful immigrants read like romances.

There is C. C. A. Baldi of Philadelphia who began with nothing and who is now one of America's foremost citizens of foreign birth. When he landed in this country thirty years ago he had only a few pennies in the pockets of his ragged trousers. He knew no English and knew nothing of American customs, but he had heard of the opportunities which America offers to a wide-awake, ambitious immigrant willing to work.

Mr. Baldi bought thirty lemons with his pennies. He peddled them and with the proceeds of sales bought more lemons and peddled them. Before long he had a cart loaded with hundreds of lemons. In time the push-cart became a store and the store grew into a great business.

Other spectacular instances of success are furnished by the careers of Louis J. Horowitz, one of America's greatest builders and S. M. Schatzkin, who came to this country twenty-five years ago with 3 dollars carefully tucked away in his clothes and began peddling coal in the East Side of New York. To-day Schatzkin has large sums invested in many big American enterprises.

Horowitz, who came here thirty years ago, built the Woolworth and Equitable buildings, one the tallest and the other the largest office building in point of floor space in the world. His first job was that of an errand boy. Later he worked as a parcel wrapper, then as a stock boy and then as a shoe salesman. After selling shoes he started selling real estate.

Witness, oh witness these lives my dainty cousins. Dear Madam: —It has often been said that one of the most interesting spots in America is the small space covered by the desk of the editor of the *Atlantic Monthly*.

All the qualities which make up the interest of life,—joy,

sorrow, romance, ambition, experience,—seem to center in this spot in turn, radiating from every nook and corner of the world.

"Adventures," remarked the talented Mr. Disraeli, "are for the adventurous," and it is to those who think of life as the supreme adventure that the *Atlantic* is most confidently addressed.

If you care for a magazine that satisfies, vexes and delights by turn, you can safely subscribe to the *Atlantic Monthly* for the coming year.

Public Service Railway Company, Newark, N. J. Amazonius 10, 1920.—To our Patrons: As a fair minded citizen, your impartial consideration of the facts set forth in subjoined letter, written by me to the Board of Public Utility Commissioners under date of Amazonius 7th, 1920, is respectfully requested. Very truly yours, Thomas N. McCarter, President.

To the Board of Public Utility Commissioners of the State of New Jersey, Trenton, New Jersey. Dear Sirs: The rate of fare of 7 cents, with one cent for a transfer, etc. . . . , etc. . . . Such large cities as Boston, New Haven, Hartford and Pittsburgh already have a 10c. flat rate. Etc. . . . etc. . . . Under the foregoing statement of facts the company is forced to file herewith a flat rate of 10c. where 7c. is now charged. Etc. . . . etc. . . .

> Now when Christmas bells ring clear
> Telling us that love is here
> And children sing
> Gifts that speak of thoughtful love
> Just like angels from above
> Glad tidings bring.

Rugs, mirrors, chairs, tables, W. & J. Sloane, N.Y., Wash., San F. Christmas Gifts Sure to be Appreciated.: Standing lamps, table lamps, book ends, Sheffield ware, desk sets, framed prints, porcelains, soft pillows, foot rests (D-2968 Rocking foot rest in Mahogany. Formerly $45.00. Sale Price $30.00!) sconces, mantel clocks, wall clocks, tall clocks, small tables, smoking stands, occasional chairs, screens, oriental rugs, Chinese embroideries, vacuum cleaners—Mirrors. Small Oriental Rugs: Mosuls, Bergamas, Beluchistans, Lilihans, Saruks, Kermanshahs.

California was peopled by the Indians first and then by the Padres who brought with them their sprigs of vine and of orange and of fig and also the art of irrigation. So that you will find today from the very northernmost part, from Klamath Lake down to the Imperial Valley in the South, the lands of California watered and made as fertile as the valley of the Nile.

That's all right. Yes Sir. But I come from the Eastern Shore of Maryland. I'm an East Sho' man. Have you ever been on the Eastern Sho'? No? Well sir, we're a strange people and we have some strange legends on the East Sho'. When Adam and Eve lived in the Garden of Eden they fell sick and the Lord was very much disturbed over them, so he called a council of his angels and wanted to know where they should be taken for a change of air.

Gabriel suggested the Eastern Sho' of Maryland but the Lord said, No, No; that wouldn't be sufficient change.

Yes sir, down at Chincoteague they have the biggest and the finest oysters in the world. Big as your hand and when you get a half dozen of them a couple of hours out of the water you know you have something.

It was at Chincoteague two Spanish galleons went ashore in the old days and some ponies swam ashore. To this day they have a yearly round-up on the island where the breed of these ponies is corralled, a short special breed of horse.

Tangier Island is another place. That's where the sheriff shot the boy who wouldn't go in off his front porch on Sunday morning during church service. Either in church or in the house during that hour. He shot him all right. They have little individual canals up to their back doors from the bay.

And the native, coming up to him suddenly with a knife as long as your arm, said,¡ *Yo soy más hombre que tú!* and

started a swing at him. Had he not been so quick to seize
a chair and bring it down on the man's head—What would
have happened?

XIX

Sometimes the men would come in and say there was a
turkey nest down in the meadow and they'd send me to
look for it.

Once I fell in the mireage up to my waist. My, they was
mad at me. "Can't tramp a meadow without falling in the
mireage?" they said.

I miss it often. At nine they let me drive the hay-hoist
with one horse and later with two. One morning I had
the young team out. It was Allie's team of greys, they was
only just no more than colts. They shied at a piece of
paper. I could hear the men up in the barn yelling. "Hey,
what's the matter down there!" But it was no use. I tried
to get to their heads. I wasn't afraid of them. Allie said
afterward he wouldn't have been surprised to have seen
me killed.

One of the women stood in the road waving a broom.
I can see her yet. I might have been able to manage them
if it hadn't been for her but they simply jumped over a
wagon and smashed the hay-fork and ran down the road
two miles. Then they came back again. My but the Old
Man was mad at me. All the black looks I got!

I used to hate the Old Man. Sometimes I'd be getting
wood and he'd ask me why I hadn't done something. I'd
say I hadn't gotten round to it yet. Maybe he'd throw a
piece of wood at me.

I can remember the churning. I wouldn't exactly like to
go back to it all but sometimes I miss it terribly. Some-
times it wouldn't take you more than five minutes to get
to the butter and sometimes you'd churn for 45 or two
hours and sometimes it would never come. We'd get four

or five pounds or more at a churning. Then it would have to be washed and salted and packed in jars in the cellar.

So now that it is raining. So now that it is Amazonius—we go to buy a metal syringe at the factory because we know the men who live on our street who own the bricks that make the walls that hold the floors that hold the girls who make mistakes in the inventories:

Every order that comes in is copied. You must rely on your help. As the orders come in they are handled by a girl who puts them on our own uniform order sheets. So right there it begins. You have to rely on a young flyaway who has perhaps been up dancing the night before. It's easy enough for her to write "with" for "without" and—that's the sort of thing that happens. There is a certain minimum of error that you must count on and no reputable house will fail to make good promptly.

The glass blowers have never in my entire experience of 17 years suffered any harm from their trade. Why we had a boy in the old factory, a cripple, a withered leg, the weakest, scrawniest lad you ever saw. He's been blowing for us for 15 or 17 years and you should see him today. Why the fat fairly hangs down over his collar.

In our thermometer work they blow the bulb then fill it with mercury which is in a special container like the cups you get at Child's restaurant say. They never have to touch the stuff. When the bulb is full they seal it. Then the mercury in the bulb is warmed by passing the bulb through a flame. This is to drive it up the capillary tube. There can be no volatilization since the mercury is in the tube and this is the only time the stuff is heated. Then when the metal rises from the heat the other end of the glass is dipped in the stuff so that as the bulb now cools the mercury is sucked up filling the thermometer completely.

Sometimes, of course, a bulb breaks in heating so that the floor is full of the stuff.

The hydrofluoric acid for marking is used under a hood with a special exhaust-blower that has nothing else to do but exhaust that hood. There is not the slightest odor of fumes in the room. The air is as good there as here.

And what is your business?

Rag merchant.

Ah yes. And what does that mean?

Our main specialty is shoddy.

Ah yes. Shoddy is made from—

From woolen rags. The whole mass is put into a vat and the cotton dissolved out. It comes out in a great wet heap of stuff that has to be washed and dried.

Sometimes they burn the cotton out with gas. For instance you'll see a piece of cloth, grey cloth. The gas will take out the black cotton and leave the wool fibres all running in one direction. One of the secrets of the trade is the selection of the colors. That is red shoddy is made from red rags and so on. But they even take the dyes out of the cloth and use it over again.

You know the army coats the boys wore. They were 70% shoddy. It's all wool but the fibre has been broken. It makes a hard material not like the soft new woven woolens but it's wool, all of it.

After the stuff from the vats is dry they put it on the donkeys which turn it into loose skeins. From that stage it goes on to the making of the yarn for weaving when any quantity of fresh wool can be mixed that you desire.

The shortest fibre, that can't be used for anything else, is made into these workingmen's shirts you see. The wool is held in a container in the loosest state possible. This is connected up with a blower in front of which a loom is set for weaving a fairly tight cotton mesh. Then as the loom is working the wool is BLOWN IN! Where the cotton warp and woof cross the shoddy is caught.

Recently a Jew came in to complain of the lightness of the shirts he was getting. All we did was to yell out, "George turn on the blower a little stronger." One washing and the wool is gone. But the Jews are the smart ones. You got to hand it to them. They invent machinery to do anything with that stuff. Why one man made a million before the government stopped him by making cheap quilts.

He took any kind of rags just as they were collected, filth or grease right on them the way they were and teased them up into a fluffy stuff which he put through a rolling process and made into sheets of wadding. These sheets were fed mechanically between two layers of silkolene and a girl simply sat there with an electric sewing device which she guided with her hand and drew in the designs you see on those quilts, you know.

You've seen this fake oilcloth they are advertising now. Congoleum. Nothing but building paper with a coating of enamel.

¡O vida tan dulce!

The Descent of Winter

The Descent of Winter

"The Descent of Winter" is total Williams—poetry, fiction, fact, criticism, personality—cast in an arbitrary shape that suited him just fine but may have confused everyone else. Except, of course, his friend Ezra Pound, who first published "The Descent of Winter" in the Autumn, 1928, issue of *The Exile*. Since then this curiosity of literary objectivism has not been reassembled and published again in its original form.

One of the important things about "The Descent of Winter" is that it contains several beautiful poems—"My Bed Is Narrow," "That Brilliant Field," "Dahlias"—meeting Williams's demand for "intense vision of the facts." But this exotic exchange between Williams and his work offers more than living poetry. It tells much about the drift of Williams's mind as he entered middle age. It suggests the difficulties he was having rationalizing everything—his art, himself, the world around him. It shows him experimenting, experimenting. The poems and prose run together because Williams was jotting them down as in a notebook. The two forms are also pressed into a single work because Williams, perhaps unconsciously, was seeking a bridge over the gap between them. He couldn't quite do it. Chasms of logic and event intervene. But the intent of union is clearly there.

Williams began "The Descent of Winter" on board the S. S. *Pennland* in the fall of 1927. He was returning from Europe, where he had left Florence Williams with their two sons, who were to attend school in Geneva. The entry dates, beginning with September 27, and ending with December 15, literally document Williams's title. Winter was coming.

As with many of his works during the 1920's, this was another of Williams's time-defined and time-defying efforts at art. It all had to happen in a given interval or it wasn't going to happen at all. Doctoring and writing must come simultaneously.

The title also states the season of Williams's emotions at that time. It was a dark time of year inside as well as outside. He tells us that "the perfect type of the man of action is the suicide." Death enters Williams's writing repeatedly, even comically: "A cat licking herself solves most of the problems of infection. We wash too much and finally it kills us." The world around Williams festers. The United States "is a soviet state decayed away in a misconception of richness." Its rivers are "polluted and defamed." Its office workers "get in a hot car, ride in a hot tunnel and confine themselves in a hot office—to sell asphalt. . . ." Williams worries over old age, poverty, loneliness, rubbish heaps, and what men and women do to one another. All are a noxious by-product, it seems, of a ravenous industrialized society. He was writing again about whatever entered his head. And what entered was occasionally as beautiful as his poem about a poet imagining himself visiting Russia after the revolution, "A Morning Imagination of Russia." More often, it was as dark as a drunk beating up his pregnant wife.

Williams was ministering to his spirit in "The Descent of Winter." He was his own therapist, getting his feelings out where he could observe them and command them to enter his art. That it worked we now know. But reading "The Descent of Winter" in 1928 we might have wondered. He sounds like a man about to take up permanent residency on a couch—or worse. His art saved him.

In his urgent, hurried way Williams also was struggling to verbalize a theory of contemporary poetry. He had to reach a clearer conception of himself as an artist. His hot pursuit of a modern style is thwarted by "the fragmentary stupidity of modern life, its lacunae of sense, loops, perversions of instinct, blankets, amputations, fullsomeness of in-

struction and multiplications of inanity. . . . To be plain is
to be subverted since every term must be forged new, every
word is tricked out of meaning, hanging with as many cheap
traps as an altar." He damns the "bastardry of the simile."
It undermines "the vividness which is poetry itself." He
feels himself flawed, a semi-literate: "Your writings are a
sea / full of misspelling and / faulty sentences. Level. Trou-
bled." Yet Williams does know that he has made essential
contact in his poetry: ". . . We have paid heavily. But we
/ have gotten—touch."

It's no caprice that leads Williams to Shakespeare in "The
Descent of Winter." It's the drive of the imagination. Wil-
liams wanted nothing except perfection as he conceived
perfection in the cold, early morning of modern American
poetry. He would come close to it later. And like the
Shakespeare he celebrates in this unclassifiable work, Wil-
liams would do it through the imagination: "By writing
he [Shakespeare] escaped from the world into the natural
world of his mind." Genius, Williams says, is not industry
or hard work. "It is to see the track, to smell it out, to know
it inevitable—sense sticking out all round feeling, feeling,
seeing—hearing, touching." Whatever his personal and emo-
tional separation from a junk society, Williams was on the
track in "The Descent of Winter." He was seeing, feeling,
hearing, touching the emerging America that later envel-
oped us.

w.s.

The Descent of Winter

9/27

*"What are these elations I have
at my own underwear?*

*I touch it and it is strange
upon a strange thigh."*

*　　*　　*

9/29

My bed is narrow
in a small room
at sea

The numbers are on
the wall
Arabic I

Berth No. 2
was empty above me
the steward

took it apart
and removed
it

only the number
remains
.2.

on an oval disc
of celluloid
tacked

to the whiteenameled
woodwork
with

two bright nails
like stars
beside

the moon

9/30

There are no perfect waves—
Your writings are a sea
full of misspellings and
faulty sentences. Level. Troubled.
A center distant from the land
touched by the wings of nearly
silent birds that never seem
to rest, yet it bears me
seriously—to land, but without
you.

This is the sadness of the sea—
waves like words all broken—
a sameness of lifting and falling mood.

I lean watching the detail
of brittle crest, the delicate
imperfect foam, the yellow weed
one piece like another—

235

There is no hope, or maybe
a coral island slowly
slowly forming and waiting
for birds to drop the seeds
will make it habitable

10/9

and there's a little blackboy
in a doorway
scratching his wrists

The cap on his head
is red and blue
with a broad peak to it

and his mouth
is open, his tongue
between his teeth—

10/10

Monday
            the canna flaunts
its crimson head

crimson lying folded
crisply down upon

            the invisible

darkly crimson heart
of this poor yard

the grass is long

            October tenth

a beard . . . not of stone but particular
hairs purpleblack . . . lies upon his stale breast

10/21

In the dead weeds a rubbish heap
in flames: the orange flames
stream horizontal, windblown
they parallel the ground
waving up and down
the flamepoints alternating
the body streaked with loops
and purple stains while
the pale smoke, above,
steadily continues eastward—

What chance have the old?
There are no duties for them
no places where they may sit
their knowledge is laughed at
they cannot see, they cannot hear.
A small bundle on the shoulders
weighs them down
one hand is put back under it
to hold it steady.
Their feet hurt, they are weak
they should not have to suffer
as younger people must and do
there should be a truce for them

that brilliant field
of rainwet orange
blanketed

by the red grass
and oilgreen bayberry

the last yarrow
on the gutter
white by the sandy
rainwater

and a white birch
with yellow leaves
and few
and loosely hung

and a young dog
jumped out
of the old barrel

10/23

I will make a big, serious portrait of my time. The brown
and creamwhite block of Mexican onyx has a poorly exe-
cuted replica of the Aztec calendar on one of its dicefacets
the central circle being a broadnosed face with projected
hanging tongue the sun perhaps though why the tongue is
out I do not know unless to taste or gasp in the heat, its
own heat, to say it's hot and is the sun. Puebla, Mexico,
Calendario Azteca, four words are roughly engraved in the
four corners where the circle leaves spaces on the square
diceface this is America some years after the original, the

art of writing is to do work so excellent that by its excellence it repels all idiots but idiots are like leaves and excellence of any sort is a tree when the leaves fall the tree is naked and the wind thrashes it till it howls it cannot get a book published it can only get poems into certain magazines that are suppressed because because waving waving waving waving waving waving tic tack tic tock tadick there is not excellence without the vibrant rhythm of a poem and poems are small and tied and gasping they eat gasoline, they all ate gasoline and died, they died of—there is a hole in the wood and all I say brings to mind the rock shingles of Cherbourg, on the new houses they have put cheap tile which overlaps but the old roofs had flat stone sides steep but of stones fitted together and that is love there is no portrait without that has not turned to prose love is my hero who does not live, a man, but speaks of it every day.

1. continued (the great law)

What is he saying? That love was never made for man and woman to crack between them and so he loves and loves his sons and loves as he pleases. But there is a great law over him which—is as it is. The wind blowing, the mud spots on the polished surface, the face reflected in the glass which as you advance the features disappear leaving only the hat and as you draw back the features return, the tip of the nose, the projection over the eyebrows, the cheek bones and the bulge of the lips the chin last.

2

I remember, she said, we had little silver plaques with a chain on it to hang over the necks of the bottles, whisky, brandy or whatever it was. And a box of some kind of wood, not for the kitchen but a pretty box. Inside it was lined with something like yes, pewter, all inside and there was a cover of metal too with a little knob on it, all inside

239

the wooden box. You would open the outer cover and inside was the lid. When you would take that off you would see the tea with a silver spoon for taking it out. But now, here are the roses—three opening. Out of love. For she loves them and so they are there. They are not a picture. Holbein never saw pink thorns in such a light. Nor did Masaccio. The petals are delicate. It is a question if they will open at all and not drop, loosing at one edge and falling tomorrow all in a heap. All around the roses there is today, machinery leaning upon the stem, an aeroplane is upon one leaf where a worm lies curled. Soppy it seems and enormous, it seems to hold up the sky for it has no size at all. We eat beside it—beside the three roses that she loves. And an oak tree grows out of my shoulders. Its roots are my arms and my legs. The air is a field. Yellow and red grass are writing their signature everywhere.

10/27

And Coolidge said let there be imitation brass filigree fire fenders behind insured plateglass windows and yellow pine booths with the molasses-candygrain in the wood instead of the oldtime cake-like whitepine boards always cut thick their faces! the white porcelain trough is no doubt made of some certain blanched clay baked and glazed but how they do it, how they shape it soft and have it hold its shape for the oven I don't know nor how the cloth is woven, the grey and the black with the orange and green strips wound together diagonally across the grain artificial pneumothorax their faces! the stripe of shadow along the pavement edge, the brownstone steeple low among the office buildings dark windows with a white wooden cross upon them, lights like fuchsias, lights like bleeding hearts lights like columbines, cherry red danger and applegreen safety. Any hat in this window $2.00 barred windows, wavy opaque glass, a block of brownstone at the edge of the sidewalk crudely stippled on top for a footstep to a carriage, lights with sharp bright spikes, stick out round them their faces! STOP in black letters surrounded by a red glow, letters with each bulb a seed in the shaft of the L of the A lights on the river streaking the restless water lights upon pools of rainwater by the roadside a great pool of light full of overhanging sparks into whose lower edge a house looms its center marked by one yellow windowbright their faces!

10/28

born, September 15, 1927, 2nd child, wt. 6 lbs. 2 ozs. The hero is Dolores Marie Pischak, the place Fairfield, in my own state, my own county, its largest city, my own time. This is her portrait: O future worlds, this is her portrait—order be God damned. Fairfield is the place where the October marigolds go over into the empty lot with dead grass like Polish children's hair and the nauseous, the stupifying monotony of decency is dead, unkindled even by art or anything—dead: by God because Fairfield is alive, coming strong. Oh blessed love you are here in this golden air, this honey and dew sunshine, ambering the houses to jewels. Order—is dead. Here a goose flaps his wings by a fence, a white goose, women talk from second story windows to a neighbor on the ground, the tops of the straggling backyard poplars have been left with a tail of twigs and on the bare trunk a pulley with a line in it is tied. A cop whizzes by on his sidecar cycle, the bank to the river is cinders where dry leaves drift. The cinders are eating forward over the green grass below, closer and closer to the river bank, children are in the gutters violently at play over a dam of mud, old women with seamed faces lean on the crooked front gates. Where is Pischak's place? I don't know. I tink it's up there at the corner. What you want?—

Here one drinks good beer. Don't tell my husband. I stopped there yesterday, really good. I was practically alone, yes.

Some streets paved, some dirt down the center. A merchant has a clothing store and looks at you wondering what he can sell. And you feel he has these people sized up. A nasty feeling. Unattached. When he gets his he'll burn it up and clear out in a day. And they do not suspect how nicely he has measured them. They need stuff. He sells it. Who's that guy I wonder. Never seen him around here before. Looks like a doctor.

That's the feeling of Fairfield. An old farmhouse in long tangled trees, leaning over it. A dell with a pretty stream in it below the little garden and fifty feet beyond, the board fence of the Ajax Aniline Dye Works with red and purple refuse dribbling out ragged and oily under the lower fence boards. No house is like another. Small, wooden, a garden at the back, all ruined by the year. Man leaning smoking from a window. And the dirt, dry dust. No grass, or grass in patches, hedged with sticks and a line of cord or wire or grass, a jewel, a garden embanked, all in a twenty foot square, crowded with incident, a small terrace of begonias, a sanded path, pinks, roses in a dozen rococo beds.

Knock and walk in: The bar. Not a soul. In the back room the kitchen immaculate, the enameled table featured. The mother nursing her from a nearly empty breast. She lies and sucks. Black hair, pencilled down the top flat and silky smooth, the palmsized face asleep, the mother at a point of vantage where under an inside window raised two inches she can govern the street entrance.

Who's that?

A woman. Oh that old woman from next door.

The father, young, energetic, enormous. Unsmiling, big headed, a nervous twitch to his head and a momentary intense squint to his eyes. She watches the door. He is in shirtsleeves. Restless, goes in and out. Talks fast, manages the old woman begging help for a bruised hand. A man who might be a general or president of a corporation, or president of the states. Runs a bootleg slaoon. Great!

This is the world. Here one breathes and the dignity of man holds on. "Here I shall live. Why not now? Why do I wait?"

Katharin, 9, sheepish, shy—adoring in response to gentleness so that her eyes almost weep for sentimental gratitude, has jaundice, leans on his knee. Follows him with her eyes. Her hair is straight and blond.

On the main river road, a grey board fence over which a grove of trees sticks up. Oaks, maples, poplars and old fruit trees. Belmont Park, Magyar Home. For rent for picnics. Peace is here—rest, assurance, life hangs on.

Oh, blessed love, among insults, brawls, yelling, kicks, brutality—here the old dignity of life holds on—defying the law, defying monotony.

She lies in her mother's arms and sucks. The dream passes over her, dirt streets, a white goose flapping its wings, and passes. Boys, wrestling, kicking a half inflated football. A grey motheaten squirrel pauses at a picket fence where tomato vines, almost spent, hang on stakes.

Oh, blessed love—the dream engulfs her. She opens her eyes on the troubled bosom of the mother who is nursing the babe and watching the door. And watching the eye of the man. Talking English, a stream of Magyar, Polish what? to the tall man coming and going.

Oh, blessed love where are you there, pleasure driven out, order triumphant, one house like another, grass cut to pay lovelessly. Bored we turn to cars to take us to "the country" to "nature" to breathe her good air. Jesus Christ. To nature. It's about time, for most of us. She is holding the baby. Her eye under the window, watching. Her hair is bobbed halfshort. It stands straight down about her ears. You, you sit and have it waved and ordered. Fine. I'm glad of it. And nothing to do but play cards and whisper. Jesus Christ. Whisper of the high school girl that had a baby and how smart her mama was to pretend in a flash of genius that it was hers. Jesus Christ. Or let us take a run up to the White Mountains or Lake Mohonk. Not Bethlehem (New Hampshire) any more, the people have ruined that like lice all over the lawns. Horrible to see. The dirty things. Eating everywhere. Parasites.

And so order, seclusion, the good of it all.

But in Fairfield men are peaceful and do as they please —and learn the necessity and the profit of order—and Dolores Marie Pischak was born.

10/28

        On hot days
the sewing machine
              whirling

        in the next room
        in the kitchen

and men at the bar
        talking of the strike
        and cash

10/28

a flash of juncos in the field of grey locust saplings with a white sun powdery upon them and a large rusty can wedged in the crotch of one of them, for the winter, human fruit, and on the polished straws of the dead grass a scroll of crimson paper—not yet rained on

10/28

in this strong light
the leafless beechtree
244 shines like a cloud

it seems to glow
of itself
with a soft stript light
of love
over the brittle

grass

But there are
on second look
a few yellow leaves
still shaking

far apart
just one here one there
trembling vividly

10/29

The justice of poverty
    its shame its dirt
are one with the meanness
    of love

its organ in a tarpaulin
    the green birds
the fat sleepy horse
    the old men

the grinder sourfaced
    hat over eyes
the beggar smiling all open
    the lantern out

and the popular tunes—
    sold to the least bidder

for a nickel
   two cents or

nothing at all or even
   against the desire
forced on us

10/30

To freight cars in the air

all the slow
   clank, clank
   clank, clank
moving above the treetops

the
   wha,   wha
of the hoarse whistle

   pah,   pah,   pah
   pah, pah, pah, pah, pah

   piece and piece
   piece and piece
moving still trippingly
through the morningmist

long after the engine
has fought by
                   and disappeared

in silence
                to the left

in almost all verse you read, mine or anybody's else, the
figures used and the general impression of the things spoken
of is vague "you could say it better in prose" especially
good prose, say the prose of Hemingway. The truth of the
object is somehow hazed over, dulled. So nobody would go
to see a play in verse if

> the salvias, the rusty hydrangeas, the ragged
> cannas

there's too often no observation in it, in poetry. It is a soft
second light of dreaming. The sagas were not like that, they
seem to have been made on the spot. The little Greek I have
read—and in translation—is not like that. Marlow, Chaucer,
el Cid, Shakespeare where he is homely, uncultured, a
shrewd guesser is not like that. Where he puts it over about
some woman he knew or a prince or Falstaff. The good
poetry is where the vividness comes up "true" like in prose
but better. That's poetry. Dante was wrestling with Italian,
his vividness comes from his escape from Latin. Don
Quixote. I don't know about the Russians or the French.

> and the late, high growing red rose
> it is their time
> of a small garden

poetry should strive for nothing else, this vividness alone,
per se, for itself. The realization of this has its own internal
fire that is "like" nothing. Therefore the bastardy of the
simile. That thing, the vividness which is poetry by itself,
makes the poem. There is no need to explain or compare.
Make it and it *is* a poem. This is modern, not the saga.

247

There are no sagas—only trees now, animals, engines:
There's that.

11/1

I won't have to powder my nose tonight 'cause Billie's
gonna take me home in his car—

The moon, the dried weeds
and the Pleiades—
Seven feet tall
the dark, dried weedstalks
make a part of the night
a red lace
on the blue milky sky

Write—
by a small lamp

the Pleiades are almost
nameless
and the moon is tilted
and halfgone

And in runningpants and
with ecstatic, æsthetic faces
on the illumined
signboard are leaping
over printed hurdles and
"¼ of their energy comes
from bread"

two
gigantic highschool boys
ten feet tall

Dahlias—
  What a red
          and yellow and white
mirror to the sun, round
              and petaled
          is this she holds?

              with a red face

      all in black
          and grey hair
          sticking out
      from under the bonnet brim

Is this Washington Avenue Mr. please

          or do I have to
      cross the track?

A Morning Imagination of Russia

The earth and the sky were very close
When the sun rose it rose in his heart.
It bathed the red cold world of
the dawn so that the chill was his own
The mists were sleep and sleep began
to fade from his eyes, below him in the
garden a few flowers were lying forward
on the intense green grass where
in the opalescent shadows oak leaves
were pressed hard down upon it in patches
by the night rain. There were no cities
between him and his desires

his hatreds and his loves were without walls
without rooms, without elevators
without files, delays of veiled murderers
muffled thieves, the tailings of
tedious, dead pavements, the walls
against desire save only for him who can pay
high, there were no cities—he was
without money—

        Cities had faded richly
into foreign countries, stolen from Russia—
the richness of her cities—

Scattered wealth was close to his heart
he felt it uncertainly beating at
that moment in his wrists, scattered
wealth—but there was not much at hand

Cities are full of light, fine clothes
delicacies for the table, variety,
novelty—fashion: all spent for this.
Never to be like that again:
the frame that was. It tickled his
imagination. But it passed in a rising calm

Tan dar a dei! Tan dar a dei!
He was singing. Two miserable peasants
very lazy and foolish
seemed to have walked out from his own
feet and were walking away with wooden rakes
under the six nearly bare poplars, up the hill

There go my feet.

He stood still in the window forgetting
to shave—

The very old past was refound
redirected. It had wandered into himself
The world was himself, these were
his own eyes that were seeing, his own mind
that was straining to comprehend, his own
hands that would be touching other hands
They were his own!
His own, feeble, uncertain. He would go
out to pick herbs, he graduate of
the old university. He would go out
and ask that old woman, in the little
village by the lake, to show him wild
ginger. He himself would not know the plant.

A horse was stepping up the dirt road
under his window

He decided not to shave. Like those two
that he knew now, as he had never
known them formerly. A city, fashion
had been between—

Nothing between now.

He would go to the soviet unshaven. This
was the day—and listen. Listen. That
was all he did, listen to them, weigh
for them. He was turning into
a pair of scales, the scales in the
zodiac.

   But closer, he was himself
the scales. The local soviet. They could
weigh. It it was not too late. He felt
uncertain many days. But all were uncertain
together and he must weigh for them out
of himself.

He took a small pair of scissors
from the shelf and clipped his nails
carefully. He himself served the fire.

We have cut out the cancer but
who knows? perhaps the patient will die
The patient is anybody, anything
worthless that I desire, my hands
to have it—instead of the feeling
that there is a piece of glazed paper
between me and the paper—invisible
but tough running through the legal
processes of possession—a city, that
we could possess—

        It's in art, it's in
the French school.

        What we lacked was
everything. It is the middle of
everything. Not to have.

        We have little now but
we have that. We are convalescents. Very
feeble. Our hands shake. We need a
transfusion. No one will give it to us,
they are afraid of infection. I do not
blame them. We have paid heavily. But we
have gotten—touch. The eyes and the ears
down on it. Close.

11/6

Russia is every country, here he must live, this for that, loss
for gain. Dolores Marie Pischak. "New York is a blight on
my heart, lost, a street full of lights fading to a bonfire—in
order to see their hats of wool on their heads, their lips to

open and a word to come out. To open my mouth and a word to come out, my word. Grown like grass, to be like a stone. I pick it. It is poor. It must be so. There are no rich. The richness is everywhere, belongs to everyone and it is hard to get. And loss, loss, loss. Cut off from my kind—if any exist. To get that, everything is lost. So he carries them and gets—himself and has nothing to do with himself. He also gets their lice.

Romance, decoration, fullness—are lost in touch, sight, a word, to bite an apple. Henry Ford has asked Chas. Sheeler to go to Detroit and photograph everything. Carte blanche. Sheeler! That's rich. Shakespeare had that mean ability to fuse himself with everyone which nobodies have, to be anything at any time, fluid, a nameless fellow whom nobody noticed—much, and *that* is what made him the great dramatist. Because he was nobody and was fluid and accessible. He took the print and reversed the film, as it went in so it came out. Certainly he never repeated himself since he did nothing but repeat what he heard and nobody ever hears the same words twice the same. Homekeeping youth had ever homely wit, Sheeler and Shakespeare should be on this soviet. Mediæval England, Soviet Russia.

It is a pure literary adjustment. The supremacy of England is purely a matter of style. Officially they are realists, such as the treaty with Italy to divide Abyssinia. Realists—it is the tactical spread of realism that is the Soviets. Imperial Russia was romanticist, strabismic, atavistic. Style. He does not blame the other countries. They fear what he sees. He sees tribes of lawyers tripping each other up entirely off the ground and falling on pillows full of softly jumbled words from goose backs.

I know a good print when I see it. I know when it is good and why it is good. It is the neck of a man, the nose of a woman. It is the same Shakespeare. It is a photograph by Sheeler. It is. It is the thing where it is. So. That's the mine out of which riches have always been drawn. The kings come and beg for it. But it is too simple. In the com- **253** plexity, when we try to enrich ourselves—the richness is lost. Loss and gain go hand in hand. And hand in hand means my hand in a hand which is in it: a child's hand soft skinned, small, a little fist to hold gently, a woman's hand, a certain woman's hand, a man's hand. Thus hand in hand means several classes of things. But loss is one thing. It is lost. It is one big thing that is an orchestra playing. Time, that's what it buys. But the gain is scattered. It is everywhere but there is not much in any place. A city is merely a relocation of metals in a certain place. —He feels the richness, but a distressing feeling of loss is close upon it. He knows he must coordinate the villages for effectiveness in a flood, a famine.

The United States should be, in effect, a soviet state. It is a soviet state decayed away in a misconception of richness. The states, counties, cities, are anemic soviets. As rabbits are cottontailed the office-workers in cotton running pants get in a hot car, ride in a hot tunnel and confine themselves in a hot office—to sell asphalt, the trade in tanned leather. The trade in everything. Things they've never seen, will never own and can never name. Not even an analogous name do they know. As a carter, knowing the parts of a wagon will know, know, touch, the parts of—a woman. Maybe typists have some special skill. The long legged down east boys make good stage dancers and acrobats. But when most of them are drunk nothing comes off but— "Nevada" had a line of cowboy songs.

11/7

We must listen. Before
she died she told them—
I always liked to be well dressed
I wanted to look nice—
So she asked them to dress
her well. They curled her hair . . .

Now she fought
She didn't want to go
She didn't want to!

The perfect type of the man of action is the suicide.

11/8

O river of my heart polluted
and defamed I have compared you
to that other lying in
the red November grass
beginning to be cleaned now
from factory pollution

Though at night a watchman
must still prowl lest some paid hand
open the waste sluices—

That river will be clean
before ever you will be

11/8

Out of her childhood she remembered, as one might re-
member Charlie Wordsworth's print shop in the rear of
Bagellons, the hinged paperknife, the colored posters of
horses (I'll bet it was for the races at Clifton where the
High School now stands). Once Pop made a big kite, five
feet tall maybe, with the horses' heads in the middle, and
it flew and I couldn't hold it without help. They fastened
it to a post of the back porch at nightfall, real rope they
had on it, and in the morning it was still there. She re-
membered the day the old man painted the mirror back

255

of the bar: He took off his coat and laid the brushes and pans from his bag on one of the barroom tables. No one else was there but Jake who sat with his head in his hands except when someone came in for something or to telephone. Then he'd unlock the inside door and sit down again watching the old man. It was a big mirror. First he painted in a river coming in over from the door and curving down greenywhite nearly the whole length of it and very wide to fall in a falls into the edge of another river that ran all along the bottom all the way across, only a little of the water to be seen. Then he put in a blue sky all across the top with white clouds in it and under them a row of brown hills coming down to the upper river banks. Green trees he made with a big brush, just daubing it on, some of it even up top over the hills on the clouds, the trunks of the trees to be put in later. But down below, under the top river and all down the right side where it curved down to the falls he painted in the trunks first like narrow dark brown bottles. Then he drew in the houses, with white sides, three of them near the falls. "A good place to fish" Jake said. The roofs were red. On the other side of the falls, between the two rivers the houses were brown, two of them on brown hills with trees all among them. Then, after the paint of the rivers was dry, he began to paint in little boats, above and below— She never saw the work finished, for the saloon had been sold and they moved away. The last thing she saw him do was paint in the boats, "Look out that boat up there don't go over those falls," Jake said. The rivers were painted flat on the glass, wonderful rivers where she wanted to be. Some day she wanted to go to that place and see it. Like the song she remembered in school and she always wanted them to sing when you could ask what song you wanted sung, "Come again soon and you shall hear sung the tale of those green little islands." She always wanted to hear the rest of it but there was never any more. They moved away.

The shell flowers
the wax grapes and peaches
the fancy oak or mahogany tables
the highbacked baronial hall chairs

Or the girls' legs
agile stanchions
the breasts
the pinheads—

—Wore my bathing suit
wet
four hours after sundown.
That's how. Yea?

Easy to get
hard to get rid of.

Then unexpectedly
a small house with a soaring oak
leafless above it

Someone should summarize these things
in the interest of local
government or how
a spotted dog goes up a gutter—

and in chalk crudely
upon the railroad bridge support
a woman rampant
brandishing two rolling pins

11/11

A cat licking herself solves most of the problems of infection. We wash too much and finally it kills us.

11/13   SHAKESPEARE

By writing he escaped from the world into the natural world of his mind. The unemployable world of his fine head was unnaturally useless in the gross exterior of his day —or any day. By writing he made this active. He melted himself into that grossness, and colored it with his powers. The proof that he was right and they passing, being that he continues always and naturally while their artificiality destroyed them. A man unable to employ himself in his world.

Therefore his seriousness and his accuracies, because it was not his play but the drama of his life. It is his anonymity that is baffling to nitwits and so they want to find an involved explanation—to defeat the plainness of the evidence.

When he speaks of fools he is one; when of kings he is one, doubly so in misfortune.

He is a woman, a pimp, a prince Hal—

Such a man is a prime borrower and standardizer—No inventor. He lives because he sinks back, does not go forward, sinks back into the mass—

He is Hamlet plainer than a theory—and in everything.

You can't buy a life again after it's gone, that's the way I mean.

He drinks awful bad and he beat me up every single month while I was carrying this baby, pretty nearly every week.

(Shakespeare) a man stirred alive, all round *not* minus the intelligence but the intelligence subjugated—by misfortune in this case maybe—subjugated to the instinctive whole as it must be, but not minus it as in almost everything— not by cupidity that blights an island literature—but round,

round, a round world *E pur si muove. That* has never sunk into literature as it has into geography, cosmology. Literature is still mediæval, formal, dogmatic, the scholars, the obstinate rationalists—

These things are easy and obvious but it is not easy to formulate them, and it is still harder to put them down briefly. Yet it must be possible since I have done it here and there.

Such must be the future: penetrant and simple—minus the scaffolding of the academic, which is a "lie" in that it is inessential to the purpose as to the design.

This will do away with the stupidity of little children at school, which is the incubus of modern life—and the defense of the economists and modern rationalists of literature. To keep them drilled.

The difficulty of modern styles is made by the fragmentary stupidity of modern life, its lacunæ of sense, loops, perversions of instinct, blankets, amputations, fullsomeness of instruction and multiplications of inanity. To avoid this, accuracy is driven to a hard road. To be plain is to be subverted since every term must be forged new, every word is tricked out of meaning, hanging with as many cheap traps as an altar.

The only human value of anything, writing included, is intense vision of the facts, add to that by saying the truth and action upon them—clear into the machine of absurdity to a core that is covered.

God—Sure if it means sense. "God" is poetic for the unobtainable. Sense is hard to get but it can be got. Certainly that destroys "God," it destroys everything that interferes with simple clarity of apprehension.

11/16

The art of writing is all but lost (not the science which comes afterward and depends completely on the first) it is to make the stores of the mind available to the pen—Wide! That which locks up the mind is vicious.

Mr. Seraphim: They hate me. Police Protection. She was a flaming type of stupidity and its resourceful manner under Police Protection—the only normal: a type. One of the few places where the truth (demeaned) clings on.

11/13 Travelling in Fast Company

As the ferry came into the slip there was a pause then a young fellow on a motorcycle shot out of the exit, looked right and left, sighted the hill, opened her up and took the grade at top speed. Right behind him came three others bunched and went roaring by, and behind them was a youngster travelling in fast company his eyes fastened on the others, and behind him an older guy sitting firm and with a face on him like a piece of wood ripped by without a quiver. And that brings it all up—Shakespeare—plays.

. . . Its hands stuck up in the air like prongs. Just sticking up in the air, fingers spread apart.

Goethe was a rotten dramatist. . . .

11/20

Even idiots grow old
 in a cap with the peak
over his right ear
 cross eyed
shamble footed
 minding the three goats
behind the firehouse
 his face is deeper lined
than last year
 and the rain comes down
260 in gusts suddenly

and hunters still return
even through the city
with their guns slung
openly from the shoulder
emptyhanded howbeit
for the most part
                    but aloof
as if from and truly from
another older world

If genius is profuse, never ending—stuck in the middle of
a work is—the wrong track. Genius is the track, seen. Once
seen it is impossible to keep from it. The superficial defi-
nitions, such as "genius is industry, genius is hard work,
etc." are nonsense. It is to see the track, to smell it out, to
know it inevitable—sense sticking out all round feeling,
feeling, seeing—hearing touching. The rest is pure grav-
ity. (The earth pull.)

Creations: —they are situations of the soul (Lear, Har-
pagon, Œdipus Rex, Electra) but so closely (subjective-
ly) identified with life that they become people. They
are offshoots of an intensely simple mind. It is no matter
what we think, no matter what we are.

The drama is the identification of the character with
the man himself (Shakespeare—and his sphere of knowl-
edge, close to him). As it flares in himself the drama is
completed and the back kick of it is the other characters,
created as the reflex of the first, so the dramatist "lives,"
himself in his world. A poem is a soliloquy without the
"living" in the world. So the dramatist "lives" the char-
acter. But to labor over the "construction" over the

"technique" is to defeat, to tie up the drama itself. One cannot live after a prearranged pattern, it is all simply dead.

This is the thing (obvious and simple) that except through genius makes the theater a corpse. To intensely realize identity makes it live (borrowing, stealing the form by feeling it—as an uninformed man must). A play is this primary realization coming up to intensity and then fading (futilely) in self. This *is* the technique, the unlearnable, it is the *natural* drama, which can't imagine situations in any other way than in association with the flesh—till it becomes living, it is so personal to a nothing, a nobody.

The painfully scrupulous verisimilitude which honesty affects drill, discipline defeats its own ends in—

To be nothing and unaffected by the results, to unlock, and to flow (they believe that when they have the mold of technique made perfect without a leak in it that the mind will be *drilled* to flow there whereas the mind is locked the more tightly the more perfect the technique is forged) (or it may flow, disencumbered by what it has learned, become unconscious, provided the technique becomes mechanical, goes out of the mind and so the mind [now it has been cut for life in this pattern]) can devote itself to that just as if it had learned it imitatively or not at all.

To be nothing and unaffected by the results, to unlock and flow, uncolored, smooth, carelessly—not cling to the unsolvable lumps of personality (yourself and your concessions, poems) concretions—

11/28

I make really very little money.
What of it?
I prefer the grass with the rain on it
the short grass before my headlights
when I am turning the car—
a degenerate trait, no doubt.
It would ruin England.

12/2

The first snow was a white sand that made the white rocks seem red.

The police are "the soldiers of the Duke." The great old names: Gaynor, Healy—

12/9

Imagine a family of four grown men, one in bed with a sore throat, one with fresh plaster dust on his pants, one who played baseball all last summer and one holding the basin, four young men and no women but the mother with small pox scars marring the bridge and the end of her nose and dinner on the table, oil and meat bits and cuts of green peppers, the range giving out a heat for coats on the backs of the chairs to dry in.

Fairfield: Peoples Loan and Service, Money to Loan: and a young man carrying a bowling ball in a khaki canvas case. The Midland and a fern in the window before the inner oak and cut glass screen. House and sign painting in all its branches. Fairfield Bowling and Billiard Academy. Architect John Gabrone Architect, U. S. Post Office, Fairfield, N. J. Branch. Commercial Barber Shop. The New Cigarette Three Castles. Real Estate and Insurance, Motor Vehicle Agency. Commercial Lunch. Fairfield Home Laundry, soft water washing.

12/15

What an image in the face of Almighty God is she
her hands in her slicker pockets, head bowed,
Tam pulled down, flat backed, lanky legged,
loose feet kicking the pebbles as she goes

12/18

Here by the watertank and the stone, mottled granite, big
as a rhinocerous head—cracked on one side—Damn fami-
lies. My grandfather was a business man, you know. He
kept the ice house in Mayaguez. They imported the ice.
He kept it and sold it. My grandmother, my mother's
mother, would make syrups, strawberry and like that. He
would sell them also. But his half brother Henriquez, there's
plenty of that in my family, would go there, to the ice
house, and drink all day long without paying anything, un-
til the man my grandfather had there complained. "You
know Henriquez comes and drinks five or six glasses of
syrup and never pays anything." He did that. Just drank,
lived at the house, took anything he pleased. That's how, as
my Mother says, she came to know Manuel Henriquez, her
half cousin, better than she did her own brother who was
away much of the time studying. Henriquez would never
work, help or do anything until my grandfather had to tell
him to stop. It was at about this time my grandfather died
and this is how my Mother came to distrust and hate the
Germans. All my grandfather's friends were German, all
but a few. "It was a man named Krug. I suppose he may
have been father's partner, anyhow he was his best friend,
I don't know. When my father died, Krug came to my
mother and asked her if she had anything because my
father owed some money. She had an *hacienda* in the coun-
try that she had had since before she was married, her own.
She gave that. Then Krug came and said it was all gone, that
there was nothing left. After that, he turned his back on
the family (the skunk). It was the Spanish druggist Mestre
who lent my mother the money to buy a few things and
sell them to make a little business. He was a Catalan—they
can't say Pepe, like a Castilian, but he would call his wife,
Papeeta. My Mother would send to Paris for a half dozen
fine shirts, but fine, fine shirts and a few things like that.

My brother was in Paris studying. When Krug told my mother she must send for him, that there was nothing left, she wrote. He answered her that he would sweep the streets of Paris rather than leave. She would send him money she made on her little business. Sometimes, he told us afterward, he would keep a sou in his pocket two weeks so as not to say he hadn't any money. The students helped each other. Barclay, an Englishman, was one of his best friends. He helped him."

That's why my own mother's education ended abruptly. Sometimes she would copy out letters for my grandmother, child that she was, to send to Paris. When her brother returned a doctor he himself sent her to Paris to study painting. But he married and he began to have children and he never collected any money—he had a wife too. So finally he sent for my mother to go back to Santo Domingo where they were living then. Mother cried for three days then she had to go and leave it all. When she got there her brother told her about his friend, Blackwell. A fine fellow, the best in the world "*pero no es musicante.*" Blackwell was in the States at the time of my mother's return from Paris having his teeth fixed.

When a little child would be bothersome they would tell her to go ask the maid for a little piece of *ten te aya*.

When my brother was happy he would sing, walking up and down kicking out his feet: *Si j'étais roi de Bayaussi-e, tu serais reine-e par ma foi!* You made me think right away of him."

A Novelette and Other Prose

Introduction

A Novelette

IN A NOTE DISPATCHING *A Novelette* to Ezra Pound, William Carlos Williams said the book was "very close to my heart." Through Pound's good offices, it was published in Toulon in 1932 in an edition of around 500 copies along with an assortment of miscellaneous prose pieces. An unpublished letter to Louis Zukofsky amplifies Williams's feelings about this short work of "automatic writing," as he was to call it much later. He said to Zukofsky, "While tearing around tending the sick I've composed a novelette in praise of my wife whom I have gotten to know again because of being thrown violently into her arms and she into mine by the recent epidemic—though not by the illness of either of us, quite the contrary."

The book is partly about the influenza epidemic that struck the U.S. in the early 1920's and the pressures Williams felt as a result. It's also about difficulties that had entered—and were resolved—in the marriage of Florence and William Carlos Williams. The only two characters of consequence are Williams and his wife, developed exclusively through conversation. The plot, if it's a plot, is their relationship. They have had familiar difficulties. They love one another very much. Here, as near the end of his life, Williams says all of his poems are for her. Through ways difficult to follow, but clear enough in Williams's own mind, the workings of his art and the progress of his marriage have common source. More than most of his contemporaries Williams was continually worrying about and testing the relationships that ought to exist between life and modern art.

In a work not especially notable for clarity of declaration, one thing stands out above all else: the practice of medicine and the craft of literature were so intertwined in William Carlos Williams he could not have succeeded (one is tempted to say he could not have stayed alive) without both. He says he must write "for relaxation, relief. To have nothing in my head,—to freshen my eye by that till I see, smell, know and can reason and be." He is writing a novelette, excited over the banality of conversation in fiction, and immediately finds his example in medicine: "Where is there any serious conversation in a novel?—except descriptions or nonsense that is not read—knowing for that comparable to a discussion with an intelligent parent over the inevitability of 'a mastoid' in an only son, where the *Streptococcus capsulatus* has been found in the ear in pure culture." He makes his calls with the familiar yellow notebook on the front seat of his car. He steals images as he drives. Williams's wandering consciousness is continually interrupted by medical notes: a child in convulsions, the ravages of the epidemic, the ringing of the telephone and the doorbell. The intensity of the epidemic heightens Williams's capacities of observation: "It is that a stress pares off the inanity by force of speed and a sharpness, a closeness of observation, of attention comes through." Rain, fire, hydrants, trees accept the transfer of energies Williams has left over from the exhilaration of the epidemic.

The circumstances of writing *A Novelette*—the epidemic surging, no advance planning, Williams firing away with his typewriter—give the work some of the spontaneity of the *Improvisations* of *Kora*. He remembers that "their excellence is, in major part, the shifting of category. It is the disjointing process." In *I Wanted to Write a Poem* Williams speaks of the influence of dadaism on *A Novelette:* "I had it in my soul." The presence of painters as exemplars of his aesthetic ambitions, Williams's casual phrasing, his continued insistence on the vitality of instinct and the impotence of science as a vehicle of enlightenment tell us he was taking dadaism more seriously than history would. His enthusiasm didn't stop to inquire whether there was anything illogical in a physician's knocking science because it couldn't write poetry. He was on the trail of something.

Williams was pursuing a synthesis of his domestic life, his personality, his profession and art, and not in an orderly fashion. The imagination of the artist and the functions of the doctor-husband had to be brought together. Like Van Gogh, he found himself unwilling merely to "represent." He lived to "create, to advance the concept of the real, the actual." And Williams's concept of the actual, during a time of stress, is this frantic, speculative, loving work. It is as rational and irrational as life itself.

The other prose pieces, many related in spirit, take Williams from fighting the reality of a 12-year-old girl's death to celebrating the poetry of Marianne Moore and the glories of tropical fruit. Mostly occasional writings first published in magazines, they were right, Williams thought, to go in a book with *A Novelette* when it first appeared. Therefore they belong here too.

They suggest the range of his interests and the intensity of his enthusiasms. But several carry more power than that. "The Venus" is pure Williams fiction about all the hot and cold things that turned him on and off. His notes on Joyce and Stein are still useful. His review of Kay Boyle is still pertinent: "There is, in a democracy, a limit beyond which thought is not expected to leap. All men being presumed equal, it becomes an offense if this dead limit is exceeded." And Williams's comments on Logan Clendening's "The Human Body" gets, then as now, to the center of things: "Love is lovelier for its lust." Time and again we see it in Williams. He believed words ought to be nails.

W.S.

I. A PARADOX

BEFORE, you could eat ice-cream out of it; after, you wouldn't spit in it. "Stride of Man." "Old Ireland." Collapse. End of the first paragraph.

Character, temperament, and desire would be the only cements of a new association. The trick is lost. Searching in the cloth the elastic band yielded before his fingers. The old fashioned trees were without a leaf. A chickadee made the pattern of three waves across the wall of the Congregational Church. Sparrows, two starlings cock fighting, a chickadee and grey breasted snow birds confuse the tense of January. And cats prowl. While she was talking the grey molly slipped out, she saw her go but made no sign. As soon as the complainer, with a fear in his heart, had backsidled away she came inside, closed the front door restrainedly, then rushed pell mell for the kitchen, out the back door and after her. The she-beast wouldn't be caught. But some people know when not to quit. It stood on the stone. It threaded the fence. It climbed the bank. It circled the shrubbery. It fled into the entry and out again. She came in with it in her arms, out of breath, eyes alive, cheeks aglow. She shook it, noozled it, held it, struggling, by the forelegs, till it spit and fought and as it broke away she slapped it on the rump and jumping to her feet stamped behind it so that it fled to turn and lick its sides. She laughed at it. You thought you could get away, young lady, did you? You did, did you? She's sweet!

John Herrmann has a good score of lines that are good in *Whoopee*.

Do you hear me? Yes, I mean you; you're crazy.

Buddy hasn't got any shirt. Buddy hasn't got any *shirt*.
Do you know what I got on?

Buddy loves Eleanor.

You shut up.

Where the drop of rain had been, there remained a deli-
cate black stain, the outline of the drop marked clearly on
the white paint, in black, within which a shadow, a smooth-
est tone faded upward between the lines and burst them,
thinning out upon the woodwork down which the rain had
come. In the tops of the screws the polishing powder could
be seen white.

Thus the epidemic had become a criticism—to begin
with. In the seriousness of the moment—not even the seri-
ousness but the single necessity—the extraneous dropped
of its own weight. One worked rapidly. Meanwhile values
stood out in all fineness. One could see at once why in
France the food is observed. *Monsieur est servi*. Manners
are to look, to smell, to weigh the matter of the cooking.
It is because the stresses of life have sharpened the sight.
Life is keener, more pressed for place—as in an epidemic.
The extraneous is everything that is not seen in detail.
There is no time not to notice.

Here food is food because there is plenty—not because
there is little. Eat—it's all good. On the street from the
car—passing hurriedly—the benign smiles of the men carry-
ing the gilt edged books—is sickly. The contentment of
blockheadedness, of plenty, of success, of obedience, of
more than enough. It is not that there is any virtue in
being lean or unprovided for or wanting. It is that a stress
pares off the inanity by force of speed and a sharpness, a
closeness of observation, of attention comes through.

O it is not realism. It is the actual—makes philosophy
cheap (though philosophy may be actual as a stone). Good
God, they tell me to turn to philosophy. It would be *like*
a poet to seek explanations in that. Let us have an edited
translation of Aldous Huxley into English.

The new moon lay reclining over the southern houses. In

a Murillo sky. One large star sparkled. From under the cloud hung an insensate red, to despair.

It's that thumping. If I could only stop that. I press my fingers into my neck to stop it for a little while said the old (par?)-purblind woman. And storm strikes Byrd's ship but the expedition is safe in snug tents. Epicurus would starve three days to enjoy the savor of a breadcrust. The epidemic rages to the same end.

We thought it was doing the split. First we thought it was stuck in the ice. We ran out to it and saw it was on its knees. When it would try to stand up its feet would slide out from under it. Its horns were broken off and its head all bloody. We touched it with our hockey sticks and pushed it toward the shore. When it got there it stood trembling and looking at us. Then it leaped into the air and ran through the woods.

Not pea NUT, pe CAN.

One of the kind who are dark skinned, dark haired, have dark eyebrows and grey eyes. Her brow was high and broad, her eyes were large and far apart. She had a large mouth with sensitive bright red lips. Her teeth were regular and white. This is so.

He lost, the sense of time. His whoreishmindedness flew off. There must have been ten thousand starlings in the leafless trees. The reason for so much noise is that each bird makes as much of an uproar as he is able to. But he hears a thousand times the clatter. Thus he feels aggrandized.

Snow changes the aspect of the world—

All this the epidemic bares. The street hydrants are green but the tops are moulded like inverted acorn saucers, red. On the oak leaves the light snow lay encrusted till the wind turned a leaf over—

No use, no use. The banality wins, is rather increased by the attempt to reduce it. Better to learn to write and to make a smooth page no matter what the incoherence of the day, no matter what erasures must be sacrificed to improve a lying appearance to keep ordered the disorder of the page-less actual.

Piecemeal excellence, related to—undesire, to anything at all: the tall barn, too tall, too weakly timbered has leaned with the wind. And the green paint shows through the red and the bare boards under all. The children have placed a barrel hoop over the door for a basket ball ring.

The rush that simpliflies life, complicates it. There is no time to stop the car to write when only the writing that comes of an intense simplification would be actual. January. January. Now actually the sun returns. Ezra Pound is already looking backward. And we, as if unborn, stare at the impossible cluttered with the temporary, the circumscribed. The composed. The inadequate. While the real, by leaves, by a table, on which lies a ten cent bottle of Aspirin tablets stands sufficiently. Under the cheap crochet table cover—the table is of stained wood, square is a yellow cloth that shows through the open-work. An electric lamp, lit, is in the center, a cloth covered cord running from it to the floor. —This is banality. The lamp is too narrow. The shade is of painted, glazed paper. On it are leaves and roses dashed in with a broad brush. Roses! Roses!

I suppose you think if the war didn't kill you nothing else can.

They imagine birth and death. The hair rises brown lined with gray, directly up and cascades two inches above his brow, forward, projecting at an angle from his head.

The compositions that are smoothed, consecutive are disjointed. Dis-jointed. They bear no relation to anything in the world or in the mind. NEXT WEEK or LATER.

Till she too appears, laughing.

II. THE SIMPLICITY OF DISORDER

RING, RING, RING, RING! There's no end to the ringing of the damned—The bell rings to announce the illness of someone

else. It rings today intimately in the warm house. That's
your bread and butter.

Is the doctor in? (It used to ring.) What is it? (Out of
the bedroom window.) My child has swallowed a mouse.—
Tell him to swallow a cat then. Bam! This is the second
paragraph of the second chapter of some writing on the
influenza epidemic in the region of New York City, Janu-
ary 11, 1929. In the distance the buildings fail. The blue-
white searchlight-flare wheels over to the west every three
minutes. Count. One.

The things—one thing I disliked about your book was
that you said that sex is beautiful. Did I? I thought I had
said the opposite. No, you said it somewhere.

She looked at me so queerly, so intently.

In this house you have to get up out of bed to get well.
You can't stay in bed with that man around. Why I believe
if he was going to my funeral he'd say to the hearse driver,
Shake it up, I've got to get back to the office.

Touch it off. She tummy, tummy (count 'em) a delight-
ful animal. Ode to a misty star.

And day comes in round the edges of the drawn shades
staining the fluted curtains green and gray. January of squir-
rels' nests and the light returning. In the exposed tops of
oaks the squirrels build—have built their round nests of
leaves. At seven the sun is not yet up—from the night clubs
—but his breath—his stain empurples. The stairs creak. The
sliding doors rumble. The thermometer also is at seven.

Her nude pinkness and familiar sex in the icy air—just
for a moment. And my own icy hands. And the bugle rests
upright on its bell.

This is Mrs. Gladis, will you come down this morning.
I've got two or three children sick. Trrrrrring. Can you
make a call this morning? I guess the half of the house is
dying again. And the cat boxes the piece of crumpled paper
over the floor.

Look out you don't get that twig in your eye. To direct,
sanctify and govern. Not too often. A pink carnation. A

sheaf of ferns. Two timeless daffodils. Two orange daisies. And three tilted salmon red and yellow tulip cups. She stopped, holding her coat close and blinked her eyes—not knowing what else to do.

Sunday

You see, dear, I pretend to be frivolous as a way of being courageous—as a sort of self-defense—but such is human nature—I'm hurt when you seem to believe it. Then, you must see, too, how I am always set to detect the slightest indication in your look or manner that you are getting tired of my friendship—and I try to have a sort of quick "getaway" ready. I'd hate to be "hard to get rid of"—and I'd never "die on your doorstep." And yet I know that your moods are variable, so I don't want to be too sensitive. Kind of complicated—isn't it?

I know it was all nonsense to blow off the other day— that was just nerves. I'm all right now. Don't believe a word I say about stunning men (with beards or without) or any of the nonsense I pull. Don't ever believe anything at all but my sincerity. I know my affection means something to you—I've seen it in your face—I know it when we are talking together.

Yes, they are here. I couldn't imagine who had left them. I'll keep them for you in my desk.

I think these days when there is so little to believe in— when the old loyalties—God, country, and the hope of Heaven—aren't very real, we are more dependent than we should be on our friends. The only thing left to believe in—someone who seems beautiful.

You like to write about love—"sweet love"—but what is it? I don't know. I only know I care about you—and what happens to you. I shall for a good many years—perhaps always.

So believe in me, dear. It's the only thing I've ever asked of you.

Photographed feeding two she-goats with bulging udders in a Mary world. A smell of paint in the hospital. The color of dogs on a gray morning, minus their shadows. They seem shadows—silently running they stop before the slow, sinister advance of a greater dog, they cower and retreat. He selects one to sniff. Looking back the other draws away. Go tell the milkman to wait a minute, the doctor is here. He's getting so big now I have to put him in a pen. I just got a packing box (lined with white oilcloth).

These (in the snow) are the prints of the small birds' feet.

And nothing—opens the doors, inserts the key, presses the starting pedal, adjusts the throttle and the choker and backs out, downhill. Sees the barberry gouts. Seize the steering wheel and turn it sharply to the left, the lilac twigs —that have lost prestige through the loss of plumage— scrape the left front fender sharply.

The tall red grass has lost its feathers too, bare stalks now, sharpened by the difficulty with the cold and the wind. The grapevines like rusty wire. The green hedge by the green signal light.

I don't know what I'd do if I had six. I'd be in an asylum or the electric chair. I'd kill 'em. *She Regained*. A short novel. Write going. Look to steer. Her ways, serious, alert, WINNING. The woolly back of a little trotting dog, his breath (her breath) standing out before him (her). The breath flittering from the other end of the cars. And now at eleven the sun is warming the air.

This house of red sandstone blocks has stood since 1797. The river is frozen overnight. The sumac clusters, snow caught in the berry red, are stiffly curled since summer. In the gutters, snow—a double pennant blue and white. And the heated air—over the car radiator the heated air dances. Dances.

In the house into which he had entered from the cold he saw a picture of Autumn, a running stream, the yellow leaves. This surprised him—in January. And another picture nearby was an old man in a beard photographed before the needles of a pine tree. But what has all this to do with general ideas if it is not the essence. Time presses.

I'm going to get undressed and get into bed and read awhile—if you don't mind my being in your private sanctum. A quick look, all that has been strangled off. The poem *Paterson* must be finished. These are his thoughts.

Keep up your courage. Get through with this awful drive. There's no way out just now—unless you quit entirely—which seems hardly possible for the moment. It will end soon (in a few years) and then you must write day and night—or as you please forever after. I'll be thinking of you and wishing I could be near you.

The firemen—unlike the cops—have six silver buttons three each side down the slit at the back and bottom of their coats—of which the lining, as they walk, shows red.

This is the essence of literature. And the concrete replica of the Palazzo Vecchio cupid in the frozen fountain hugs still his dolphin. It was damned clever, making a diagnosis like that and saving a baby's life, worth more than any poem, I think. But I'll do anything you say—anything, only make up your mind.

Why?

Doctrinaire formula-worship—that is our real enemy. The rustle of her book is in his ear.

III. A BEAUTIFUL IDEA

IT HAS the same effect—the epidemic—as clear thought. It is like the modern advent of an old category supplanting a stalemate of information. A world of irrelevancies in the doing of one thing. But the intense haste is raised, wholly unforeseen, to a higher power: the birth of a female baby (colored) under a mustard-colored ceiling, by a cracked wall, to a turkey wishbone, in the shivering cold.

This morning, eh, will you stop in to see Mamie Jefferson, eh, she's having pains, eh, quite often.

And they have added a new brick front to the old brick house, coming out to the sidewalk edge for a store. Writing should be like that, like the world, a criticism of ideas; a thought implied in trees, the storm grown vocal: One thing supplanting all things—the flu, summing all virtues. A lardy head—new brick joined to the old—the corner of the street in a wind that's driven them all indoors.

Take the surrealists, take Soupault's *Les Dernières Nuits de Paris,* take—You think I take no interest in you? It is not so. I avoid your eye merely to avoid interruption. Gladly, were I able, would I serve you and listen to you talk of your sore toe. But, unless I apply myself to the minute— my life escapes me. You must pardon me. I love you as I hope that you will notice by all that I have done to make you comfortable. Talk is the most precious thing in the world. I know that and I will find a way to secure it for you also but my interest in writing is so violent an acid that with the other work, I must pare my life to the point of silence—though I hope surliness may never intervene— in order to get to the paper.—Take the work of Eric de Haulleville, in *transition:* Well, take it.

Want alone is what makes poverty tolerable, impressing unity and seriousness. And the old, aged, seventy-five-year-old woman: all she does is pray that she be taken. What makes you shake like that, Grandma? I don't know. The pain catches her. Thus the effect of poverty that makes it tolerable.

So the surrealists. So the enlivening scurry. So the injected birth of a black child breaking the simplicity to a patient—to the five bare eyes.

Language is in its January. How shall I say it? The surrealists are French. It appears to be to them to knock off every accretion from the stones of composition. To them it is a way to realize the classical excellences of language, so that it becomes writing again, and not an adjunct to science, philosophy and religion—is to make the words into sentences that will have a fantastic reality which is false.

By this the falseness of the piecemeal (when language is subservient to the sale of old clothes and ideas and the formulas for the synthetic manufacture of rubber) is made apparent and the triumphant of an old category that will liberate all ands and thes is—as you shall see.

Did the academicians but know it, it is the surrealists who have invented the living defense of literature, that will supplant science; and it is they who betray their trust by allowing the language to be enslaved by its enemies; the philosophers and the venders of manure and all who cry their wares in the street and put up signs: "House for sale."

Language, which is the hope of man, is by this enslaved, forced, raped, made a whore by the idea venders. It has always angered me that other classes of men write their books in words which they betray. How can a philosopher, who is not an artist, write philosophy in words? All he writes is a lie.

Surrealism does not lie. It is the single truth. It is an epidemic. It is. It is just words.

But it is French. It is *their* invention: one. That language is in constant revolution, constantly being covered, merded, stolen, slimed. Theirs.

It is in the kind that we should see it. In that diversity of the mind which is excellence, like a tree—one single tree —French—it is surrealism. It is of that kind which is the actual.

There rested her bum. The heat lingers. In the moment of admiration, she leaned back her head and he saw up to her left nostril a THING, entangled in hairs. Oh, wipe out the stain. The memory lingers on. A delicate false balance. We see too much.

Theirs is a simplicity of phrase emphasizing the elusive reality of words. Mine is in pink pants, she hanging my coat in the closet.

Take the enormous Joyce brandishing his classic symbols. Nothing could be further from Paris. Yet it is the one thing. And I'll say this for myself that in spite of obvious defects of learning I have never known differently.

Never known differently. It is this which, in all, is the one that from the viewpoint of intelligence criticizes religion as bad writing. Which is to state that Shakespeare, were he to be read aright, would have an identical relation to a pair of shoes—in the mind—that on paper distinguished his plays from a press dispatch.

This is the alphabet q w e r t y u i o p a e d f g h j k l z x c v b n m. The extraordinary thing is that no one has yet taken the trouble to write it out fully. And what is a beautiful woman?

She is one.

Over and over again, she is one.

Look at her bare feet. You will see the effects of wearing shoes—unless she be used to going barefoot. Sometimes the toenails will be round, sometimes square and at others long. At the ankle the foot is joined to the leg. From here to the knee is usually sixteen inches. The knee is important. Let us describe the thigh of a beautiful woman. Most literature is now silent. The physiognomy of the joint between the torso and the thighs is as various as the faces of dogs. In literature the necessity for a constant freshness of praise— of words that will have a fresh distinction of cut, of tint, of texture—must be felt as one feels instantly a dereliction in the selection of covers for this joint. Other than that— The corner of the street became, not indifference, but a cold stone-edged place of the winds.

So all things enter into the singleness of the moment and the moment partakes of the diversity of all things. And so starting, stopping, alighting, climbing, sitting—a singleness lights the crocheted edge of the heavy white sheets in the houses of the Umbrian peasants in Lyndhurst, N.J. And so it makes her also one, combining them all in her composite necessity, doing all honor—as Joyce by one means honors surrealism and the others, him.

So she—building of all excellence is, in her single body, beautiful; enforcing the mind by imperfections to a height. Born again, Venus from the confused sea. Summing all the virtues. Single. Excellence. Female.

What happened last night? I must never go to sleep before you again.

Who shall say differently? Edison who invented the electric bulb—of which I have two in this room—is still alive. And in self-defense—Jo. No, I mean. Where I am and what I am, under the time that I am—Who shall say differently?

IV. JUAN GRIS

BECAUSE HE was not Picasso—nor discouraged by him—but a Spaniard full of admiration for French painting and lived in Paris where he worked: like you. This is exceptional praise.

I am the Paris of your eyes: it is not in what you say but that you say it.

If I am indifferent to the extraneous: so little does it matter what we wear.

—faults of patients, I should have said.

That singleness I see in everything—actual—which has been my life, because of the haste due to the epidemic, I see in you and so you become beautiful partly because you are so but partly because of other women.

Did you ever see squirrels making love? He stands near her and chatters and his tail gets big. She was smelling around for a nut. He followed her chattering and his tail got big. She ran up the tree and he after her. That's all I saw.

Do you remember the Black Tom explosion? You were away. That's right. I was asleep on the porch. I awoke out of bed standing on my feet. It must have been the first blast. I couldn't imagine what had taken place. The night was intensely still. Then came the second blast.

Can they not see and why not? but for lethargy—that literature is and must be constantly in revolution, being reborn and that exactly *that* is the only classic. That the aberrant is the classic: as she.

What will become of the poems of Miss Loy? The impression that remains is of an Italian peasant, a woman's pockmarked face and tempered voice, and quiet ways.

Phaugh, hougfh, pfaugh, ka woof! said the fat dog. Oh, he's just got a hair in his nose. He sleeps with his nose buried in his side. That's all right.

The Jews, you know, go everywhere and very seldom pay for it. It's not the Jews alone, of course, but they are typical. They pay but they bring suit against the company afterward and try to recover damages for every sort of ridiculous thing. The company has it all tabulated, everything that they are likely to pull off. So they are watched constantly. To see which it will be.

Do not think you can get away with anything, on a ship, that the company doesn't know of. There was one woman who came into the office with two men—you know the kind she was. She wanted eight hundred to a thousand dollars for a set of false teeth which she claimed had been thrown out when her tray was emptied.

She said she had been humiliated and found herself unable to leave her stateroom for the balance of the trip.

It had been a joke among the stewards where her teeth would be found next.

Oh, they were thrown out all right, with the things from her tray.

As the gates closed and the bridge slowly swung open wasting his time—enforcing a stand-still, he thought again of "Juan Gris," making a path through the ice. That was the name of the approaching tug boat seen through the branches of a bare beech tree. It had a white cabin and a black stack with a broad yellow band around it.

A patch of snow lay on the sand nearby and the ice of the river was behind the green hemlock's very short branches, from a tall tree growing up from below the high bank.

The bridge tender wore spectacles and used a cane. And the rotary movements of the bridge was a good example of simple machinery. Write, said he to himself taking up the yellow pad from the seat of the car and beginning to scratch with—

In the city the cold had driven the people from the streets; nothing (much) remained outdoors in the wind but the bedclothes of the wives of the Polish factory workers— on the railings of the second story porches.

To unlearn is as hard as to learn. —Aristotle.

In the development of the human mind a fertile error is of infinitely more value than a sterile fact. —Luciani.

Thank her for the tickets—Jeritza's gonna sing—and tell her we can't use them.

I'm afraid so, the work is terrible. It can't last much longer.

It can't or I can't.

Oh well, make hay while the sun shines.

Feather your nest, eh?

I suppose so.

Dearest, I'm hungry as hell. Dearest, I wish you were here. I'm hungry as hell.

So'm I.

What are we gonna do about it?

Let's wait for you.

Aw right.

Kindly note that all I have ever done has been the one thing. Pound will say that the improvisations are—etc. etc. twenty, forty years late. On the contrary he's all wet. Their excellence is, in major part, the shifting of category. It is the disjointing process.

Now I can say: There is no one else in the world but you: in sum.

Even the hot bath and the body returning.

Shall I turn off the heat?

Yes, shall I help you—to turn it tighter, so it won't leak?

Nothing leaks around here.

Don't you think we better open it wide a minute. To air it out?

Ea.

At night everything looks blackest. Always at night. Don't the air feel good? I've just had a hot bath.

Shall I close them?

No, wait till the room cools off a little more.

There is no conversation in novels, the novel soaks it all up. There is the story, the timbre.

There is no conversation in the papers, one must convey the timbre of the news.

Always the one thing in Juan Gris. Conversation as design. Were it not so—it is less than actual, it is covered, dull, a makeshift. I have always admired and partaken of Juan Gris. Singly he says that the actual is the drawing of the face—and so the face borrowing of the drawing—by lack of copying and lack of a burden to the story—is real.

Were it not a single monotonous repetition like the one hill of Eze continuously repeated without wit—so that every variety of what is actual is continuously made fresh since the design is never weighted with smartness, nor real paint—but—never falters.

V. CONVERSATION AS DESIGN

By THIS SINGLENESS do you, my dear, become actually my wife.

By design do you become bright, purely what you are (and visible), not to bear me a message—but as a wife you carry me the freshness of all women. There is no necessity for witty fingers. The solidity of the pure lends itself by pure design in which you are accomplished.

That would be a writing.

What's that?

In which the conversation was actual to the extent that it would be pure design.

How?

Till death do us part.

Do you like it?

It is the one thing I admire in his drawings—since there is nothing else.

When writing is not witty it is dull.

Take a guitar.

Nonsense.

Really, I wish I could believe that.

You are copying.

Always.

But that's not original nor is it design.

Purely.

Purely what?

Conversation of which there is none in novels and the news.

Oh, yes, there is.

Oh, no, there is not. It is something else. To be conversation, it must have only the effect of itself, not on him to whom it has a special meaning but as a dog or a store window.

For this we must be alone.

It must have no other purpose than the roundness and the color and the repetition of grapes in a bunch, such grapes as those of Juan Gris which are related more to a ship at sea than to the human tongue. As they are.

As you by becoming pure design have become real. In the singleness of this epidemic which is like the singleness of Juan Gris?

You are copied after all wives and all women but by the papers or a novel no one could possibly guess it. And just because the lack has never been described means nothing in the sense of it, or the uncertainty.

It takes writing such as unrelated passing on the street to rescue us for a design that alone affords conversation. Do you see?

What's your husband's job?

Let's see, what shall I say? he just drives cars.

He can't even vomit in the spittoon. It came from him

from the front, from the sides, from the back. He didn't know what he was doing. Just like I don't know what is doing in Paris.

There is no conversation in marriage as there is none in a novel for it is all sold first.

What is pure in marriage unless it be the actual? And what is actual if it rely on wit merely to outwit? In that surely there is no wit. Not even a cyclamen for the window.

By all means give him an enema and I'll be there as soon as I can.

And so you become actual.

I can't see that. It seems to me I become a copy.

Exactly, and so purely yourself, real. I really think I'd better examine you.

Come on, thrill of a lifetime.

Suddenly within fifteen minutes, everywhere in the town and in the whole section, a light drizzle fell upon the packed snow of the streets making the roads impossible, that's what I mean. Cars were caught everywhere without chains—by the swiftness. All were alike affected. It was as if at a signal the cars had been all deprived of their brakes.

Where is there any serious conversation in a novel?—except descriptions or nonsense that is not read—knowing for that comparable to a discussion with an intelligent parent over the inevitability of "a mastoid" in an only son, where the *Streptococcus capsulatus* has been found in the ear in pure culture.

Since in a novel conversation is not actual (as you are) and never can be—but a pale reflection—never can be real, as conversation or design.

But conversation in a novel can be pure design.

Yes, if it doesn't have to tell a story. That would be difficult: a novel that is pure design—like the paintings of Juan Gris.

That's what I like about the best writing of McNutt. It is actual. Thucydides. Remind the boy.

The trouble was that she was run down. You see, they

made her an angel just before Christmas and she did quite a little running round in her bare feet and she's not used to that.

But the thing is that the actual sentences of conversation simply do not exist in literature—and can never do so; Since they have doffed their actuality: One thing, they could eat regularly.

Save in relation to a new interest.

There is damned little else to say: I regret the necessity of—forgotten what I was going to say.

But in the very room. What could I do? He wouldn't say anything but that he respected every hair of my head. He sat there in my room and said that. That he said sitting in the very room of the hotel. He pays no attention to me. Everything that you can imagine has long since taken place between a man and a woman.

The sparkles of red and yellow light in the wet ink of his script as he made notes rapidly delighted him.

If you don't be a husky around here, she said swinging her ten-year-old son over on his back, you don't get no-where.

Eliot's Tivoli Underwear, he read on a tag sticking up over the edge of the boy's trousers. I do a little peddling, fruits and vegetables, two days a week, but there's too many in it. It's a shame what the workingman has to put up with, you can't save nothing.

Why do you write?

For relaxation, relief. To have nothing in my head,—to freshen my eye by that till I see, smell, know and can reason and be.

VI. THE WALTZ

How ARE YOU?
   I'm all right.
   Sleeping?

A hm.

The car was too heavy for him anyway. It being icy and dark and a mist up, he saw a thing of branches, the mist, a single yellow lamp—

I'm gonna have another drink. I don't care, I've got a *man* in my room.

—like a woman on her knees who had just been beaten up and was looking through her fallen hair with one eye.

It being slippery, drunk with the mist and the night and success—and escape from the eyes and bells; wanting to turn—he spun the wheel around to the left in the narrow street—in the dark. The big car skidded as he intended it should, the front end riding up over the curb on the candied grass to a tree, not quite touching it. Then he kissed it with his bumper—for no reason in the world but idleness and pleasure, before he backed out.

The hundred pages have become twenty-five. I can do no more just now. I simply cannot.

Possibly you will find even what I have done senseless. I should worry. You say you want experiment. I tried for a single thing.

Good luck. I ask only that the pages be printed as written—correcting the spelling if you care to—or I will correct it later on.

Hello, Bill.

I am alone only while I am in the car. What then? Take a pad in the car with me and write while running.

Humanity? It is inhuman to write badly.

Into the middle of the twelfth afternoon chance and the end of the term throw another female agony.

Madonna Mia, che cosa bruta

Humanity, general ideas where? In the garbage.

Me moria!

Well, what do you know?

He did not realize that he could so step up his energy. Suddenly he increased it by two and did not feel fatigue. So he came to observe the stairs.

A drumming in my head and pain under my arm and in my groins.

Speak of the lack of general ideas—Jesu! in the writing. It is the writing. This is the theme of all I do. It is the writing. Speak of a flight by plane to Europe, of the two hundred inch telescopic reflector that discovers the nebula on the obscure outskirts of the milky way travelling at the incredible speed—away from the earth—of 2500 miles a second: it is the actual writing that embodies it, as the king in a chair—or a flea on a cat.

The general ideas—are over the writing. No. They are the writing. The writing is not carrying—their jackass. It is essential to all exposition that the writing be as discreet as the flight, the nebula, the telescope. It is and embodies them all. Actual.

In front walks Don Quixote; Sancho follows.

First, shall one say "the stairs" or the flight of steps, or a pair of stairs or the steps, or *Voyez l'escalier*.

Peaceful, significant, not like me, devoted, rhythmic—leading down as well as up. I beg to call attention to the stairs. All that I have wanted to say—succinctly—and could not, is here exhibited in quiet verse. This is in fact my intimate, my musician, my servant, my wife.

I imagine each step enlarged to a plain. Poetry is on the second floor. Above that the future and the past. Beyond that day and night. In the cellar you may imagine what. Science and philosophy have no reason but to lead us to bed and to sleep.

And if I work at this epidemic—by my advice and skill and care—if I work devotedly and work long. And even if I myself were taken with the flu and died. It has no significance whatever. But that I write and write actually—and well,—outweighs all the rest. Therefore, I stop and write.

That is its humanity.

On the other hand, I could not—if I would: I cannot not work.

In this fierce singleness—intensifies the ash fallen from a

cigar. The electric bulb unlit through which one sees the metal support. The gold fish double, one through the side of the bowl a smaller one under the water surface. A pile of rubbish of which the catalogue should be made.

And the January sunlight on Guinea Hill. Sunlight over the world over the black overgrown scene of the explosion of the ammunition works. Sunlight on the shiny mud. Making the houses black camouflage on the metal east. A boy on a bike kicking his foot at a bounding dog.

Seclusion and peace.

I guess you'll have me examined for my sanity. I dream of such things as an animal saying something. I guess I was born crying. I wept when I went to school. If I read anything and it is even patriotic I weep. I know he was dirty. He got on the dining room table and did it against the fruit dish. They wanted me to get rid of him. I made up my mind and let them take him away. But I see him all long. I know I'm silly but he was such a baby. I cannot stand it.

Crude, oil-stained hands on the fancy furniture fumble with the cheap lock.

You can't win.

Thus it is broken apart. Nothing swims. End the obscure with the actual. End the obscure allusion, the involved symbolism. Here none. The intention was to quit. But the impetus continued. This last chapter is too much. But the intensity of the interruption was trebled.

Tock qui chock qui fardoe: The fracture being greater the meaning must be thereby clarified.

Chapter after chapter presented itself. But at the same moment—as if called into being by the desire for clarification, just as the mind clicked and the illumination was released:

He fell to laughing so hard that he had no recourse but to gobble his supper and rescue a child in convulsions.

But dullness comes with eating.

The brilliance lasts only during the mating season. The significance is related to something else. The cat rubs against the tableleg. The effect is missed in a confusion that is continuously misinterpreted.

It is warm as summer outside. Voices come from the street dulling the edge of understanding that is ingrained in unrelease. Sleep intervenes upon fatigue just at the moment when confusion becomes significant so that it seems to be a mirage.

America, especially the United States—is the China of the future.

I could not do better because when the thing was in my mind clearly I simply could not find the minute to put it down. The dullness of this chapter is due to the difficulty.

It is bad merely because I was not able to do differently. Therefore, it remains actually the thing that it is. And thus is exactly what I mean and could not be said more clearly.

VII. FIERCE SINGLENESS

AT FORTY-FIVE there is no quitting. Now especially must the thing be driven through. So he argued wanting to write at night.

Begin again.

It is, sweetheart, a culmination of effort. Can you not see? What I conceive is writing as an actual creation. It is the birth of another cycle.

In the past the excellence of literature has been conceived upon a borrowed basis. In this you have no existence. I am broken apart, not so much with various desire—but with the inability to conceive desire upon a basis that is satisfactory to either.

The common resort is to divorce. What is that? It is for the police.

But to me it has always been that until a new plane of understanding has been established—or discovered, all the values which we attempt are worthless.

This is literature. Say there are ten men in love with you,

perhaps an exaggeration. To five women it will be inconceivable.

What is humanity to this, whether you do or whether you do not? All present day writing is upon such a basis. But should we succeed in deciphering the difficulty; should there be a mode by which to discover a common basis on which to act without cataclysm feeling—

This would be humanity itself.

On this basis only is it possible to conceive the work of James Joyce and to predict the future. The analogy with radium is inadequate. So is the analogy with essences. It is the complete establishment of a new category of understanding in which writing will deal with—

You, I, we, cannot you see how in the singleness of these few days marriage and writing have been fused so that the seriousness of my life and common objects about me have made up an actuality of which I am assembling the parts?

I blunder not at all. But the difficulty is immense, not to be solved by quietness, but by greater fracture. In the haste, stillness: It is fused.

Try as I will the thing comes only when I have one stocking on, the telephone is ringing, my mind is full of difficulties and you have asked me a question. In a flash it comes and is gone. Words on a par with trees. A humane matter that will sweep through the confusions of the world as the thought of the new world swept Europe—and ended in the Great Pox—perhaps.

It is a thing so penetrant, so powerful, so inclusive of all good that I cannot believe the difficulty real. It will blast a million difficulties. It is so simple, so easy that once it is caught it will be common as flesh or stupidity. It is entirely new and will include all that has been sought under the name of—conscience and what you will.

Imagine then that I see you in such a light. Imagine then why I cling to you. It is a fierce singleness that the epidemic has stepped up to a mountain.

Imagine then why I have—why it has been impossible for

me to think of not being married. Because in that is a key. The old terminology intervenes. In every poem that I have writing is one thing. So in you. In you is everything, in you is a piece of paper—

This sounds transcendental. One must come to the point. I begin, finally, to sound like an American.

But to leave the difficulty, is not to solve it. There is a single significance in every minutest gesture of my life of which I am a part only.

Practically, let me put down examples—

There are birds of two sizes on the brush pile.

What has this to do with our marriage or our love? Wait and see.

A storm coming drives dead leaves. Well, what of it? It is that you are laboring in an old category so that it is impossible for you to see either the leaves or the storm. It is likewise impossible to draw a simple inference from these things and to come to a salutory conclusion.

Dogs by multiples follow a single bitch. Never have I seen two bitches together.

Frozen ground cracks open. A tree with a split that admits water will show fresh wood when it freezes.

A stone is darker when wet than when dry. Water falling free in the air is, however, white.

The pipe emits steam which, freezing, coats the roof with ice, which, melting runs from the roof edge and freezing, forms icicles there which, melting, the water drips in the sun and catches the light as it falls.

It is necessary to put these things down not for scientific purposes, nor for their practical information nor for their originality or their wit.

Mercury shrinks with the cold, as water, when it freezes expands and floats.

When these things were first noted categories were ready for them so that they got fast in corners of understanding. By this process, reinforced by tradition, every common thing has been nailed down, stripped of freedom of action and taken away from use. This is the origin of trips to the poles, trips of discovery, suicides and the inability to see clearly.

Writing that would solve this by being actually itself would be in itself a general idea of the most concrete, as art (without just honor) has always been. But artists are dupes and idiots. They have not known how to lift what they have to a tremendous level that will outdistance everything else.

They have allowed men to demean them by speaking of the "philosophy of art." It is to break through that, to establish the tremendous idea and human significance of understanding of which my life is a moment that I welcome you.

Such then is this novel. You willing by a original force of understanding which by fierce singleness liberates on a fresh plane to perform in a new way that will include the world. It is the promise of the future.

Can you not see how this excludes the criticisms of the meanest critics and includes my meanest action? It is the only possible theme for a novel.

As to say: rhododendron leaves shrivel in the cold making thus a very serviceable thermometer. One can judge of the cold merely by looking at them through glass to within five degrees, after a little practice.

After the flu a weakness persists that is out of all proportion to the coincident anatomical changes, proving the effects of an evanescent poison of great intensity. Also proving that all the information that is static in the liberal arts and sciences can, by intelligent understanding, be made active—loosed from a cupboard of dullness—Thus fatigue, so called, dulls the perception. It is hard to keep on a basis of actuality.

Sycamore trees shed their bark differently from most others, by patches, leaving a green or yellow freshness for the beginning year. Nijinski's tights.

The boulder, pocked, is marked by times past. Thus I

could not stop at the twenty-fifth page. I had to go on. I realized anything less than a full development would be an ineptitude, a disloyalty.

These and other things have a relationship with each other simply because both are actual.

VIII. ANTI-ALLEGORY

THUS I PUT DOWN, to explain to you and to be absolutely clear and for its actual value—as grapes in a painting by Juan Gris—which by other means could be in no way related to marriage, this account:

"Non canimus surdis: respondent omnia silvae."

The wintry landscape is a museum of dried vegetation, bearing much the same resemblance to the verdant wealth of summer that a mummy does to a living human being, yet with the difference that the vegetable mummy often retains the most graceful elegance; and this it is to be feared, can scarcely be said of any Egyptian princess, however distinguished in her time. Indeed I may go so far as to assert that some plants are positively more elegant as mummies than they were when the sap circulated in all their vessels. There is the common teasel, for example, which in winter acquires a quite remarkable perfection of curvature in all its leaves. There is a clump of them not far from the Val Ste. Veronique, of which the tallest is nearly eight feet high, and so very perfect and delicate that if some skillful goldsmith were to copy it as it stands in pure Australian gold (silver would be too chilly in tint) all Paris would wonder at its loveliness. Not a leaf of it but is fit to be modeled for an archbishop's crozier, and round the head rise the thin bracts like guards, still perfect, every one of them, though the tall stem has swayed in the autumn storms. As to that head itself, what a miracle of texture! Warm reddish brown in the sun, and at a short distance seeming soft as fur, but nearer a delicate network.

Another very fine plant in winter, happily very common in many places, is the great mullein, which, though it does not equal the teasel in elegance, far surpasses it in the expression of melancholy ruin. Still it retains some rich, thick, pale, dusty, cottony leaves, between the earth and the blackened raceme where the pale yellow flowers once clustered so gaily in the sunshine, but the large outer leaves have faded and lost form, and become mere brown rags, like the tatters of miserable poverty, drenched in the rains of winter, and draggled on the mud of the cold inhospitable earth. Of all the plants that grow, the mullein in its decay comes nearest to that most terrible form of human poverty when the victim has still, to his misfortune, vitality enough for mere existence, yet not enough to make existence either decent or endurable.

The ferns and grasses bear the season better, and—

Aviation started in when the Wright brothers after several attempts to fly like the birds succeeded.

If what I have said so far is clear and true and strange to unaccustomed ears, let me see if I can make it still more lucid.

The night offers no explanation for its sound of winds or its lights. Yet it is accepted simply as if it were a common occurrence. It is accepted—yet the explanation is full of the greatest suggestion.

Love songs have always looked flat to me. Since what else is there to be written? But to attempt to state what is in effect the statement requires a subtlety that is rare—or an understanding which I have not yet found outside the difficulties which involve the expression I am detailing.

Forced close to you, the effect is to me of trees, cups and people. The theatre is muffled. Likewise the "like" songs.

Would you consider a train passing—or the city in the icy sky—a love song? What else? It must be so.

And if I told you the dark trees against the night sky

and the row of the city's lights beyond and under them—
would you consider that a love statement?

This is what my poems have been from the first.

It is simple. There is no symbolism, no evocation of an
image.

It is so.

Or a lit church. *There* is something you must under-
stand, coming from me, in all frankness. What I would say
has no relation to the effect of a church on the mind. It is
so. It is, therefore, solely a song—when it is set down to be
what is actually of no consequence in itself.

Deschanel, in his clever and amusing *"Essai de critique
naturelle,"* gives a description of an English landscape-
painter addicted to botanical study; a description slightly
caricatured, yet probably drawn from some living instance,
and accurate in the main: *"Il s'en va herboriser par champs,
s'assure que tel vegetable a les feuilles pointues ou découpées
de telle façon que telle fleurette a une telle corolle et tant
de pétales; qu'il y a d'ailleurs, dans la nature des rouges
violents, des verts crus, des jaunes impitoyables, beaucoup
de violet,"* etc. Well, this may be true with reference to
some painters of that young realist school which was
flourishing in England when M. Deschanel wrote his book,
and he may have met some English artists who were also
botanists; but the harm is not in the study of plants, it is in
the forgetfulness of large relations to which minute observa-
tion of Nature has occasionally led those who are addicted
to it.

As in this so every detail of the day—the lights of the
city—in the distance that seem to close in together at the
end of the dark street as the car swiftly advances: in them-
selves equal in detail the existence of affection—the fact of
love and so, deciphered, intensely seen become in themselves
praise and a song.

A natural example is the memory of moonlight in youth.
Daring no more we sat hand in hand. The moon rose over
the water.

Every motion of the cars in the half light had its effect upon the motion of the eye.

It is a great advantage of the winter season for the study of the sylvan nature that it enables us to see the structure of trunks and branches so much better than we can do when they are laden with summer foliage. Of all trees at this season of the year my favorite is decidedly the walnut. Its bark is magnificent in the strength of the deeply furrowed lines which mark it (tempting beyond measure to an etcher), and its fine pale grays exhibit to perfection that wealth of dark mosses which the landscape painter knows and values. Besides this, there is so much grandeur in its far-spreading, powerful arms, that it is well for us to see them during part of the year without their voluminous green sleeves. Happily for the beauty of many a village the walnut is productive during life, so that it is allowed to come to full maturity. The oak is inferior both in form and color, and expresses only a sturdy strength. The ash shows her grace of structure, her tall, elegant limbs.

Fatigue is like a tree.

The work that is being done by many writers is so much of one—The sound of her book as she turns the pages sums the substance of summer. The click of the keys. The squeal of the car on the hill.

But to return to the passing of the railroad train. Its shape squatted upon the ground in its habitual mode scoots over the ground. It appears to live of itself and to be unrelated to all other things.

IX. IN SUM

WHAT CAN I SAY? Who shall describe the light? It is like an epidemic; it is like your love.

There is no other way than that which I have adopted.

Any writer has mentioned the light, how it lies like a darker sediment, yellow at the bottom of a blue bottle upon the dark glass of the city. It fades weakly up as if Man Ray had painted it.

Or they pick out various objects to describe: how it touches the trees, how against it the branches lie flattened. Three squirrels race in the dim light over the frozen ground. There is no flower, no leaf. The ground is hard and pale, pale as the face.

Or they grow impassioned. Upward leaps the flaming disc. Night is defeated. The shadows drop. The triumphant orb steadily mounts into his serene demesne.

This is the depression we feel in the middle of our excitement over the classics. Marvellous, we say. And isn't it after all too bad that there are no writers like that today.

But that which is the dawn is—a face, a look. It is a man on a ship. It is the successful termination of an experiment. It is discovery. At this a light does penetrate without announcement everywhere. It is indeed like the epidemic, in its humanity, the fullness of its rise. It is indeed a love that willynilly mounts.

So is writing that is not infused with a light which is already at the edge of our understanding—dark.

It is a complete day, to interpenetrate every activity, so that though we enjoy and shout about—anything at all, when it shall be re-valued in this light,—All manner of new works, in painting, in literature, in music—until they be conceived in the manner which I have expressed, as a unit, all touching various phases of a rise in the intelligence which will stand out beyond the concepts of science and the reflective images of philosophy.

It is that literature has been also scientific and philosophic in its conception. The foreign categories have imposed themselves giving a sense of falseness which is intolerable in the face of the actual. It is no chance that men do not now paint portraits of the sun rising any more than they do a fire in the forest. The whole conception of these things was wrong—But going a step further, in just that way, everything we read now is uncleanly.

Even the unfortunate moralists are not entirely stupid. They crave no replica but the real. Yet they cannot, by the impossibility of the distance, stretch from their sink of morality to the heights reached by a Van Gogh. Or to the works of any painter who is no longer content to "represent" but lives to "create" as they say, to advance, that is, the concept of the real, the actual. It is this everywhere in the arts that is not copying science, which must be dealt with separately, but realizing its own grandeur.

Van Gogh, realizing the light, fought blindly to paint it and to live it. But died, naturally. One cannot eat sand—and the world would not give itself to be eaten.

To formulate these things in pseudo-prose, or verse is as impossible as for me to say "I love you." If the intelligence must wait to have its ticket punched before it dares to acknowledge that the train is waiting—it must walk. And walking is delightful.

Van Gogh would paint the light.

Again and again, the sun makes day in every backyard. These thing are interrelated in the painters, in the—

There will be an objection, many, from every side. From those who will not be related to anyone. That I mean a progress upward. Nonsense. I mean a progress downward to the beast. To the actual. To the devil with silks. But there cannot be an objection to an intelligent cutting away of obscurity that is not a return to an old cesspool. Violent nonsense. It must continue to reveal its body, its body, unclothed—unclothed, that is, save as it pleases.

Syphilitic, afraid, cloistered in a library. One could catalogue, but only if it were a catalogue to be a catalogue, not for ready reference for "useful purposes."

The snow lies on the branches in patches, as in an old drawing.

This way, doctor, that's the locked-up room.

As an infant loves paper, to crumple in the hand.

When I have nothing in my stomach I don't feel so good.

There are no valid conceptions, outside of the modern, of

sufficient size: as that *all* writing is a waste of time, as practiced *now* and *earlier* conceived.

This game of who buries whom; this double solitaire.

G. Fracastoro (1484-1553). Physician and poet. The first to recognize the nature of syphilis. He was the author of numerous medical poems.

The grey sky is rifted and intermediate; crushed ashes and broken glass on the frozen ground are identical with it.

The snow—as in Joyce but actual, this time, as his new work.

What more delightful than to acquire the strength of an elephant, to be actually the locomotive (this is the charm of big business—foretelling what deceptions) to uproot and push down oak trees with the lip of a steam shovel.

First, of course, were the fields, fertile or otherwise, or first, if you prefer, was the idea of the thing. Then the small houses. Then the people. Young. Then trouble, pain. Dejection of false ideals. Consolation. Never a light. The fields were golden rod, excellent and actual—an odor rather pungent, irritating and altogether curious. At most, now, a beautiful (i. e. young) troubled woman, with full, milky breasts, quite detached.

My friends, intense action—isolation—goes with writing. But it separates friends: a gain, quite definitely. D. says he is bringing a painting to New York and wants me to see it with him. When? Nothing would please me better than to run up to Westchester to see S. Z's letter lies unanswered. A cat running, not galloping, seems to have eight legs.

Far better to drink alcohol than to distress the mind with tyrannical prohibitions. Far better for a man to smoke tobacco than to eat crackers and candy between meals.

The camouflaged cannon in the park seems ten thousand years old—or infinitely past—compared to the boulder with the glacier scratches upon it, which seems new, fresh by comparison—its secret undrained.

It's all very well for this one to speak of general ideas and the content of literature, but the only conception that is worth entertaining is that which includes them all.

Hello Sweetness. These are the inexpressible gestures of love. Secretive. Undiscovered. Here lies the difficulty of talk. Everything has a tail of difficulties that swamps the mind before the expression.

Thank God that's about finished.

What's that, dear?

This thing I wanted to do. This is, after all, the substance, therefore, the explanation, of my poems and my life in which *there exists* (instead of "*you exist*").

The snow continues to fall. Calls begin to come in from the outside: not professional. The epidemic is over.

The following is to fill in the space between the last words, "The epidemic is over" and the paragraph beginning "It must be that the devotees of philosophy, etc." There must be five or six letters lying around unanswered from as far back as four weeks ago. Someone wants me to write an article about my view on the conflict between art, science and philosophy. Things like that. Often the mail is received while I am at breakfast and I have no time between telephone calls, etc. to more than glance at the place from which the letters have been mailed.

It must be that the devotees of philosophy have a valuable thing between them since they appear—barring certain general characteristics of the class—essentially intelligent.

There have been geniuses among them as among adepts in other categories of the intelligence. It is wise to note that there have been also those less than geniuses. Which is to point a range within a certain space of the intelligence, that philosophy has no more to do with the absolute, that it is no more inclusive of other categories of the intelligence than the concept of a tree or a stone—which includes truly a conception of the whole, by necessity, as does any thing or category by virtue of its nature as a part, but without any pretense toward absoluteness.

The excellence and perfection of philosophy are within a circumscribed area and its successes are the perfect interrelationships of its parts. Thus one may stand within or outside, without onus or necessity for doing otherwise, and retain the full privileges and prerogatives of the intelligence. This is the first necessity for a conception of the function of art and the antagonism which is implied in such a mixed, therefore, impure and so untrue delineation as "the philosophy of art."

The category of art is incapable of correct definition in terms of philosophy. The category of art is another thing with its own particular function the time for the full exercise of which is now approaching, a function beyond the scope of philosophy.

Science is cruder, more directly useful, more intimate to our lives, more imbedded in our errors of perception and so harder to eradicate from the mind. It is a category of the understanding, just as philosophy is and in the same way—inferior to the not so well developed though equally well practiced category of art.

Science is impotent from all the viewpoints from which in its inception it seemed to promise enlightenment to the human mind. It is going nowhere but to gross and minute codification of the perceptions. It means nothing to us more than bread does though as much. It bears, that is, the same relationship to us as meat to a dog. It has no future but multiplication—the 200 inch telescopic reflector. It has, on the other hand, deterrent effects on the imagination which are severe bars to a humane and intelligent understanding of man in his life and world. Pure, it achieves its design; less than pure it serves its purpose—no more can be said for it.

The actual is another field, the field of art, which must liberate from the defects of philosophy and science, body, mind and morals. There are extraordinary recesses of the understanding still untouched by any generally practiced mode of approach—which artists have found accessible since the beginning of time—more fully to be appreciated and explored.

This sense of the actual is destructive to much that is overbearing in S. and P. The antagonism between the actual and them must exist for an indefinite period or until the intelligence liberates itself from the fetishism mainly perpetuated by academies and our present recognized intellectual leaders.

Meanwhile men are brought nearer to starvation out of respect for these things; and others accumulate profits by the millions of dollars through neglecting them for pay.

These things also are actual qualities of writing.

Or to sum it all up there's the legend in gold letters on the window of the abandoned saloon:

O L   M P I

Other Prose (1921–1931)

The Accident

DEATH IS DIFFICULT for the senses to alight on. There is no help from familiarity with the location. There is a cold body to be put away but what is that? The life has gone out of it and death has come into it. Whither? Whence? The sense has no footspace.

After twelve days struggling with a girl to keep life in her, losing, winning, it is not easy to give her up. One has studied her inch by inch, one has grown used to the life in her. It is natural.

She lies gasping her last: eyes rolled up till only the whites show, lids half open, mouth agape, skin a cold bluish white, pasty, hard to the touch—as the body temperature drops the tissues congeal. One is definitely beaten.

—Shall I call you when it happens or will you come again?

—Call me.

It is the end!

It is spring. Sunshine fills the out-of-doors, great basins of it dumped among factories standing beside open fields, into back lots, upon a rutted baseball field, into a sewage ditch running rainwater, down a red dirt path to four goats.

What are you stopping here for! To show him the four goats. Come on. No? Ah? —She blushes and hides her face. Down the road come three boys in long pants. Good God, Good God! How a man will waste himself. She is no more than a piece of cake to be eaten by anyone. Her hips beside me have set me into a fever, I was up half the night last night, my nerves have the insulation worn off them. But— Fastened in her seat because three boys may pass near her!

They may even look at her. She knows that they will. She will pick one and play him against the rest. They will try to remain three; she will try to make them one and one and one. And I? Am I mad or starved—or tired out? What is fatigue but an opportunity for illuminating diversions? It is like sickness, a sign of normality. Like death, a sign of life.

The path follows above the gully, red in the flamy green of the new grass. The goats are tied by long cords, one to each of two solitary old trees at the path's end, one to the right, one to the left. The others, a white and a black, are in the rough ground beyond. The white one has its tether fastened to a circular block of turned steel with a hole in the center—the railroad is hard by; the other's is tied to an irregular brown stone.

—See the nanny goats! —I approach the smallest goat timidly. It is the one fastened to the large tree to the left of the path. It has small but sharp black horns. It draws away, beginning to wind its tie rope around the tree. Its hair is long, coarse, fawncolored, fading into white over the face and under the belly where the udder hangs, the two pinkish teats pointing slightly forward. I back the creature around the tree till it can go no further, the cord is all wound up. Gingerly I take it by the ear. It tries to crowd between me and the tree. I put out my right knee to stop it. It lowers its head. I seize a horn. It struggles. I find I can hold it. I call the baby.

He isn't afraid. He lays his face against the goat's hairy cheek Ah! I warn him away watching the sharp point of the free horn. I think of the child's moist gelatinous eyes. I look at the goat's eyes. They are round, large and gray, with a wide blue-black slit horizontal in the center, the striae of the iris folded into it like threads round a buttonhole.

The child strokes the goat's flanks. The hair is not smooth, there is straw and fragments of dried leaves between the horns, an awkward place for a goat to get at. The nozzle is hairy, the nose narrow, the moist black skin at the tip, slit either side by curled nostrils, vibrates sensitively. A goat.

I push the baby away and drive the goat around the tree again until the rope is entirely unwound. The beast immediately finds new violent green tufts of grass in some black mud half under some old dried water-soaked weedstalks. Thrusting down her slender face she starts to crop away unreflectively at that which a moment before she did not know to achieve.

To the right of the path the other goat comes forward boldly but stops short and sniffs, stretching out its neck; prop for the nose. It ventures closer. Gan-ha-ha-ha-ha! (as in hat). Very softly. The small goat answers. Also gray eyes but the body is marked in a new fashion. Zebra-like two black stripes down the two jowls between which, tawny and black bands down forehead and nozzle. Ears black fringed. A broad and shaggy black stripe down the backbone to the tail. Starting down from this on either flank a broad white band round and under from side to side. Behind and in front of which the flanks are the same tawny yellow as the face.

The baby goes up to the goat and pats its face before I can get to him to draw him back. The goat is impassive, her eyes fixed on me. I take the baby's hand and draw him away. He strains to touch the goat.

The two other goats look up from time to time from a distance then go on nibbling, pulling at the grass with short jerks of the head.

I grip the child's wrist and hand and drag him back between the fields of green flames and the painted gully along the red dirt path.

As we approach the car, the baby stumbles on a flange of the gutter. He falls forward on his hands. For a moment his feet leave the ground and he remains poised with feet and buttocks in the air as if he were about to stand on his hands as a circus performer would. Then his arms give way and his face goes in the dirt.

He cries. His mouth is circled with grit. Fortunately the front of his heavy wool cap has spared his brow from injury.

I sit on the step of the car and, taking out my clean handkerchief, I wipe his face. In the windows of the Franco-American Chemical Company across the way six women have appeared in the two windows, four in one and two in the other. They watch the baby, wondering if he is hurt. They linger to look out. They open the windows. Their faces are bathed with sunlight. They continue to strain out at the window. They laugh and wave their hands.

Over against them in an open field a man and a boy on their hands and knees are planting out slender green slips in the fresh dirt, row after row.

We enter the car. The baby waves his hand. Good bye!

Marianne Moore

THE BEST WORK is always neglected and there is no critic among the older men who has cared to champion the newer names from outside the battle. The established critic will not read. So it is that the present writers must turn interpreters of their own work. Even those who enjoy modern work are not always intelligent, but often seem at a loss to know the white marks from the black. But modernism is distressing to many who could at least, due to the necessary appearance of disorder in all immediacy, be led to appreciation through critical study.

If one come with Miss Moore's work to some wary friend and say, "Everything is worthless but the best and this is the best," adding, "only with difficulty discerned" will he see anything, if he be at all well read, but destruction? From my experience he will be shocked and bewildered. He will perceive absolutely nothing except that his whole preconceived scheme of values has been ruined. And this is exactly what he should see, a break *through* all preconception of poetic form and mood and pace, a flaw, a crack in the bowl. It is this that one means when he says destruction and creation are simultaneous. But this is not easy to accept. Miss Moore, using the same material as all others before her, comes at it so effectively at a new angle as to throw out of fashion the classical conventional poetry to which one is used and puts her own and that about her in its place. The old stops are discarded. This must antagonize many. Furthermore, there is a multiplication, a quickening, a burrowing through, a blasting aside, a dynamization, a flight over—it is modern, but the critic must show that this is only to reveal an essential poetry through the mass, as always, and with superlative effect in this case.

A course in mathematics would not be wasted on a poet, or a reader of poetry, if he remember no more from it than the geometric principle of the intersection of loci: from all angles lines converging and crossing establish points. He might carry it further and say in his imagination that apprehension perforates at places, through to understanding—as white is at the intersection of blue and green and yellow and red. It is this white light that is the background of all good work. Aware of this, one may read the Greeks or the Elizabethans or Sidney Lanier even Robert Bridges, and preserve interest, poise, and enjoyment. He may visit Virginia or China, and when friends, eager to please, playfully lead him about for pockets of local color—he may go. Local color is not, as the parodists, the localists believe, an object of art. It is merely a variant serving to locate acme point of white penetration. The intensification of desire toward this purity is the modern variant. It is that which interests me most and seems most solid among the qualities I witness in my contemporaries; it is a quality present in much or even all that Miss Moore does.

Poems, like painting, can be interesting because of the subject with which they deal. The baby glove of a Pharaoh can be so presented as to bring tears to the eyes. And it

need not be bad work because it has to do with a favorite
cat dead. Poetry, rare and never willingly recognized, only
its accidental colors make it tolerable to most. If it be of a
red coloration, those who like red will follow and be led
restfully astray. So it is with hymns, battle songs, love
ditties, elegies. Humanity sees itself in them, it is familiar,
the good placed attractively and the bad thrown into a
counter light. This is inevitable. But in any anthology it
will be found that men have been hard put to it at all times
to tell which is poetry and which the impost. This is hard.
The difficult thing to realize is that the thrust must go
through to the white, at least somewhere.

Good modern work, far from being the fragmentary,
neurotic thing its disunderstanders think it, is nothing more
than work compelled by these conditions. It is a multipli-
cation of impulses that by their several flights, crossing at
all eccentric angles, *might* enlighten. As a phase, in its
slightest beginning, it is more a disc pierced here and there
by light; it is really distressingly broken up. But so does
any attack seem at the moment of engagement, multiple
units crazy except when viewed as a whole.

Surely there is no poetry so active as that of today, so
unbound, so dangerous to the mass of mediocrity, if one
should understand it, so fleet, hard to capture, so delight-
ful to pursue. It is clarifying in its movements as a wild
animal whose walk corrects that of men. Who shall separate
the good Whitman from the bad, the dreadful New Eng-
land maunderers from the others, put air under and around
the living and leave the dead to fall dead? Who? None
but poems, such as Miss Moore's, their cleanliness, lack of
cement, clarity, gentleness. It grows impossible for the
eye to rest long upon the object of the drawing. Here is
an escape from the old dilemma. The unessential is put
rapidly aside as the eye searches between for illumination.
Miss Moore undertakes in her work to separate the poetry
from the subject entirely—like all the moderns. In this
she has been rarely successful and this is important.

Unlike the painters the poet has not resorted to distortions or the abstract in form. Miss Moore accomplishes a like result by rapidity of movement. A poem such as "Marriage" is an anthology of transit. It is a pleasure that can be held firm only by moving rapidly from one thing to the next. It gives the impression of a passage through. There is a distaste for lingering, as in Emily Dickinson. As in Emily Dickinson there is too a fastidious precision of thought where unrhymes fill the purpose better than rhymes. There is a swiftness impaling beauty, but no impatience as in so much present-day trouble with verse. It is a rapidity too swift for touch, a seraphic quality, one might have said yesterday. There is, however, no breast that warms the bars of heaven: it is at most a swiftness that passes without repugnance from thing to thing.

The only help I ever got from Miss Moore toward the understanding of her verse was that she despised connectives. Any other assistance would have been an impoliteness, since she has always been sure of herself if not of others. The complete poem is there waiting: all the wit, the color, the constructive ability (not a particularly strong point that, however). And the quality of satisfaction gathered from reading her is that one may seek long in those exciting mazes sure of coming out at the right door in the end. There is nothing missing but the connectives.

The thought is compact, accurate and accurately planted. In fact, the garden, since it is a garden more than a statue, is found to be curiously of porcelain. It is the mythical, indestructible garden of pleasure, perhaps greatly pressed for space today, but there and intact, nevertheless.

I don't know where, except in modern poetry, this quality of the brittle, highly set-off porcelain garden exists and nowhere in modern work better than with Miss Moore. It is this chief beauty of today, this hard crest to nature, that makes the best present work with its "unnatural" appearance seem so thoroughly gratuitous, so difficult to explain, and so doubly a treasure of seclusion. It is the white of a clarity beyond the facts.

There is in the newer work a perfectly definite handling of the materials with a given intention to relate them in a certain way—a handling that is intensely, intentionally selective. There is a definite place where the matters of the day may meet if they choose or not, but if they assemble it must be there. There is no compromise. Miss Moore never falls from the place inhabited by poems. It is hard to give an illustration of this from her work because it is everywhere. One must be careful, though, not to understand this as a mystical support, a danger we are skirting safely, I hope, in our time.

Poe in his most-read first essay quotes Nathaniel Willis' poem "The Two Women," admiringly and in full, and one senses at once the reason: there is a quality to the *feeling* there that affected Poe tremendously. This mystical quality that endeared Poe to Father Tabb, the poet-priest, still seems to many the essence of poetry itself. It would be idle to name many who have been happily mystical and remained good poets: Poe, Blake, Francis Thompson, et cetera.

But what I wish to point is that there need be no stilled and archaic heaven, no ducking under religiosities to have poetry and to have it stand in its place beyond "nature." Poems have a separate existence uncompelled by nature or the supernatural. There is a "special" place which poems, as all works of art, must occupy, but it is quite definitely the same as that where bricks or colored threads are handled.

In painting, Ingres realized the essentiality of drawing and each perfect part seemed to float free from his work, by itself. There is much in this that applies beautifully to Miss Moore. It is perfect drawing that attains to a separate existence which might, if it please, be called mystical, but is in fact no more than the practicability of design.

To Miss Moore an apple remains an apple whether it be

in Eden or the fruit bowl where it curls. But that would be hard to prove—

"dazzled by the apple."

The apple is left there, suspended. One is not made to feel that as an apple it has anything particularly to do with poetry or that as such it needs special treatment; one goes on. Because of this, the direct object does seem unaffected. It seems as free from the smears of mystery, as pliant, as "natural" as Venus on the wave. Because of this, her work is never indecorous as where nature is itself concerned. These are great virtues.

Without effort Miss Moore encounters the affairs which concern her as one would naturally in reading or upon a walk outdoors. She is not a Swinburne stumbling to music, but one always finds her moving forward ably, in thought, unimpeded by a rhythm. Her own rhythm is particularly revealing. It does not interfere with her progress; it is the movement of the animal, it does not put itself first and ask the other to follow.

Nor is "thought" the thing that she contends with. Miss Moore uses the thought most interestingly and wonderfully to my mind. I don't know but that this technical excellence is one of the greatest pleasures I get from her. She occupies the thought to its end, and goes on—without connectives. To me this is thrilling. The essence is not broken, nothing is injured. It is a kind hand to a merciless mind at home in the thought as in the cruder image. In the best modern verse, room has been made for the best of modern thought and Miss Moore thinks straight.

Only the most modern work has attempted to do without *ex machina* props of all sorts, without rhyme, assonance, the feudal master beat, the excuse of "nature," of the spirit, mysticism, religiosity, "love," "humor," "death." Work such as Miss Moore's holds its bloom today not by using slang, not by its moral abandon or puritanical steadfastness, but by the aesthetic pleasure engendered where pure craftsmanship joins hard surfaces skilfully.

Poetry has taken many disguises which by cross reading or intense penetration it is possible to go through to the core. Through intersection of loci their multiplicity may become revelatory. The significance of much reading being that this "thing" grow clearer, remain fresh, be more present to the mind. To read more thoroughly than this is idleness; a common classroom absurdity.

One may agree tentatively with Glenway Wescott, that there is a division taking place in America between a proletarian art, full of sincerities, on the one side and an aristocratic and ritualistic art on the other. One may agree, but it is necessary to scrutinize such a statement carefully.

There cannot be two arts of poetry really. There is weight and there is disencumberedness. There can be no schism, except that which has always existed between art and its approaches. There cannot be a proletarian art— even among savages. There is a proletarian taste. To have achieved an organization even of that is to have escaped it.

And to organize into a pattern is also, true enough, to "approach the conditions of a ritual." But here I would again go slow. I see only escape from the conditions of ritual in Miss Moore's work: a rush through wind if not toward some patent "end" at least away from pursuit, a pursuit perhaps by ritual. If from such a flight a ritual results it is more the care of those who follow than of the one who leads. "Ritual," too often to suit my ear, connotes a stereotyped mode of procedure from which pleasure has passed, whereas the poetry to which my attention clings, if it ever knew those conditions, is distinguished only as it leaves them behind.

It is at least amusing, in this connection, to quote from *Others*, Volume 1, Number 5, November 1915—quoted in turn from J. B. Kerfoot in *Life:* "Perhaps you are unfamiliar with this 'new poetry' that is called 'revolutionary.' It is the expression of democracy of feeling rebelling against an aristocracy of form."

> As if a death mask ever could replace
> Life's faulty excellence!

There are two elements essential to Miss Moore's scheme of composition, the hard and unaffected concept of the apple itself as an idea, then its edge-to-edge contact with the things which surround it—the coil of a snake, leaves at various depths, or as it may be; and without connectives unless it be poetry, the inevitable connective, if you will.

Marriage, through which thought does not penetrate, appeared to Miss Moore a legitimate object for art, an art that would not halt from using thought about it, however, as it might want to. Against marriage, "this instituion, perhaps one should say enterprise"— Miss Moore launched her thought not to have it appear arsenaled as in a textbook on psychology, but to stay among apples and giraffes in a poem. The interstices for the light and not the interstitial web of the thought concerned her, or so it seems to me. Thus the material is as the handling: the thought, the word, the rhythm—all in the style. The effect is in the penetration of the light itself, how much, how little; the appearance of the luminous background.

Of marriage there is no solution in the poem and no attempt to make marriage beautiful or otherwise by "poetic" treatment. There is beauty and it is thoughtless, as marriage or a cave inhabited by the sounds and colors of waves, as in the time of prismatic color, as England with its baby rivers, as G. B. Shaw, or chanticleer, or a fish, or an elephant with its strictly practical appendages. All these things are inescapably caught in the beauty of Miss Moore's passage through them; they all have at least edges. This too is a quality that greatly pleases me: definite objects which give a clear contour to her force. Is it a flight, a symphony, a ghost, a mathematic? The usual evasion is to call them poems.

Miss Moore gets great pleasure from wiping soiled words or cutting them clean out, removing the aureoles that have been pasted about them or taking them bodily from greasy contexts. For the compositions which Miss Moore intends, each word should first stand crystal clear with no attachments; not even an aroma. As a cross light upon this, Miss Moore's personal dislike for flowers that have both a satisfying appearance and an odor of perfume is worth noticing. With Miss Moore a word is a word most when it is separated out by science, treated with acid to remove the smudges, washed, dried and placed right side up on a clean surface. Now one may say that this is a word. Now it may be used, and how?

It may be used not to smear it again with thinking (the attachments of thought) but in such a way that it will remain scrupulously itself, clean perfect, unnicked beside other words in parade. There must be edges. This casts some light I think on the simplicity of design in much of Miss Moore's work. There must be recognizable edges against the ground which cannot, as she might desire it, be left entirely white. Prose would be all black, a complete black painted or etched over, but solid.

There is almost no overlaying at all. The effect is of every object sufficiently uncovered to be easily recognizable. This simplicity, with the light coming through from between the perfectly plain masses, is however extremely bewildering to one who has been accustomed to look upon the usual "poem," the commonplace opaque board covered with vain curlicues. They forget, those who would read Miss Moore aright, that white circular discs grouped closely edge to edge upon a dark table make black six-pointed stars.

The "useful result" is an accuracy to which this simplicity of design greatly adds. The effect is for the effect to remain "true"; nothing loses its identity because of the composition, but the parts in their assembly remain quite as "natural" as before they were gathered. There is no "sentiment"; the softening effect of word upon word is nil; everything is in the style. To make this ten times evident is Miss Moore's constant care. There seems to be almost too great a wish to be transparent and it is here if anywhere that Miss Moore's later work will show a change, I think.

The general effect is of a rise through the humanities, the sciences, without evading "thought," through anything (if not everything) of the best of modern life; taking whatever there is as it comes, using it and leaving it drained of its pleasure, but otherwise undamaged. Miss Moore does not compromise science with poetry. In this again, she is ably modern.

And from this clarity, this acid cleansing, this unblinking willingness, her poems result, a true modern crystallization, the fine essence of today which I have spoken of as the porcelain garden.

Or one will think a little of primitive masonry, the units unglued and as in the greatest early constructions unstandardized.

In such work as "Critics and Connoisseurs," and "Poetry," Miss Moore succeeds in having the "thing" which is her concern move freely, unencumbered by the images or the difficulties of thought. In such work there is no "suggestiveness," no tiresome "subtlety" of trend to be heavily followed, no painstaking refinement of sentiment. There is surely a choice evident in all her work, a very definite quality of choice in her material, a thinness perhaps, but a very welcome and no little surprising absence of moral tone. The choice being entirely natural and completely arbitrary is not in the least offensive, in fact it has been turned curiously to advantage throughout.

From what I have read it was in "Critics and Connoisseurs" that the successful method used later began first to appear: If a thought presents itself the force moves through it easily and completely: so the thought also has revealed the "thing"—that is all. The thought is used exactly as the apple, it is the same insoluble block. In Miss Moore's work the purely stated idea has an edge exactly like a fruit or a tree or a serpent.—

To use anything: rhyme, thought, color, apple, verb—so

as to illumine it, is the modern prerogative; a stintless inclusion. It is Miss Moore's success.

The diction, the phrase construction, is unaffected. To use a "poetic" inversion of language, or even such a special posture of speech, still discernible in Miss Moore's earlier work, is to confess an inability to have penetrated with poetry some crevice of understanding; that special things and special places are reserved for art, that it is unable, that it requires fostering. This is unbearable.

Poetry is not limited in that way. It need not say either

> Bound without,
> Boundless within.

It has as little to do with the soul as with ermine robes or graveyards. It is not noble, sad, funny. It is poetry. It is free. It is escapeless. It goes where it will. It is in danger; escapes if it can.

This is new! The quality is not new, but the freedom is new, the unbridled leap.

The dangers are thereby multiplied—but the clarity increased. Nothing but the perfect and the clear.

A Matisse

ON THE FRENCH grass, in that room on Fifth Ave., lay that woman who had never seen my own poor land. The dust and noise of Paris had fallen from her with the dress and underwear and shoes and stockings which she had just put aside to lie bathing in the sun. So too she lay in the sunlight of the man's easy attention. His eye and the sun had made day over her. She gave herself to them both for there was nothing to be told. Nothing is to be told to the sun at noonday. A violet clump before her belly mentioned that it was spring. A locomotive could be heard whistling beyond the hill. There was nothing to be told. Her body was neither classic nor whatever it might be supposed. There she lay and her curving torso and thighs were close upon the grass and violets.

So he painted her. The sun had entered his head in the color of sprays of flaming palm leaves. They had been walking for an hour or so after leaving the train. They were hot. She had chosen the place to rest and he had painted her resting, with interest in the place she had chosen.

It had been a lovely day in the air.—What pleasant women are these girls of ours! When they have worn clothes and take them off it is with an effect of having performed a small duty. They return to the sun with a gesture of accomplishment. —Here she lay in this spot today not like Diana or Aphrodite but with better proof than they of regard for the place she was in. She rested and he painted her.

It was the first of summer. Bare as was his mind of interest in anything save the fullness of his knowledge, into which her simple body entered as into the eye of the sun himself, so he painted her. So she came to America.

No man in my country has seen a woman naked and painted her as if he knew anything except that she was naked. No woman in my country is naked except at night.

In the French sun, on the French grass in a room on Fifth Avenue, a French girl lies and smiles at the sun without seeing us.

An Essay on Virginia

BEGIN WITH A to remain intact, redundant not even to the amount of a reflective title. Especially today is it necessary to be academic, the apology for academic precision—which is always essential in realistic ages—being that this has no relation to facts. To essay is to try but not to attempt. It is to establish trial. The essay is the most human literary form in that it is always sure, it remains from first to last fixed.

Nothing affects it. It may stop, but if it stops that is surely the end and so it remains perfect, just as with an infant which fails to continue. It suffers disclosures, up and down, but nothing can affect it. It is as a man: a lunatic or not; no matter. Whatever passes through it, it is never that thing. It remains itself and continues so, pure motion.

Perhaps one should say that it is only an essay when it is wholly uncolored by that which passes through it. Every essay should be, to be human, exactly like another. But the perfect essay should have every word numbered, say as the bones in a body and the thoughts in the mind are fixed, permanent and never vary. Then there could be no confusion, no deception and the pleasure of reading would be increased.

Naturally, that which is sure to remain intact is the only thing to which experience is sufferable. So it is said "to essay" to stand firm, that is, during penetration by a fluid.

"The only thing that changes is man" it is said. This false-hood is true. Its vitality is the same as that of fashions: changelessness. Without one there is not the other. Periods and places by their variety function as do the fashions, to establish man who essays. Geography and history deal wholly with fashion. But the rigidity of the essay is in itself human.

After this description of Virginia it would be impossible to go on were it not for vanity which, the essence of science, enforces accuracy and thoroughness. Not only is it necessary to prove the crystal but the crystal must prove permanent by fracture. This is an essay: the true grace of fashion. The essay must stand while passion and interest pass through. The thing must move to be an engine; this in an essay means the parts are infinitely related to each other—not to "unity" however. It is the crossing of forces that generates interest. The dead centers are incidental. But the sheer centrifugal detail of the essay, its erudition, the scope of its trial, its vanity or love, its force for clarity through change is not understood except as a force that is in its essence centripetal. The motion is from change to the variety of changelessness.

Each essay rings the changes of its range, the breadth, the penetration moving inward about the fashionable brick of all styles, unity. Unity is the shallowest, the cheapest deception of all composition. In nothing is the banality of the intelligence more clearly manifested. There is no less significant matter for the attention. Every piece of writing, it matters not what it is, has unity. Inexpert or bad writing most terribly so. But ability in an essay is multiplicity, infinite fracture, the intercrossing of opposed forces establishing any number of opposed centres of stillness. So the history of Virginia has gone, even more so than in most of the states.

The varied intellectual and moral phases of Virginia are disclosed in a seacoast, a plain and a great valley, taken from east to west. It is covered by holly and wild turkeys. At least there are a few turkeys. You get a turkey dog. He flushes the covey. You then build a blind of brushwood and hide in it, the dog too, since his work is done. Take out the turkey-call and blow it skillfully. The birds will then come creeping in to be killed. Here and there on the old estates there are even a few great holly trees they brought from Carolina. All these things come originally from England. The women are charming. But the men still carry firearms generally and keep the bull in the pasture behind the hill, preferring witticisms with quail or the fox to the sexual breakdown.

The opalescent, sluggish rivers wander indeterminately about the plain. Africans, corn, tobacco, bull-bats, buzzards, rabbits, figs, persimmons are the common accompaniments of these waters. There are no lakes. Oaks and yellow pine are the usual trees. These are essentially the component moments of all essays, hams, anecdotes of battles, broken buildings—the materia are the same. It is their feudal allocation in Virginia that is important. But the essay is essentially modern.

Of Virginia, especially, among the other states, one may
say, the older it is the newer it has become. Oaks and
women full of mistletoe and men. Hollow trunks for pos-
sums and the future. It clings and slips inside. Hunt for it
with hounds and lanterns under the "dying moon" crying
rebel yells back and forth along the black face of the ridge
—from sunset to 1 A.M.: the yelp of the hounds, the shouts,
now a horse neighing, now a muffled gunshot. The black
women often have the faces of statesmen and curiously per-
fect breasts—no doubt from the natural lives they lead.

Often there will appear some heirloom like the cut-glass
jelly stand that Jefferson brought from Paris for his daugh-
ter, a branching tree of crystal hung with glass baskets that
would be filled with jelly—on occasion. This is the essence
of all essays. Or there will be the incident of John Paul,
a Scotch gardener's son whom Governor Jones, who owned
the most of North Carolina, built into his name. Or there
will be an Indian war club; a cylindrical rod of stone en-
crusted with natural garnets. Or a bronze ax of Spanish
make which they found in the hole they dug in removing
the old pear tree from the garden. Or, by Willis mountain,
a converted Negro cabin: the man who owned the ground
on which a great part of Richmond stands—lives here alone
a millionaire—on whom the rest draw inexhaustibly. An
essay in himself.

In Virginia there is the richest gold mine known to the
country before the rush of '49. In the cornfields almost any-
where you'll pick up Indian arrowheads of quartz.

The country is still largely argricultural.

A Memory of Tropical Fruit

THE GUAVA you find growing more in the country, like a
plum. Yes, they eat them raw—they are very good. The
mango they plant in yards like our apple-trees or peach-

trees. I remember there was a whole double row of them at Mme. Christi's along the road up to the *hacienda*, the boys coming home from school would pick them up from the ground. Then there is the *caimito*. It is round like an apple and bright green but inside it is pure white, like milk. Toledo always called me, *cara de caimito*, because when I was young my face was round like that. The *níspero* is about the same size only it is brown and soft inside—fluffy. They say.

> *El que níspero come*
> *y esparrego chupa*
> *bebe cerveza*
> *y besa una vieja*
>
> *ni come, ni chupa,*
> *ni bebe, ni besa*

When a child eats the *caimito* he must be a little careful because the inside near the skin sticks all around the mouth all white and you cannot get it off, it is like glue.

Then there is the *corazon*, red and shaped like a heart and the *quenepa*, small like a plum and green, it comes in bunches and you bite it and open it, tac! and suck the inside. It leaves a pit that rattles inside the skin when you shake it. There is a bean too, the *guama*, that, when you open it, has little things like cotton and inside of each is the seed. It is very sweet. You take each one and suck it. There is, too, a grape that grows by the sea, a seaside grape. But it is different from the grapes here. It is more the shape of those torpedoes that the children throw down, tac! and they explode. They are pinkish and very good.

We never went bathing in the sea. What! take off our clothes where men could see us! No. Once I remember I went with my mother, perhaps at five o'clock in the morning, before anybody was up, to bathe. Then we came back before anybody could see us. When the Americans went there and went bathing in their suits with the men, the people were scandalized but now that there has been time for the children to grow up and get used to it—they are Americans, too.

When I first knew your father in Puerto Plata, he lived in a long low house, what they would call here a bungalow. It was not more than from here to the street from the sea. He would go down there and bathe. Your grandmother would go too sometimes. But there were *baracutas* there. When the little Negro boys would be swimming someone would watch, then there would be a cry. Here comes a *baracuta!* and everybody would scramble to get on shore. Once your father was just going to dive in when he looked down and saw one quiet in the water looking up at him and—and waiting.

Rosita would say, Oh Elena, I wish you would marry Willie.

The Venus

WHAT THEN is it like, America?

It was Fräulein von J. talking.

They were on their way to take the train to Frascati, the three of them—she, her companion, and Evans.

In reply, he shook his head, laughing—and they hurried on to catch the car.

She could speak English well enough, her companion could not, Dev's German was spasmodic coming in spurts for a moment or two but disappearing as suddenly leaving him tongue-tied. So they spoke English and carried their lunch. A picnic. He was delighted.

This day it was hot. Fräulein von J. seemed very simple, very direct, and to his Roman mood miraculously beautiful. In her unstylish long-sleeved German clothes, her rough stockings and heavy walking-shoes, Evans found her, nevertheless, ethereally graceful. But the clear features, the high forehead, the brilliant perfect lips, the well-shaped nose, and best of all the shining mistlike palegold hair unaffectedly drawn back—frightened him. For himself he did not know where to begin. But she looked at him so steadily, for some strange reason, as if she recognized him, that he was forced at last to answer her.

The tram was packed to the doors with passengers. Just before starting three tree-like Englishwomen had come rushing up calling out distractedly in English that the tram must not go, that somebody was coming—Do you see her? Oh, what can have happened? She had the correct information, et cetera—until finally Clara arrived just in the moment of the tram's departure and clambered aboard desperately, not a minute too soon. So that now they stood in the aisles, the four of them, sweating and glowering at the Italian men, who oblivious to such violence had long since comfortably settled themselves in their seats.

Fräulein von J. was placed immediately before Evans looking at him absorbedly like a child. Not knowing what else to do or to say, he too looked (as the tram went through some bare vineyards) straight back into her clear blue eyes with his evasive dark ones. She lifted her head a little as if startled, flushed (he thought) just a trifle but did not change her gaze. So they continued to look fixedly among the backs and across the coats of the Englishwomen in the aisle, who were jabbering away disturbedly about the threatening weather. She did not stir to look away but seemed to rest upon his look with mild curiosity and no nervousness at all. It was, as usual, his look which faltered.

Hearing the talk of the Villa this and the Villa that, about to be visited, Evans felt that he wished he could lose this crowd and was more than pleased when Fräulein von J. suggested that as soon as they should get to Frascati they head for the open country, delighted to find that her mood suited his own as well.

At the market place of Frascati, where a swarm of guides and carriages swooped down upon them, the three picnickers moved off at right angles to the direction taken by the rest, up a road that led between two walls around behind the town. They did not know where they were or indeed anything about the place or its beauties—they didn't care. Fräulein wanted to see the Italian springtime, that was the most definite of their spoken desires and Dev, sick of antiquities and architectural beauties, was more than willing to follow. The companion disliked Italian gardens anyway, lacking as they do the green profusion of the northern trees. With this they started, beginning at once to see violets along inside the fences, violets they could not reach. Following a brook which ran beside them, contrariwise down the hill, they trampled on, heading for open country.

What is it like, America? And so Dev began to tell her— Not like this—and all the time somehow he was thinking of his sister. Where is Bess? I wish she were here! till walking and talking, leaving the town behind them, they came quite out into the fields with a hill on the left and a little village off in the distance across the valley before them. They were in a worn dirt gully high hedged on both sides with banks cut into narrow paths by goats' hoofs. Before them four absorbed children gathering violets rushed forward in the path by ones and twos rivalling each other in their efforts to pounce upon the finer groups of flowers.

The children paid no attention whatever to the three hikers, not even by so much as one glance. Running ahead with cries of delight, each racing to exceed the others, they soon disappeared through gaps in the hedge. Evans was over and over startled by the German girl's delicate coloration and hair and eyes. Also, her hands were lovely, her ankles firm—like the Venus, thicker than the stage or dance-hall type, but active too—just suggestive enough of the peasant to be like a god's.

You have not told me yet, what it is like, America.

It is like. Dev began, something muffled—like a badly trained voice. It is a world where no man dare learn anything that concerns him intimately—but sorrow—for should we learn pleasure, it is instantly and violently torn from us as by a pack of hungry wolves so starved for it are we and so jealous of each of us is our world.

I think I know what you mean, she replied, it is that we are all good citizens on top and very much better than that inside. It makes me think of the *Johannisfeuer*. You know Sudermann's play?

America is a pathetic place where something stupefying must always happen for fear we wake up. Yes, I have read the play.

By this time they had come quite around behind Frascati hill. Here they had lunch in a diminutive, triangular grove of oaks where there was a grassy bank with a few daisies on it, and the tall trees bending overhead. Then climbing through a fence they took the road again up to the right around the hill climbing steeply now on a stony path. It was a hard walk this part of the way and before long they were tired, especially Frau M. who was glad to stop near the top and rest.

But after a few words in German which Dev missed, Fräulein von J. cried, Come on! and they two went on alone about two hundred yards ahead up to the woody summit, to a place from which they could see Frau M. below them lying under an ash-tree. Here there were a few stones of some ancient construction almost gone under the wood soil and rotted chestnut leaves. It was a chestnut grove cut and counter cut by innumerable paths which led north over the brow of the hill—to Frascati, no doubt. But now at this early season, the place was deserted. The random, long, dart-shaped dry leaves covered the ground all about them, two foreigners resting on the old stones. Elsa waved to Frau M. from where she sat, then she turned again to Evans, Tell me what you are. You do not mind? I want to know everything. What is America? It is perhaps you?

No, Dev shook his head.

Is it something to study? What will it do? Shall we go there to learn? she asked in rapid succession.

Dev shook his head.

But you will return to it?

Yes.

Habit?

No, it is something.

It is that I may the better hide everything that is secretly valuable in myself, or have it defiled. So safety in crowds—

But that is nothing. That is the same as in Europe.

America seems less encumbered with its dead. I can see nothing else there. It gives less than Europe, far less of everything of value save more paper to write upon—nothing else. Why do you look at me so? Dev asked her.

Because I have seen no one like you in my life, few Americans, I have talked to none. I ask myself, are you an American?

And if I am—

Then it is interesting.

He said, To me it is a hard, barren life, where I am "alone" and unmolested (work as I do in the thick of it) though in constant danger lest some slip send me to perdition but which, being covetous not at all, I enjoy for the seclusion and primitive air of it. But that is all—unless I must add an attraction in all the inanimate associations of my youth, shapes, foliage, trees to which I am used—and a love of place and the characteristics of place—good or bad, rich or poor.

No, she continued, it is not that.

Evans felt at that moment, that there was very little in America. He wanted to be facetious but the girl's seriousness was not a thing to be fooled. It made him pensive and serious himself.

He could say that it was just a place.

But you must not tell me that America is nothing, she anticipated him, for I see it is something, and she looked at him again with her little smile. You seem to me a man like I have not seen before. This is America?

I am a refugee, Dev continued, America is or was a beginning, to clean out the—

Then, she replied, it is as in Germany. I did not think so when I saw you.

And I, Dev answered, did not think so when I saw you.

Why am I in Rome, do you think? she queried next.

He did not know.

To become a nun.

And with a shock he remembered the German youths in their crimson gowns whom he had seen filing down the Quirinal, down the long steps; the Scotch youths playing soccer in the Borghese gardens Sunday afternoon with their gowns tucked up, or doffed, garters showing and running like college athletes for the ball. He remembered too, the Americans with the blue edge to their gowns, the Spanish, the French.

Yes, she continued, that is it. I am in Rome to feel if the church will not offer me an answer. I was fourteen years old when the war ended. I have seen the two things—to throw myself away or to take hold again. I have seen the women running in the stadiums, I have seen them together. If we were peasants, we could be nearer—but we must lose it all, all that is good. I am a German, an East Prussian. My mother is dead. My father is a general—of course. What shall I do? I do not want anything—Tell me what is America. You must say. Is it just a place to work?

Dev nodded.

You see that I am young—I am young, of course. You come to me carrying a message. I do not know what to do. I believe you will tell me. I am not a fool—and I am not gifted either. There is nothing for me. Is there? I cannot walk about letting my hair loose to surprise men because it is so yellow. You perhaps, yes, if you please—and she smiled —but not those whom I do not want. I cannot marry. It makes me sick to marry. But I want, I want. I do not care that I am virgin or not. No. No. That is childish. I cannot remain as I am—but I must—until this (and she tapped her forehead) is satisfied. You have said something to me. What do I say to you?

Dev thought "running wild" that if they should do as
he wished they would both end that night in the jail at
Frascati hungry and very much disturbed—possibly—but
no more than that. Fool.

They speak to me of my body. It is beautiful. For what?
Of what use to me?

She talked quite coolly.

Within a few years I must lose this. Why not? and I
have nothing else unless it is a mind to have, to have and
nothing that I want. Not painting, not music, philosophy,
tennis—for old men, young men, for women? No. America,
that seems something new.

You would find nothing in America, Evans quickly inter-
posed. The girls there cannot go half a mile out of town
for fear a Negro might rape them, or their complexions be
spoiled by the weather, or the Japanese come too close or
they be buried in snow or baked in summer; or they marry
business managers or become secretaries and live together
two or three in apartments. Their thoughts are like white
grass so heavily have they been covered by their skins—
and so heavily covered are they to protect them from the
weather that when they are uncovered they do not exist.
One must snatch another up quickly from the general sup-
ply, from a patent container.—Evans was ashamed of this
speech of which as a fact Fräulein von J. understood not
one word. But the few women he had admired were not
pretty and the pretty ones he did not admire.—Never
think of America, he concluded. The men are worse than
the women.

Are you then one?

Evans had no reply.

When I saw you, I saw something unusual, I am never
mistaken. I saw something different from what I see every
day, neither throwing away nor taking hold to the old
horrible handle, all filthy—Is it America? I asked, but you
tell me nothing. It is because you will not do so.

America, he began again haltingly, is hard to know.

Yes, she answered, because she had made him serious so that he must speak his mind or say nothing.

I think it is useful to us, he continued, because it is near savagery. In Europe, you are so far from it that maybe you will have to die first before you will live again.—But Dev was not such a fool.—Europe, I do not know, he corrected himself, I am seeing a few superficial moments only.

But he had a quick pupil.—That is enough, replied Fräulein von J. I see now what I saw at the beginning. You are a savage, not quite civilized—you have America and we have not. You have that, yes, it is something.

It is very difficult, said Dev. I am not a typical American. We have a few natives left but they would not know me—

You are holding on to something, she said.

It is very difficult, Dev went on—something very likely to be lost, this is what—So he took out the flint arrowhead he had in his pocket and showed it to her.

She was impressed. She held it hard in her hand as if to keep its impression there, felt the point, the edge, tried it, turned it over.

Yes, she said, I have seen the same thing from our own fields, more finished work—but it is very far, very far. No one believes it is real. But this you carry in your coat? It is very strange. Where did you find it?

In a corn-field in Virginia, there are many of them there.

Are there many Americans who know this that you are saving?

Dev shook his head. I have seen but a few. There are pictures pressed into my mind, which have a great power of argument. Summer pictures mostly, of my part of the country, one of the old pioneer houses fast to the ground. There is nothing like them in Europe. They were not peasants, the people who built them, they were tragic men who wasted their wits on the ground—but made a hard history for me—not for me only, I think; they were like all earlier peoples but it has been so quick and misplaced in America, this early phase, that it is lost or misinterpreted —its special significance.

You think then it might be useful to—me? Yes, that was what I saw in your eyes—She looked again. Yes, it is so.

She shook her head gently from side to side in marveling realization. Come, she said, I was right. What an America is that! Why then did you not look at me all this week? I was troubled. I wondered what was the matter with me.

Dev said he had been excited studying something he wanted among the antiquities.

But a feeling almost of terror, Dev thought, mixed with compassion perhaps, came now into her eyes as she continued to look at him.

It must be even more lonesome and frightening in America than in Germany, she said. She shook her head. She seemed as if looking off into a new country and to be feeling the lonesomeness of it.

America is marvelous, replied Dev, grossly prosperous— She shuddered, No. So were we. So will we be soon again. —She was frightened.—How can you stay where you are? Why do you stay there? You make the church impossible— but you are alone. I will pray for you.

They started to get up quietly from their serious mood and were rather startled to find themselves still in the surroundings of the pagan grove. Not too sure were they that they knew each other as well as they had been feeling they did for the few moments of hard sympathetic understanding just past, projecting themselves out; each feeling, each trying hard, to get at the other's mood. They laughed, and Dev gave her his hand but she did not move away.

It is very difficult, she said, for us to support ourselves after we have passed the semi-consciousness of the peasant, and his instincts. We fall back, do we not? You are brave, she said, to want to find some other way—and one that is American. It seems curious to me.

Moving to rejoin Frau M. they saw that it was getting on

into the afternoon and that they must be stepping along if they would be back in Rome by nightfall.

You believe in America like a church, mused Fräulein von J. almost to herself.

Dev did not think so.

Do you believe then that the church is an enemy to your belief?

Yes.

She looked away.

Oh come on, said Dev, let's get out of this.

A Note on the Recent Work of James Joyce

A SUBTITLE to any thesis on contemporary reputations might well be: How truth fares among us today. I see no other approach, at least, to the difficulties on modern literary styles than to endeavor to find what truth lies in them. Not in the matter of the writing but in the style. For style is the substance of writing which gives it its worth as literature.

But how is truth concerned in a thing seemingly so ghostlike over words as style? We may at least attempt to say what we have found untrue of it. To a style is often applied the word "beautiful"; and "Beauty is truth, truth beauty," said Keats; "that is all ye know and all ye need to know." By saying this Keats showed what I take to have been a typical conviction of his time consonant with Byron's intentions toward life and Goethe's praise of Byron. But today we have reinspected that premise and rejected it by saying that if beauty is truth and since we cannot get along without truth, then beauty is a useless term and one to be dispensed with. Here is a location for our attack; we have discarded beauty; at its best it seems truth incompletely realized. Styles can no longer be described as beautiful.

In fact it would not be stretching the point to describe all modern styles in their grand limits as ways through a staleness of beauty to tell the truth anew. The beauty that clings to any really new work is beauty only in the minds of those who do not fully realize the significance. Thus tentatively, James Joyce's style may be described, I think, as truth through the breakup of beautiful words.

If to achieve truth we work with words purely, as a writer must, and all the words are dead or beautiful, how then shall we succeed any better than might a philosopher with dead abstractions? or their configurations? One may sense something of the difficulties by reading a page of Gertrude Stein where none of the words is beautiful. There must be something new done with the words. Leave beauty out or, conceivably, one might begin again, one might break them up to let the staleness out of them as Joyce, I think, has done. This is, of course, not all that he does nor even a major part of what he does, but it is nevertheless important.

In Joyce it began not without malice I imagine. And continued, no doubt, with a private end in view, as might be the case with any of us. Joyce, the Catholic Irishman, began with English, a full-dressed English which it must have been his delight to unEnglish until it should be humanely Catholic, never at least sentimental. This is purely my imagination of a possible animus. And again a broken language cannot have been less than affectionately fostered since it affords him a relief from blockheaded tormentors. Admirably, of course, Joyce has written his words to face neither customs officials nor church dignitaries, Catholic or Protestant, but the clean features of the intelligence. Having so suffered from the dirtiness of men's minds—their mixed ideas, that is—suffered to the point of a possible suppression of all he puts upon paper, there is a humane, even a divine truth in his appeal to us through a style such as his present one which leaves nothing out. Much that he must say and cannot get said without his brokenness he gets down fully with it. But this is, again, merely a fancy. It is nothing and

I put it down to show that it is nothing, things that have very little general value.

We are confronted not by reasons for its occurrence in Joyce's writings but by his style. Not by its accidental or sentimental reasons but its truth. What does it signify? Has he gone backward since *Ulysses?* Hish-hash all of it?

To my taste Joyce has not gone back but forward since *Ulysses.* I find his style richer, more able in its function of unabridged commentary upon the human soul, the function surely of all styles. But within this function what we are after will be that certain bent which is peculiar to Joyce and which gives him his value. It is not that the world is round nor even flat, but that it might well today be Catholic; and as a corollary, that Joyce himself is today the ablest protagonist before the intelligence of that way of thinking. Such to my mind is the truth of his style. It is a priestly style and Joyce is himself a priest. If this be true to find out just what a priest of best intelligence intends would be what Joyce by his style intends. Joyce is obviously a Catholic Irishman writing English, his style shows it and that is, less obviously, its virtue.

A profitable beginning to going further is to note the kinship between Joyce and Rabelais. Every day Joyce's style more and more resembles that of the old master, the old Catholic and the old priest. It would be rash to accuse Joyce of copying Rabelais. Much more likely is it that the styles are similar because they have been similarly fathered.

Take what is most obviously on the surface in both of them, their obscenity. Shall we object to Joyce's filth? Very well, but first answer how else will you have him tell the truth. From my own experience I am perfectly willing to venture that Joyce's style has been forced upon him, in this respect at least, by the facts, and that here he has understated rather than overstated the realistic conditions which compel him. One might even go on to say that in this respect of obscenity all other present styles seem lying beside his. Let his words be men and women; in no other way could so much humanity walk the streets save in such hiding clothes. Or put it the other way: in no other way could the naked truth hidden from us upon the streets in clothes be disclosed to us in a way that we could bear or even recognize save as Joyce by his style discloses it. We should praise his humanity and not object feebly to his fullness, liars that we are. It would be impossible for Joyce to be truthful and accurate to his understanding by any other style.

This it is, let us presume, to be a Catholic of the world, or so Joyce has impressed me by his style. They say Joyce fears that were he to return to Ireland it would be seen to that they excommunicate him. I cannot believe such foolishness. They are wiser than that in the church today. Joyce writes and holds his place, I would assure them, solely by the extreme brilliance of his Catholicism.

And all this is no more than a reflection of the truth about Rabelais now common property. He was not at all the fat-headed debauchee we used to think him, gross, guffawing vulgarly, but a priest "sensitized" to all such grossness. Else his style would not have assured his lasting out a year.

Joyce is to be discovered a catholic in his style then in something because of its divine humanity. Down, down it goes from priesthood into the slime as the church goes. The Catholic Church has always been unclean in its fingers and aloof in the head. Joyce's style consonant with this has nowhere the inhumanity of the scientific or protestant or pagan essayist. There is nowhere the coldly dressed formal language, the correct collar of such gentlemen seeking perhaps an English reputation.

Joyce discloses the X-ray eyes of the confessional, we see among the clothes, witnessing the stripped back and loins, the naked soul. Thoughtfully the priest under the constant eyes of God looks in. He, jowl to jowl with the sinner, is seen by God in all his ways. This is Joyce. To please God it is that he must look through the clothes. And therefore the privacy of the confessional; he must, so to speak, cover the ache and the sores from the world's desecrating eye with a kindly badinage. Yet he must tell the truth, before God.

Joyce has carried his writing this far: he has compared us his reader with God. He has laid it out clean for us, the filth, the diseased parts as a priest might do before the Maker. I am speaking of his style. I am referring to his broken words, the universality of his growing language which is no longer English. His language, much like parts of Rabelais, has no faculties of place. Joyce uses German, French, Italian, Latin, Irish, anything. Time and space do not exist, it is all one in the eyes of God—and man.

Being Catholic in mind, to blatantly espouse the church, that is the superficial thing to do. The sensible thing is to risk excommunication by stupidity if it come to that in order to tell the truth. Therefore I rate Joyce far above such men as G. K. Chesterton, that tailor, or even Cocteau, if he has turned Catholic as I have heard, though in the case of the latter it chimes well with his acknowledged cleverness to be anachronistic.

And why should we fear, as do so many Protestants, that all the world turn Romanist? What in that conglomerate is out of date would even there be finally corrected by the sovereign power of the intelligence than which nothing is greater including as it must at work the instincts and emotions, that is the round brain and not the flat one. And this is once more Joyce's style.

To sum up, to me the writings of James Joyce, the new work appearing in *transition*, are perfectly clear and full of great interest in form and content. It even seems odd to me now that anyone used to seeing men and women dressed on the street and in rooms as we all do should find his style anything but obvious. If there is a difficulty it is this: whether he is writing to give us (of men and women) the aspect we are most used to or whether he is stripping from them the "military and civil dress" to give them to us in

their unholy (or holy) and disreputable skins. I am inclined
to think he leans more to the humaner way.

1927

The Somnambulists*

THERE IS, in a democracy, a limit beyond which thought is
not expected to leap. All men being presumed equal, it be-
comes an offense if this dead limit be exceeded. But within
the opacity which encloses them the American people are
bright, active and efficient. They believe in science and
philosophy and work hard to control disease, to master the
crime in their cities and to prevent the excessive drinking of
alcohol. Alcohol is the specific for their condition, thus
they fear it; to drink to excess breaks the shell of their lives
so that momentarily, when they drink, they waken. Or
they drink, under subterfuge, as much as they may desire,
but it is a public offense, for all that, which the very drink-
ers themselves acknowledge.

When one wakes from that sleep, literature is among the
things which confront him, old literature to begin with and
finally the new. In the United States let us say first Emily
Dickinson and then Kay Boyle. To waken is terrifying.
Asleep, freedom lives. Awake, Emily Dickinson was torn
apart by her passion; driven back to cover she imprisoned
herself in her father's garden, the mark of the injury she
deplored, an opacity beyond which she could not penetrate.
And in literature, since it is of literature that I am writing,
it is the mark of our imprisonment by sleep, the continuous
mark, that in estimating the work of E. D., still our writers
praise her rigidity of the sleep walker—the rapt gaze, the
thought of Heaven—and ignore the structural warping of

* A review of *Short Stories* by Kay Boyle. Black Sun Press, Paris, 1929.

her lines, the rhymelessness, the distress marking the place at which she turned back. She was a beginning, a trembling at the edge of waking—and the terror it imposes. But she could not, and so it remains.

It remains with us the wilderness, the Indians, the forest, the night, the New World,—as already pointed out. Kay Boyle was quick to take up this realization. A woman, as fully impassioned as was her famous compatriot, but trembling today on the other side of waking, her short stories assault our sleep. They are of a high degree of excellence; for that reason they will not succeed in America, they are lost, damned. Simply, the person who has a comprehensive, if perhaps disturbing view of what takes place in the human understanding at moments of intense living, and puts it down in its proper shapes and color, is anathema to United Statesers and can have no standing with them. We are asleep.

In some moods it may be charming, a breaking and holding that reminds one of surf on rocks. But good God, it is the breaking of the barriers to our lives that is human, not the dashing of ourselves to pieces on granite that we should praise. We try and yet we do not lift a finger. In what country will such freedom of intercourse exist among school children? And in what country, on the other hand, is the fear of genius so pronounced in the midst of such overpowering wealth? In what other country, its potential home, could a jazz opera by a German composer be received and paid for while not the faintest flick of support and encouragement is accorded to a man like George Antheil, an outstanding genius among us, whose works Germany and France both have honored? The German work which we have accepted is pale, abstract, removed from direct contact with our lives, an opera in a foolish dream. Antheil's work hits home. It is one of our characteristics that we distrust each other and are rivals to show how appreciative we are of foreign distinction. Antheil is antipathetic to us. It is that we fear to awaken and in sleep all are equal.

The phenomenon of our attitude toward the work of George Antheil and what must be Kay Boyle's reception; the brilliant newspapers actively trembling under a veil; the work of the poet H. D.; the young wife that walked six blocks asleep in her husband's pajamas one winter's night, the pants' bottoms trailing in the mud; the boy that, thinking himself in an airplane, dived from a window in a dream head down upon the gravel path—this is America accurately delineated. It is the School Board which, to make a rule, made a rule that forbids themselves from smoking at their evening meetings in the school building in order that they might prevent the janitors from smoking in the buildings while cleaning up the dirt after school. Fear to vary from the average, fear to feel, to see, to know, to experience—save under the opacity of a mist of equality, a mist of common mediocrity is our character.

The quality of Kay Boyle's stories has in it all of this strain. They are simple, quite simple, but an aberrant American effect is there in the style. There is something to say and one says it. That's writing. But to say it one must have it alive with the overtones which give not a type of statement but an actual statement that is alive, marked with a gait and appearance which show it to be the motion of an individual who has suffered it and brought it into fact. This is style. Excellence comes from overcoming difficulties. Kay Boyle has the difficulty of expression by Americans firmly in her mind and at the same time the female difficulties to make them more difficult. And yet, showing all this, the work may be done simply and directly; not with the horrible contortions, the agony of emission, the twisting and groaning and deforming effort of statement, seeking to disclose what it dare not acknowledge, the style of the repugnant Jurgen, tortured without relief in his quiet Richmond library—free from interruption. Kay Boyle has succeeded in writing of difficult matters clearly and well and with a distinction that is outspoken and feminine—not resorting to that indirection and tortured deformity of thought and language, that involved imagery which allows us to lie and hide while we enjoy, the peep style of a coward.

Why do American artists go to France and continue to do so and when there to drink, if they are wise, heavily? It is not postwar hysteria as the newspapers and monthly reviews would make us believe—for it has always been the same. It is not, to repeat, postwar hysteria. We do not go there out of courtesy to the French. We go out of our direct need. Paris is the one place in the world that offers the West its compensation, an opportunity, in all its deformity of spirit to awaken. Drink breaks the savage spell of nonentity, or equality as they call it, which chokes them in the great western republic. In France, they find themselves, they drink and they are awakened, shocked to realize what they are, amazed loosed—as, in fact, they on their part shock and arouse the tenderest sentiments of astonishment and tolerance among the French. They are, in fact, for the first time in their lives—and it is curious—with the sound frequently of slops emptied from a bucket. Not always; however. Possibly, it will be enlightening, if something of spiritual worth is uncovered. But most that appears is stale, mediocre, not equal to the continental. The women, Americans, get to show their bodies—I don't mean the contours only—and American women in Paris have been anonymously very successful in latter years. At their best they are perhaps always anonymous. They seem delightfully exotic with their natural faces, pretty legs and feet and shoes.

Kay Boyle, in her stories, reveals herself, her body, as women must in any art and almost never do in writing, save when they are exceptionally distinguished. It is France again and she, partly from her own tragic history, more by France and alcohol, is awake. She has shown more than the exterior of her purely American female body. I don't know any other place where this has occurred. I speak of a work of art as a place where action has occurred as it occurs nowhere else. Kay Boyle has profited by her release to do a stroke of excellence which her country should honor her for. It never will.

It is a false hope, pathetic and amusing at the same time—like an old woman dying of a worn-out heart, broken over the loss of a pet dog, who refuses treatment but keeps a chicken wish-bone between her swollen feet under the bed-clothes—that a man should think he can solve the everlasting and everpresent problem of making of literary excellence in a quiet, sane and orderly manner, using the same old wordbound ideas that have been successful with writers in the past, by the virtuous exercise of reason alone. The new is disorderly and lacks, it may be, all correlation with a ready body of listeners—who must be sacrificed—but it does not at least pretend to believe that out of old wrecks of thought, once successful, it can constitute by substitution and rearrangement alone that which is living, young and able.

Surely excellence kills sales. Why is an outspoken statement of this plain fact, known the world over to publishers and writers, always so carefully avoided? I know it is a cover in which writers hide their pique and, naturally, just because a work does not sell does not prove it good. But it certainly is known that even when excellence has a market, such a success is rarely its own but must be suspect, from the artist's viewpoint. Nearly always some quite accidental and therefore unimportant genre which such a work shows will be found to be the cause of its popularity. It is worth-while in considering the extraordinary modeling and sure technique of Kay Boyle's work, what she has avoided and what included, to know that she has also written two novels (being hard pressed for cash) which two prominent New York publishers (one of them had given her his word that he would print her first novel) with typical cupidity have turned down.

This is the sum and sum again of the publishing situation in America. Plain it is and has always been and must be to anyone that the best is untimely as well as rare, new and therefore difficult of recognition, without immediate general interest (any more than a tomato was until prejudice had been knocked down) therefore, dependent on discerning support (without expectation of money benefit) from the able; scantily salable—and without attraction for the book trade. While wonders are advertised. And it is at the same time true that the only thing of worth in writing is this difficult, priceless thing that refreshes the whole field which it enters, perenially, when it will, the new.

The great and blackguardly American publishers, catering to the somnolence, think always and only of cash and, bat-blind, (seeking to seem to favor the new out of fear lest they must) toot for new that which is first salable, new in appearance only, but mediocre and trite in fact. There is nothing to be done about it, nothing except to continue to envision the fact and to continue, difficult as it may be, to build a new means of access to new work separate from the agents in control and their fashionable pimps.

Few women have written like this before, work equal in vigor to anything done by a man but with a twist that brings a new light into the whole Sahara of romanticism, a twist that carries the mind completely over until the male is not the seeing agent but the focus of the eye. The dirty tradition of women's modesty and the cringing of women behind law and tradition gets an airing that certainly calls for a protest from the corrupt puritans. The usual reader will not be used to fairness from a woman, this straightforward respect for the writer's trade. Nearly all the noteworthy women writers of the past that I can think of, or nearly all, have been men, essentially. Perhaps I should have said, all the women writers acceptable to the public.

The Work of Gertrude Stein

Would I had seen a white bear!
(for how can I imagine it?)

LET IT BE granted that whatever is new in literature the germ of it will be found somewhere in the writings of other times; only the modern emphasis gives work a present distinction.

The necessity for this modern focus and the meaning of the changes involved are, however, another matter, the everlasting stumbling block to criticism. Here is a theme worth development in the case of Gertrude Stein—yet signally neglected.

Why in fact have we not heard more generally from American scholars upon the writings of Miss Stein? Is it lack of heart or ability or just that theirs is an enthusiasm which fades rapidly of its own nature before the risks of today?

The verbs auxiliary we are concerned in here, continued my father, are am; was; have; had; do; did; could; owe; make; made; suffer; shall; should; will; would; can; ought; used; or is wont . . . —or with these questions added to them;—Is it? Was it? Will it be? . . . Or affirmatively . . . —Or chronologically . . .— Or hypothetically . . . —If it was? If it was not? What would follow?—If the French beat the English? If the Sun should go out of the Zodiac?

Now, by the right use and application of these, continued my father, in which a child's memory should be exercised, there is no one idea can enter the brain how barren soever, but a magazine of conceptions and conclusions may be drawn forth from it.—Didst thou ever see a white bear? cried my father, turning his head round to Trim, who stood at the back of his chair.— No, an' please your honour, replied the corporal.—But thou couldst discourse about one, Trim, said my father, in case of need?—How is it possible, brother, quoth my Uncle Toby, if

the corporal never saw one?—'Tis the fact I want, replied my
father,—and the possibility of it as follows.

A white bear! Very well, Have I ever seen one? Might I
ever have seen one? Am I ever to see one? Ought I ever to have
seen one? Or can I ever see one?

Would I had seen a white bear! (for how can I imagine it?)

If I should see a white bear, what should I say? If I should
never see a white bear, what then?

If I never have, can, must, or shall see a white bear alive; have
I ever seen the skin of one? Did I ever see one painted?—de-
scribed? Have I never dreamed of one?

Note how the words *alive, skin, painted, described,
dreamed* come into the design of these sentences. The feel-
ing is of words themselves, a curious immediate quality
quite apart from their meaning, much as in music different
notes are dropped, so to speak, into a repeated chord one
at a time, one after another—for itself alone. Compare this
with the same effects common in all that Stein does. See
Geography and Plays, "They were both gay there." To
continue——

Did my father, mother, uncle, aunt, brothers or sisters, ever
see a white bear? What would they give? . . . How would
they behave? How would the white bear have behaved? Is he
wild? Tame? Terrible? Rough? Smooth?

Note the play upon *rough* and *smooth* (though it is not
certain that this was intended), *rough* seeming to apply to
the bear's deportment, *smooth* to surface, presumably the
bear's coat. In any case the effect is that of a comparison re-
lating primarily not to any qualities of the bear himself but
to the words *rough* and *smooth*. And so to finish——

Is the white bear worth seeing?
Is there any sin in it?
Is it better than a black one?

In this manner ends Chapter 43 of *The Life and Opinions
of Tristram Shandy*. The handling of the words and to some

extent the imaginative quality of the sentence is a direct
forerunner of that which Gertrude Stein has woven today
into a synthesis of its own. It will be plain, in fact, on close
attention, that Sterne exercises not only the play (or music)
of sight, sense and sound contrast among the words them-
selves which Stein uses, but their grammatical play also—
i.e. for, how, can I imagine it; did my . . . , what would, how
would, compare Stein's "to have rivers; to halve rivers," etc.
It would not be too much to say that Stein's development
over a lifetime is anticipated completely with regard to sub-
ject matter, sense and grammar—in Sterne.

Starting from scratch we get, possibly, thatch; just as they
have always done in poetry.

Then they would try to connect it up by something like
—The mice scratch, beneath the thatch.

Miss Stein does away with all that. The free-versists on
the contrary used nothing else. They saved—The mice,
under the . . . ,

It is simply the skeleton, the "formal" parts of writing,
those that make form, that she has to do with, apart from
the "burden" which they carry. The skeleton, important
to acknowledge where confusion of all knowledge of the
"soft parts" reigns as at the present day in all intellectual
fields.

Stein's theme is writing. But in such a way as to be writ-
ing envisioned as the first concern of the moment, dragging
behind it a dead weight of logical burdens, among them a
dead criticism which broken through might be a gap by
which endless other enterprises of the understanding should
issue—for refreshment.

It is a revolution of some proportions that is contem-
plated, the exact nature of which may be no more than
sketched here but whose basis is humanity in a relationship
with literature hitherto little contemplated.

And at the same time it is a general attack on the scholastic
viewpoint, that medieval remnant with whose effects from
generation to generation literature has been infested to its

lasting detriment. It is a break-away from that paralyzing vulgarity of logic for which the habits of science and philosophy coming over into literature (where they do not belong) are to blame.

It is this logicality as a basis for literary action which in Stein's case, for better or worse, has been wholly transcended.

She explains her own development in connection with *Tender Buttons* (1914). "It was my first conscious struggle with the problem of correlating sight, sound and sense, and eliminating rhythm;—now I am trying grammar and eliminating sight and sound" (*transition* No. 14, Fall, 1928).

Having taken the words to her choice, to emphasize further what she has in mind she has completely unlinked them (in her most recent work) from their former relationships in the sentence. This was absolutely essential and unescapable. Each under the new arrangement has a quality of its own, but not conjoined to carry the burden science, philosophy and every higgledy-piggledy figment of law and order have been laying upon them in the past. They are like a crowd at Coney Island, let us say, seen from an airplane.

Whatever the value of Miss Stein's work may turn out finally to be, she has at least accomplished her purpose of getting down on paper this much that is decipherable. She has placed writing on a plane where it may deal unhampered with its own affairs, unburdened with scientific and philosopic lumber.

For after all, science and philosophy are today, in their effect upon the mind, little more than fetishes of unspeakable abhorrence. And it is through a subversion of the art of writing that their grip upon us has assumed its steel-like temper.

What are philosophers, scientists, religionists, they that have filled up literature with their pap? Writers, of a kind. Stein simply erases their stories, turns them off and does without them, their logic (founded merely on the limits of the perceptions) which is supposed to transcend the words, along with them. Stein denies it. The words, in writing, she discloses, transcend everything.

Movement (for which in a petty way logic is taken), the so-called search for truth and beauty, is for us the effect of a breakdown of the attention. But movement must not be confused with what we attach to it but, for the rescuing of the intelligence, must always be considered aimless, without progress.

This is the essence of all knowledge.

Bach might be an illustration of movement not suborned by a freight of purposed design, loaded upon it as in almost all later musical works; statement unmusical and unnecessary, Stein's "They lived very gay then" has much of the same quality of movement to be found in Bach—the composition of the words determining not the logic, not the "story," not the theme even, but the movement itself. As it happens, "They were both gay there" is as good as some of Bach's shorter figures.

Music could easily have a statement attached to each note in the manner of words, so that C natural might mean the sun, etc., and completely dull treatises be played—and even sciences finally expounded in tunes.

Either, we have been taught to think, the mind moves in a logical sequence to a definite end which is its goal, or it will embrace movement without goal other than movement itself for an end and hail "transition" only as supreme.

Take your choice, both resorts are an improper description of the mind in fullest play.

If the attention could envision the whole of writing, let us say, at one time, moving over it in swift and accurate pursuit of the modern imperative at the instant when it is most to the fore, something of what actually takes place under an optimum of intelligence could be observed. It is an alertness not to let go of a possibility of movement in our fearful bedazzlement with some concrete and fixed present. The goal is to keep a beleaguered line of understanding which has movement from breaking down and becoming a hole into which we sink decoratively to rest.

The goal has nothing to do with the silly function which logic, natural or otherwise, enforces. Yet it is a goal. It moves as the sense wearies, remains fresh, living. One is concerned with it as with anything pursued and not with the rush of air or the guts of the horse one is riding—save to a very minor degree.

Writing, like everything else, is much a question of refreshed interest. It is directed, not idly, but as most often happens (though not necessarily so) toward that point not to be predetermined where movement is blocked (by the end of logic perhaps). It is about these parts, if I am not mistaken, that Gertrude Stein will be found.

There remains to be explained the bewildering volume of what Miss Stein has written, the quantity of her work, its very apparent repetitiousness, its iteration, what I prefer to call its extension, the final clue to her meaning.

It is, of course, a progression (not a progress) beginning, conveniently, with "Melanchtha" from *Three Lives*, and coming up to today.

How in a democracy, such as the United States, can writing which has to compete with excellence elsewhere and in other times remain in the field and be at once objective (true to fact), intellectually searching, subtle and instinct with powerful additions to our lives? It is impossible, without invention of some sort, for the very good reason that observation about us engenders the very opposite of what we seek: triviality, crassness and intellectual bankruptcy. And yet what we do see can in no way be excluded. Satire and flight are two possibilities but Miss Stein has chosen otherwise.

But if one remain in a place and reject satire, what then? To be democratic, local (in the sense of being attached with integrity to actual experience) Stein, or any other artist, must for subtlety ascend to a plane of almost abstract design to keep alive. To writing, then, as an art in itself.

Yet what actually impinges on the senses must be rendered
as it appears, by use of which, only, and under which, un-
touched, the significance has to be disclosed. It is one of
the major problems of the artist.

"Melanctha" is a thrilling clinical record of the life of a
colored woman in the present-day United States, told with
directness and truth. It is without question one of the best
bits of characterizaion produced in America. It is universally
admired. This is where Stein began. But for Stein to tell a
story of that sort, even with the utmost genius, was not
enough under the conditions in which we live, since by
the very nature of its composition such a story does vio-
lence to the larger scene which would be portrayed.

True, a certain way of delineating the scene is to take
an individual like Melanctha and draw her carefully. But
this is what happens. The more carefully the drawing is
made, the greater the genius involved and the greater the
interest that attaches, therefore, to the character as an in-
dividual, the more exceptional that character becomes in
the mind of the reader and the less typical of the scene.

It was no use for Stein to go on with *Three Lives*. There
that phase of the work had to end. See *Useful Knowledge*,
the parts on the U.S.A.

Stein's pages have become like the United States viewed
from an airplane—the same senseless repetitions, the endless
multiplications of toneless words, with these she had to
work.

No use for Stein to fly to Paris and forget it. The thing,
the United States, the unmitigated stupidity, the drab tedi-
ousness of the democracy, the overwhelming number of the
offensively ignorant, the dull nerve—is there in the artist's
mind and cannot be escaped by taking a ship. She must
resolve it if she can, if she is to be.

That must be the artist's articulation with existence.

Truly, the world is full of emotion—more or less—but
it is caught in bewilderment to a far more important degree.
And the purpose of art, so far as it has any, is not at least to

copy that, but lies in the resolution of difficulties to its own comprehensive organization of materials. And by so doing, in this case, rather than by copying, it takes its place as most human.

To deal with Melanctha, with characters of whomever it may be, the modern Dickens, is *not* therefore human. To write like that is not, in the artist, to be human at all, since nothing is resolved, nothing is done to resolve the bewilderment which makes of emotion an inanity: That, is to overlook the gross instigation and with all subtlety to examine the object minutely for "the truth"—which if there is anything more commonly practiced or more stupid, I have yet to come upon it.

To be most useful to humanity, or to anything else for that matter, an art, writing, must stay art, not seeking to be science, philosophy, history, the humanities, or anything else it has been made to carry in the past. It is this enforcement which underlies Gertrude Stein's extension and progression to date.

George Antheil and the Cantilène Critics

A Note on the First Performance of Antheil's Music in New York City (April 10th, 1927)

EVERY MAJOR musical critic of New York reacted unintelligently to Antheil's first presentation of his compositions in Carnegie Hall last April. I do not mean that they reacted stupidly, for they were shrewd in listening to and sensing the immediate expressions of feeling among certain of the audience rather than to have paid attention to what was going on within the limits of the musical problem itself confronting them. I mean they found nowhere in their minds an apposite thing to say musically about the object for criticism, or nothing of importance, so that their "columns" in the papers the next morning were totally blank to a person seeking musical information concerning the event. They completely failed to place, musically, what had gone on.

Of Antheil they said, of course, a great deal. Small, ill-mannered, silly, they were. But what of that if they had actually heard anything even to defame. Naturally, they claimed that they had heard nothing, which was probably quite true. Certainly, I did not seek to have them favor Antheil. I really did not. But I did expect their criticism to be about music. I did expect them to say at least somewhere what the works might have been about even if they were failures. It is their inability even to come in contact with the problem and not their unfavorable comments which disturbed me.

For music is changing in character today as it has always done. Where is it going? Did Antheil's work cast any light on that? No answer. And why? No answer. Was the work seeking a track and what track and why, if it did not attain it, why did it not do so? No answer. All they wrote was fillgap, and dirty fillgap too, some of it, showing their nervousness under stress of the occasion—always the result of failure to focus.

I say they were dirty since having nothing else in their heads they must attack Antheil in the qualities of his person saying catty things of his press-agenting, his appearance on the stage, etc., etc. This in New York, the musical center of America. They described the noises at the back of the auditorium and counted (later to lie about it) the number of people who, overborne by the avalanche of sound, walked out. The critics had time for that.

I myself remember one lantern-jawed young gentleman somewhat resembling the pictures we used to see of Alfred Dreyfus, who rose to his feet in the middle of the parquet seats during the long ringing of the electric bells in the "Ballet Mécanique," and shaking his head like a tormented young bull, stumbled blindly out over the feet beyond him whilst his lady smilingly and protestingly followed after.

I can understand the unhappiness, even the madness, of such a defeat. He was stuck and ran off bellowing. But neither this sort of thing, nor even its frozen counterpart, is musical criticism and offers no escape from the dilemma of making apposite comment when the mind is empty.

As a fact, the audience stayed almost to a person until the end of the concert, even applauding wildly at the success of the final "Jazz Symphony." Who has a right to say what was in their minds as Lawrence Gilman offered to do; or to interpret their reactions in the mass from the noise of a few disturbers? No one who uses his mind musically, surely. For myself, I am sure that many a one went away from Carnegie Hall thinking hard of what had been performed before him. It is to present one of these thoughts, or possible thoughts that I am writing. Not praise, not senseless derogations but—what could one, not being a musical critic, really think about that music?

One thing Gilman did say was that in respect of "*cantilène*" Antheil was deficient. Now that is something at any rate. It means roughly that a hat is not much like a banana unless we try to make it so, which was quite patently not Antheil's purpose. Or most likely "*cantilène*" was not one of the qualities Antheil was after.

But just why does a critic pick out just this detail of style for comment? Perhaps because when among listeners to music the wearying body fails in its following of the mind it drags all down more and more to that, asking to be rocked, "inspired" as they say. But there is an operation for that. But the alert mind outspreads the dull song, goes any way it can from point to point, brokenly if it must.

But the habitual music writers having mentioned this and some other "flaws" in Antheil's work (without respecting the critic's function to inquire why) the way is at least opened for a note on the facts of the case. I, too, saw the empty phrases, the failure to come up to a grand summary of the age in the climaxes and the "childish" rhythms. This requires depth in a critic, I wonder if anyone missed those things. And the resemblance of some of the tonality to Schönberg. And the "Jazz Symphony" not being epic must, of course, be flat, not being lyric it must of course be trite, though if ever there were anything more exquisitely lyric of present-day "new world" than the saxophone cadenza in that symphony, surely I have never heard it.

The question, I think, resolves itself to this, as always with contemporaneous criticism: Shall we (from our free *fauteuil*) knock a man down as hard as we can whenever we are given an unpoliced (by opinion) opportunity, hitting him personally when we have nothing to say about his music? Or do we perhaps find in the music something we wish to hold up (or to condemn) in particular that it may (or may not) go on to develop into that unique thing of vast importance "the future of music"? I think there is something in Antheil that should be saved.

For myself I am willing to let most of the works performed at the concert remain out of the discussion or to say very little of them. To bring such work up to the mind at a single hearing is most difficult. And the music is hard. I am not a trained critic. Hardest of all for me was the quartet where Gilman say Antheil resembles Schönberg. I do not know. Perhaps that's the trouble, maybe that's where he needs to work hardest. Men do have to work, even to be critics. Yet in the quartet the *allegro–andante* oscillation was a most welcome innovation not at all to be condemned because of its simplicity, which Gilman does without the faintest reason. But to cry out that this "is not music" is simply futile. "It's all wrong, it's all wrong," kept repeating the woman back of me. Of course it is. We are not used to it, therefore, it must be so. But we are not quite yet dead. Everything new must be wrong at first since there is always a moment when the living new supplants that which has been and still is right and is thus sure to be wrong in transit, or until it is seen that that which was right is dead.

I myself have but one bit of observation worth anything

to present: Here is Carnegie Hall. You have heard something of the great Beethoven and it has been charming, masterful in its power over the mind. We have been alleviated, strengthened against life—the enemy—by it. We go out of Carnegie into the subway and we can for a moment withstand the assault of that noise, failingly! as the strength of the music dies. Such has been its strength to enclose us that we may even feel its benediction a week long.

But as we came from Antheil's "Ballet Mécanique" a woman of our party, herself a musician, made this remark: "The subway seems sweet after that." "Good," I replied and went on to consider what evidences there were in myself in explanation of her remark. And this is what I noted. I felt that noise, the unrelated noise of life such as this in the subway had not been battened out as would have been the case with Beethoven still warm in the mind but it had actually been mastered, subjugated. Antheil had taken this hated thing life and rigged himself into power over it by his music. The offense had not been held, cooled, varnished over but annihilated and life itself made thereby triumphant. This is an important difference. By hearing Antheil's music, seemingly so much noise, when I actually came upon noise in reality, I found that I had gone up over it.

Kenneth Burke

WRITING IS MADE of words, of nothing else. These have a contour and complexion imposed upon them by the weather, by the shapes of men's lives in places. Their combined effect is not sculptural; by their characters they are joined to produce a meaning. This is termed good writing. By success with the words, the success of the composition is first realized.

Writing otherwise resolves itself into trite sentences of occasional grace, the idea becomes predominant, the craft becomes servile. Kenneth Burke is one of the few Americans who know what a success of good writing means—and some of the difficulties in the way of its achievement. His designs are difficult, possibly offensive, at times recondite.

From the shapes of men's lives imparted by the places where they have experience, good writing springs. One does not have to be uninformed, to consort with cows. One has to learn what the meaning of the local is, for universal purposes. The local is the only thing that is universal. *Vide* Juan Gris, "The only way to resemble the classics is to have no part in what we do come of them but to have it our own." The classic is the local fully realized, words marked by a place. With information, with understanding, with a knowledge of French, a knowledge of German, I do not hear Burke calling out, Good-bye New Jersey!— No place is important, words.

I know Burke would like to go to Paris if he could afford it. He doesn't have to listen to the dialect of some big Swede or other to paste up a novel. Words will come to him just as they come to them, but of a different order. Writing.

This is rather negative in the way of praise, but in a starving country one might as well at least talk of food. This will be at least important to American literature, though negatively, if there will ever be an American literature. And when there is, that will be important to French literature, English literature, and so finally to the world. There is no other way. Burke seems to me to be stalled in the right place. But that doesn't finish him.

For me, his life itself is a design, gives me a satisfaction enough, always from the viewpoint of an interest in writing. He is one of the rarest things in America: He lives here: he is married, has a family, a house, lives directly by writing without having much sold out.

Any cricket can inherit a million, sit in a library and cook up a complicated or crotchety style. Plenty of Americans who know the importance of the word, if it is French or British, can be taught to do smooth puttying. But damned few know it and know the reward and would rather work with the basic difficulty to what end is not apparent.

Kenneth Burke (and family, very important) found a place out in the country where they could live. That's all.

The White Oxen is a varied study, as any book where writing is the matter, must be. American beginning—in the sense of the work of Gertrude Stein, difficult to understand, as against, say the continuities of a De Maupassant. It is a group of short accounts, stories, more or less. They vary from true short stories to the ridiculousness of all short stories dissected out in readable pieces; writing gets the best of him, in the best of the book: "The Death of Tragedy" and "My Dear Mrs. Wurtlebach." "Then they were all gone. They had all gone ahead, leaving the log behind them, and the fresh rips in the ferns growing out of the rotten leaves. Wurtlebach had avoided the cow-flops, as well as the eyes of the girls."

Water, Salts, Fat, etc.*

THE WAY of the world is stupid and obscure and must be so to fit man's intelligence. Therefore, we love show and hate the truth. Somewhat in refutation of this, Dr. Logan Clendening has written a book for us about the human body that is lucid, engaging and full of valuable information. It seems really the body itself speaking, a very old, very certain, distinctly Rabelaisian and absolutely unflustered body, looking out through two eyes, a quick brain back of them, at some of the shows of the world.

This definite and well sustained viewpoint, as from within the hide, amounting at times to the effect of a vigorous and convincing style, holds the book close to the reader's attention from beginning to end. This it is which permits Dr.

* A review of *The Human Body*, by Logan Clendening, M. D.

Clendening, in crisp sentences which have an actual critical
force to them, to make flashing remarks upon the many men
and things mentioned among his pages. It is the body speak-
ing. We see Hippocrates, Vesalius, Galen, Shaw, Maude
Slye, Hilaire Belloc, Hugh Chamberlin, Louis XIV, and a
company of others, but it is the light which falls upon them
that is the book's merit. Because of this, no unfavorable
complex will be created in the mind of the reader, as is
often the case with similar works from which, however, all
style is lacking.

Anecdotes and illustrations are used freely—both draw-
ings and photographs. But the book is primarily informa-
tive in a practical way. "I was asked to write it in order
to make intelligible some of the intricacies of the human
body for the adult and otherwise sophisticated reader."
This is exactly what Dr. Clendening has succeeded in doing.
There are paragraphs on sex psychology, which I shall
point out to my wife. I'd like my brother to read one or
two other sections, particularly the one on—oh, well, no
need to mention it. And as soon as he cares to, my elder
son may look for what he pleases in it. The book is a capital
outline of that thing which from the beginnings of objective
science men have brought up step by step through great
sacrifice, by force of superb intelligence and with unflinch-
ing courage to be what Dr. Clendening prefers still to speak
of as the "art of healing." Nothing could be finer than this
book as a feeler, for the young man or woman contemplat-
ing the study of medicine. It will give him a capital idea of
the history of that study and of many of its humane possi-
bilities. Dr. Clendening is a tremendous enthusiast for the
art he loves and practices.

The book presumes knowledge of the body itself as the
source of all knowing; which should come as a refreshing
novelty to post-Freudian man and woman.

It begins with the body as a unit. This is the one place
where I should like to add something. I should have liked
the doctor to have been much more the philosopher of the

body as a whole before he went on to other things, for we
greatly need that emphasis today. This is, of course, what
he does emphasize but not sufficiently. It would have been
something to this effect, that whatever we see of worth in
the world the generation of it has been crude, corpor as
the sexual itself. Then that force begins to fan out, grows
thinner, more fragile as it gets further and further from
the fountain head.

One thing, such an understanding would at once resolve
the wonder we experience when "fine souls" as we speak
of them, revert so we say, to low practices. When we think
of the body as the sole source of all our good the return of
an attenuated or spent "culture" to that ground can never
after be seen as anything but a saving gesture—perverted
only by surrounding stupidity. These things interest me. I
should have liked Dr. Clendening to go on in this way
before taking up the more detailed stuff. A "fine" man or
woman, let us say, goes down. If this be not a necessary
terminal act is it not then in itself a work of art, an evoca-
tion of the true procreative process which is at the back
of all genius and all worth? So, or as he might have pleased,
would I have liked to have had the doctor enlarge this
first section.

The body is a thing which when we see it roundly as the
source of all good we see well, and when we see it cut up
for this or that special set of purposes, we see badly and
(if uncorrected) degenerately—in the manner of a puritan.
It is just such amputated concepts which clutter up the
world to its everlasting bewilderment and frustration, be-
cause it is so easy to present a pretty case for them. This
is exactly the appeal of a Ziegfield Follies exhibition, let us
say, when we think it after all aesthetic and rather fine. The
girls themselves, however, know damn well differently.
Take men, take an athlete or an iron worker or a Negro
teamster in July. Anyone watching them in action must
be struck by their beauty—anyone watching them in an
uninvolved way from the outside that is. But there again

we have it. That these men's bodies are related to sources, to all kinds of generative processes within the understandings of the men themselves that inhabit them, to be used with a crude or trained energy designed to be destructive of ideas. . . . were we to feel this and act upon such a conception, that *would* be dangerous. So we invent games and the ideal of work for them. Work! My God, for what reason? Work is the great mystifier for most men. Anyhow, "beautiful." Such things concern the body as a whole.

Or he might have classified bodies: some a sort of hanging rind for the brain, some fit only to bear offspring, some absolutely not, some flowers, some this and some that, etc. and all requiring refertilization, both male and female, one way or another at frequent intervals.

The rest of the book, and of course the greater part, is divided into three major sections: (1) The human body as an organism for the conversion of food and air into energy and into tissues: (2) the human body as an organism for the reproduction of its own kind, and (3) the human body and disease. This is detail work, but far from uninteresting. It is characterized by excellent physical descriptions and sound advice. Once more, it is the body speaking, weaning the man away from many phobias, putting him on a straight road to understanding of his commoner functions and consoling him over many of his inevitable deficiencies —as much as one can console a man by telling him the truth. Read of constipation and "Epsom's Old Well," read of height, weight and the span of life. The book is serious and abounds in references.

But the book is not a compendium; it is the straight opinion of Dr. Clendening wherein at times he differs sharply from the dicta of some authorities. In particular, does he object to the modern insistence upon periodic physical examinations of the circulatory system, the gall bladder, etc., by so-called health extension clinics, when there are no symptoms whatever to make a man seek medical advice. "To balance this," he says, "it is acknowledged that some cases of symptomless diabetes and early tuberculosis of which the owner is unaware are discovered. Also latent syphilis may be discovered, though the owner usually is not unaware. I know of no other common disease likely to be detected by routine examination." Every older man playing the game should read what he has to say about golfer's heart. It is decidedly encouraging.

There is some excellent reading upon "high blood pressure" though I do think he goes a bit strong here on heredity. When it comes to baldness and "weak stomach," however, I agree with him completely. It is time someone got inside the hysteria built around us today by damnable half-knowledge and systematically pernicious advertising which would force on us all sorts of "health" practices, tooth pastes and other nostrums. And it is sweet music to have some one who knows what he is talking about stand up and speak for the dignity of the great study of physiology as against the asininity of those who fill our children's minds with long and lying dissertations on the evils of alcohol and tobacco in school books. Yes, Dr. Clendening is outspoken.

He is courageous, too. And "love is lovelier for its *lust.*" The emphasis is mine.

There are excellent chapters on Coordination and Control, Nutrition, the Nervous System and Six Senses, the Relations of Mind to Body, the Venereal Diseases, Pregnancy and Labor, Secondary Tissue Changes, Neoplasms, Tumors, Cancers, etc., and *De Senectute* and Death.

An example of his good sense is what he says in speaking of the intestinal flora, relative to the *Lactobacillus acidophilus,* its name now pasted on nearly every milk wagon we see in the streets; "a normal inhabitant of the colon, whose increase can be stimulated by using an exclusive lactose or milk-sugar diet for a few days."

Discoveries in medicine of far reaching importance have been ridiculously simple in their inception; such was the birth of percussion, the method of tapping the chest to determine the state of its contents, a procedure ascribed to the Viennese innkeeper's son Auenbrugger, later a famous physician, who used to see his father practice it on casks of beer and wine. Similarly came about the birth of the stethoscope at the hands of Laënnec. It seems incredible how slow men were to understand the working of heart and blood vessels aright. And so with this and that it has gone. Slowly in reading Dr. Clendening's book it begins to dawn on us what knowledge is and what we are really made of. We see a play of slow and solid understanding gradually coming about through vague apprehension followed by a careful rejection of the inessential until we arrive at last at a very simple and throughly physical explanation of everything. The body it is which stands guard not only over our comings and goings, but over our wits also. It is there. We gloss it over with unresolved suppositions, the result of too hasty conclusions, then a century or so later, the body emerges like a rocky peak out of a cloud to reassure and tranquilize us. Dr. Clendening has caught this mood firmly in what he says so that it pervades everything—even his own mistakes. It is the principal enjoyment for me in such a writing.

Statement

THE GREATEST WORK of the twentieth century will be that of those who are placing literature on a plane superior to philosophy and science. Present day despairs of life are bred of the past triumphs of these latter. Literature will lay truth open upon a higher level. If I can have a part in that enterprise, I shall be extremely contented. It will be an objective synthesis of chosen words to replace the common dilatoriness with stupid verities with which everyone is familiar. Reading will become an art also. Living in a backward country, as all which are products of the scientific and philosophic centuries must be, I am satisfied, since I prefer not to starve, to live by the practice of medicine, which combines the best features of both science and philosophy with that imponderable and enlightening element, disease, unknown in its normality to either. But, like Pasteur, when he was young, or anyone else who has something to do, I wish I had more money for my literary experiments.